Latin American Women
and the Literature
of Madness

Latin American Women and the Literature of Madness

Narratives at the Crossroads of Gender, Politics and the Mind

ELVIRA SÁNCHEZ-BLAKE
and LAURA KANOST

McFarland & Company, Inc., Publishers
Jefferson, North Carolina

LIBRARY OF CONGRESS CATALOGUING-IN-PUBLICATION DATA

Sánchez-Blake, Elvira E. (Elvira Elizabeth)
    Latin American women and the literature of madness : narratives at the crossroads of gender, politics and the mind / Elvira Sánchez-Blake and Laura Kanost.
       p.   cm.
    Includes bibliographical references and index.

    ISBN 978-0-7864-7485-1 (softcover : acid free paper) ∞
    ISBN 978-1-4766-2110-4 (ebook)

    1. Women—Latin America—21st century. 2. Women—Latin America—Social conditions. 3. Women authors, Latin American—Latin America. 4. Allegory. I. Kanost, Laura, 1980– II. Title.

HQ1460.5.S356 2015
305.4098—dc23
                                                        2015013515

BRITISH LIBRARY CATALOGUING DATA ARE AVAILABLE

© 2015 Elvira Sánchez-Blake and Laura Kanost. All rights reserved

No part of this book may be reproduced or transmitted in any form or by any means, electronic or mechanical, including photocopying or recording, or by any information storage and retrieval system, without permission in writing from the publisher.

Front cover image © 2015 Shutterstock

Printed in the United States of America

McFarland & Company, Inc., Publishers
  Box 611, Jefferson, North Carolina 28640
  www.mcfarlandpub.com

Elvira
A Roberto, por acompañarme en esta aventura.
To Robert, for accompanying me on this journey.

Laura
To my parents, my most important teachers.

Table of Contents

Acknowledgments		ix
Preface		1
Introduction		3
One.	A Dialogical Journey: Cristina Peri Rossi's *La nave de los locos* (Elvira Sánchez-Blake)	29
Two.	Homesickness: Lya Luft's *Exílio* (Laura Kanost)	52
Three.	Dissonance on Display: Diamela Eltit and Paz Errázuriz's *El infarto del alma* (Laura Kanost)	69
Four.	See the World Through My Lens: Cristina Rivera Garza's *Nadie me verá llorar* (Elvira Sánchez-Blake)	82
Five.	A Poetics of Madness: Laura Restrepo's *Delirio* (Elvira Sánchez-Blake)	102
Six.	Literary Agency: Irene Vilar's Life-Writing (Laura Kanost)	122
Conclusions		144
Chapter Notes		157
Bibliography		163
Index		171

Acknowledgments

First of all, I thank Laura, my co-author, for embarking on this adventure.

To Annette Pasapera and Emily Holley, who offered constructive suggestions on earlier versions of this project. To my mentor, colleague and friend, Jonathan Tittler, who read the final draft and provided fruitful commentaries and suggestions. To my daughter Victoria for her understanding, and especially to my husband Robert for his moral support and for sharing this journey with me.

—Elvira

I thank Elvira for inviting me to collaborate on this project. I am grateful to Danny J. Anderson, Marta Caminero-Santangelo, Jill S. Kuhnheim, Jonathan Mayhew, and Vicky Unruh for their mentorship in the earliest phase of my research on this subject. Many thanks to my family and to my colleagues at Kansas State University for their support.

—Laura

Preface

This book is the result of a long process of research and interactions while teaching in the U.S. and Latin America. Elvira began studying these issues while teaching a course on "locura and literatura" (madness and literature) at the Universidad Autónoma de Yucatán (Mérida, Mexico) in the summer of 2008. Interactions with students when discussing some of the texts that would later be selected for this project fostered many of its fundamental questions. At Michigan State, Elvira has offered two graduate seminars on a related subject, "Latin American Postmodernisms" (2010 and 2012). Her approach further developed as she presented her research at conferences, becoming the source of collaborations with colleagues at other institutions. Laura's 2007 Ph.D. dissertation at the University of Kansas examined the cultural imagination of mental illness in late 20th-century Latin America by focusing on representations of the space of the psychiatric hospital. This dialogue with the field of disability studies has continued through her subsequent publications and conference presentations, especially her participation in the forthcoming volume on disability studies in Latin America, *Libre Acceso* (State University of New York Press), edited by Susan Antebi and Beth Jorgensen. In 2014, she taught a course on narratives of disability and illness in contemporary Spanish American narratives at Kansas State University. After originally conceptualizing this book as a single-author monograph, Elvira saw the potential for collaboration when she met Laura at a 2014 Latin American Studies Association conference panel on Madness and Mental Health in Latin American Literature and Culture. It has been an enriching and productive partnership.

Preface

This volume explores contemporary Latin American realities through madness narratives written by prominent women authors. Included are Cristina Peri Rossi (Uruguay), Lya Luft (Brazil), Diamela Eltit (Chile), Cristina Rivera Garza (Mexico), Laura Restrepo (Colombia), and Irene Vilar (Puerto Rico). These authors use madness in literature to explore women's social roles and to expose sociopolitical issues in their respective countries. The selected narratives compose a textual cartography tracing transformations and challenges during the last three decades in a territory marked by individual domestic battles, participation in political activism and commitment to social causes. What we call a poetics of madness emerges from this gender-politics dynamic in a continuous flow of transformation and change.

This study is the first book devoted to representations of madness in Latin American women's narratives that establishes a dialogue between theories from the Anglo-European tradition and Latin American perspectives on the region's own realities. We began to develop this approach through the following journal articles and chapters, some of which include earlier versions or excerpts from chapters in this book. Sánchez-Blake is the author of "La mirada de la locura: Naves, manicomios y delirantes en las letras femeninas latinoamericanas," *Cuaderno Internacional de Estudios Humanísticos y Literatura* (Universidad de Puerto Rico, Humacao, 2015); "Behind the Mirror: Narratives of Madness in Latin American Feminine Literature," *Twenty-First Century Latin American Narrative and Postmodern Feminism* (Cambridge Scholars, 2014); "Narrativas de locura. *La nave de los locos* de Peri Rossi y *Nadie me verá llorar* de Rivera Garza," *Hispanic Journal* (2011); "Locura y literatura en la narrativa femenina latinoamericana: la otra Mirada," *La manzana de la Discordia* (Universidad del Valle, Colombia, 2009); and "La frontera invisible: Razón y sin razón en *Delirio*" in the anthology *El universo literario de Laura Restrepo* (Taurus, 2007). Kanost has published "Re-Placing the Madwoman: Irene Vilar's *The Ladies' Gallery*," *Frontiers: A Journal of Women Studies* 31.3 (2010), which has been revised for inclusion in Chapter Six, and "Pasillos sin luz: Reading the Asylum in *Nadie me verá llorar* by Cristina Rivera Garza," *Hispanic Review* 76.3 (2008), referenced briefly in Chapter Four.

Introduction

The dynamics of reason and unreason in the history of the world through the arts and literature reveal a great deal about societies in different periods and times. From the ship of fools and mythic allegories to asylums and politics of marginalization, relations of power and exclusion have intersected in the definitions of madness and social control. This topic, widely addressed and studied by 20th-century scholars in Europe and North America, has received little attention in Latin America, a void we begin to fill in this book.

This volume examines narratives of madness written by women in the context of postmodern Latin American literature. It explores a diverse selection of emergent and canonical writers: Uruguayan Cristina Peri Rossi, Brazilian Lya Luft, Chilean Diamela Eltit, Mexican Cristina Rivera Garza, Colombian Laura Restrepo, and Puerto Rican Irene Vilar. This book studies and analyzes a corpus of representative literary texts by Latin American women writers who use madness to raise critical awareness about social and political issues affecting their home countries at the turn of the 21st century. Through this selection of texts, we compare, contrast and analyze insanity as a literary device that intersects with postmodern and feminist critical theories. Specifically, we explore how figures of the mad and mentally disturbed have been a tool to denounce marginalization and to reflect changes in Latin American women's positioning at both the individual and collective levels. At the individual level, we refer to marginalization of women with mental illness, who outnumber their male counterparts due in part to unequal cultural and sociopolitical stressors.[1] At the collective level, we emphasize the exclusion of women who have been part of social and political movements, and who have been labeled as "locas" (mad) for their activism.

Following Michel Foucault, the concept of madness is approached here as a cultural construct. Foucault defined the literature of madness as a medium for raising the critical consciousness of humanity in his seminal account, *History of Madness* (1961). He demonstrated that the experiences of madness throughout history reveal more about society's deviations than about inherent characteristics of the human self (Rogers 25). This explains why the "madman" has become both a symbol of crisis and a mirror reflecting critical consciousness of contemporary realities. Accordingly, for the present analysis, madness is understood as the disorders associated with emotions, thoughts, and behaviors perceived as pathological within the accepted social codes and cultural norms in a given society. The poetics, defined by Aristotle as the ontology (the being) of poetic arts and their textual representation (11), and madness, understood as a cultural construct that defines deviant behaviors from the norm, are the cornerstones of this study. Thus, the analytical approach will focus on the discursive strategies and narrative techniques used to represent the dynamics of reason and unreason in the selected texts. For example, many of these writers juxtapose multiple discourses that clash to destabilize marginalizing clichés and open up a new space to talk about the intersections of experience, culture, and politics. Physical images of the body and exterior spaces are employed to represent psychic pain and trauma, contesting the assumption that madness is housed in language or is intangible, exploring the intersections of word and image, and highlighting the potential for the invisible to change reader perception of the visible. Riddles and puzzles are posed to readers, requiring active participation and forming an expectation for a definitive answer that often remains frustrated when the text comes to a close. Strategies such as these, aligned with their postmodern literary context, create uncertainty about what is knowable or tellable and about the power relationship between the reader, the text, and contemporary Latin American social concerns.

Many scholars have examined the relevance of madness as a cultural signpost that indicates shifts in a given culture. That is the case of 16th-century works portraying madness through art and literature (Bosch, Brueghel, Erasmus, Cervantes, Shakespeare), marking the onset of modernism and the Renaissance in Europe. In Latin America, narratives of madness are blooming today just as they did in Europe's fifteenth and sixteenth centuries. This phenomenon is evident among women writers who use the figure of the mad to convey messages of social and political significance. Cristina Peri Rossi represents madness through characters traveling on a ship of fools to denounce exclusion and marginalization by military regimes in South America. Lya Luft's depressed protagonist stands as a representative of contemporary Brazilian women whose mental health is strained by multiple and sometimes clashing societal expectations. Diamela Eltit and Paz Errázuriz's portrayal of the utter marginalization of psychiatric hospital residents alludes to oppression by military dictatorships in Chile.

Cristina Rivera Garza renders madness as a reflection of gender, class and nation struggles in Mexico at the turn of the 20th century. Laura Restrepo portrays a woman suffering from delirium to depict a Colombia under siege by violence, political corruption and social decay. Irene Vilar constructs a family narrative of mental illness that is inextricably linked to the neocolonial status of Puerto Rico. These narratives represent allegories in which madness represents a social ill on one level. Furthermore, they explore power relationships affecting the realities experienced by people considered mentally ill. They address the relationship between madness (marginalization) and intellectual discourse (power). The intersection of these issues will form the core of this project to demonstrate how power relations, gender exclusions and social marginality result from cultural constructs and reflections of politics over the body and the self. An important element of this study focuses on the dynamics of gender and political struggles in the selected narratives that reflect historical events affecting Latin American countries in the late 20th century and turn of the millennium. This component differs from North American and European studies on madness and literature, which have focused mostly on the individual battle with mental illness within a given social context.

The next section of this introduction begins by contextualizing madness in literature. It presents some of the canonical works that have studied women and mental illness in Western literature, focusing lastly on critical works dealing with narratives of madness by Latin American women at the turn of the millennium. In the process, we establish the cultural framework in which ideas of madness, literature and femininity are constructed in the context of Latin America and its connection to the world.

Introduction

Madness and Literature

In *History of Madness in the Classical Period*, Michael Foucault introduces readers to the image of a Ship of Fools, "a drunken boat that glides along the calm rivers of the Rhineland and the Flemish Canals" (8). This is the vessel that Sebastian Brant depicted in his 1494 literary satire. The vessel carried within it the insane, expelled from towns in Europe and condemned to wander from place to place with no clear destination in sight, a powerful signifier of the complexities of exclusion. Foucault relates how at the end of the 15th century, the fear of death and madness turns on itself to mockery and satire. Erasmus's *In Praise of Folly* (1509) was inspired by Brant's text, transforming madness into a spectacle of life. Many other literary, theatrical and artistic works followed the model. Henceforth, madness became wisdom and knowledge—a kind of forbidden knowledge—as illustrated by Foucault:

> While the man of reason and wisdom sees only fragmentary figures that are all the more frightening for their incompleteness, the madman sees a whole unbroken sphere. For him the crystal ball empty for others is filled with invisible knowledge. [...] This knowledge, so inaccessible, so formidable, the Fool, in his innocent idiocy, already possesses [*History of Madness* 19–20].

Foucault considers Erasmus to be the milestone marking when the medieval concept of "mad and horror" turned into one of satire and mockery in times when people began to gain access to knowledge and humanism. Following Erasmus, literary and philosophical expression becomes the domain of madness in the 15th century. Both Cervantes and Shakespeare use mad characters to reflect a moral satire of the world they live in. Both testify to a critical and moral experience of reason and unreason developing in their era. For Foucault, the entire humanist tradition of the 15th century revealed that madness unmasked the truth, and its discourse was bound up with a critical consciousness: "the vision of madness as an experience within the domain of language, where man was confronted with his moral truth, the laws of human nature and human truth" (*History of Madness* 27).

By the 17th century, the experience of madness was driven away by Descartes's discourse of rationalism. Reason prevailed over madness. It traced a dividing line that would make it impossible to distinguish *unreasonable reason* and *reasonable unreason*. Oblivion falls upon the world navigated by the free Ship of Fools, which loses its mystical romanticized

Introduction

aura. Madness is reduced to silence and confinement in the form of asylums and hospitals. The asylum was then considered the great continuity of social morality, the values of family and work. It became an instrument of formal uniformity and of social denunciation (*History of Madness* 494–95). The relationship between physician and patient was founded upon powers of domination based on moral and social order. The physician became the father, judge, family and law, the supreme authority exercising order and punishment. Life in the asylum, according to Foucault, reproduced in a microcosm the dominant structures of bourgeois society and its values: family, justice, and social order. Confinement was also a convenient resource for social cleansing and control on moral issues and for maintaining patient-doctor dependence. According to Foucault, Freud later transformed the powers that had been distributed in the asylum. On the one hand, he freed the patient from the asylum, but on the other, he confined the patient to the alienation of the physician. Therefore, for Foucault, "psychoanalysis can untangle some forms of madness, but it is a perpetual stranger to the work of unreason" (*History of Madness* 511).

An essential component in Foucault's discussion is the dynamics of language and silence, reason and unreason. Foucault's assertion, "Language is the primary and ultimate structure of madness" (*History of Madness* 237), has spawned great controversy among thinkers of different periods.[2] At the same time, it has promoted intellectually rich debate over the constitution of mental illness beyond clinical and psychiatric discourses.

Michel Foucault's genealogy of madness through different historical periods provides four pivotal elements for this study. First, madness is seen as a human experience that builds on the consciousness of humankind. The influence of madness in the arts and literature in the 16th century, when madness as a tragic experience turns into critical consciousness, provides a lens for reading turn-of-the-millennium Latin American literature. Presenting the world as a spectacle permits raising awareness about a society where both authors and readers mirror themselves onto the literary text.

The second element is the emphasis on the eye and the gaze, which according to Foucault, allows the insane to see what is concealed by the eyes of the "sane." This resource opens up the vast spectrum between vision and blindness, a recurrent motif in the literature of madness. It also unfolds the subject of perception: who decides what is real or illusory. This takes us to the third consideration: the blurry line between reason and unreason, an interrogation that is constantly present throughout Foucault's study. A

Introduction

final consideration is the relation of power between the insane and physicians, which could be extended to the mad and society and projected onto the networks of authority, control and repression derived from this relationship. These four elements will guide the reading of madness in literature through the texts selected for this volume.

Cultural Representations of Mental Illness

Subsequent studies of cultural representations of mental illness take into account Foucault's approach to mental illness as neither a fixed identity nor a constructed human experience, but as part of a greater apparatus of socioeconomic control. Shoshana Felman, in *Writing and Madness* (originally published in French in 1978 and in English in 1985), explores ways that the language of literature reclaims the language of madness, defining it through its contradictions. Felman observes that literary language closely resembles the discourse labeled as mad and therefore equivalent to silence, describing the latter as "nonsense, alienating strangeness, a transgressive excess, an illusion, a delusion, a disease" (2). When taken up in literature, however, Felman claims that the discourse of madness gains cultural legitimacy and is no longer considered a form of silence. Felman even suggests that "literature becomes the only recourse for the self-expression and the self-representation of the mad" (4). For Felman, the special discourse of madness lies at the very heart of literature: "this reclaiming of the margins both of knowledge and of power come[s] to represent the literary claim par excellence" (2–3). Felman presents literature as the necessary meeting space between madness and reason. Focusing on the interplay of literature, philosophy and psychoanalysis, she affirms that "while madness has been recognized as a burning contemporary question, it is as though the question of literature has become anachronistic and irrelevant" (15). However, Felman appropriates Foucault's claim that "throughout our cultural history, the madness that has been socially, politically and philosophically repressed has nonetheless made itself heard, has survived as a speaking subject only in and through literary texts" (15). Her approach to literature and madness is defined by an essential kinship "as gravitational poles for the very energy of repression as it is activated within a shifting but ultimately irreducible field" (17). Felman's rhetorical perspective will be essential for the texts considered for this volume, by the link established between madness as a signifier and its role in textual

Introduction

discourse. According to Felman, madness as a signifier inquires not so much at the meaning of that signifier, as its power. "It asks not what it is (or what it signifies), but, what it does—what are the textual acts and speech events it activates and sets into motion" (32). This connection will be applied in particular to the analysis of *La nave de los locos* by Cristina Peri Rossi, a novel in which madness constitutes a main signifier from an allegorical perspective.

Following Felman, two relevant psychoanalytical approaches consider the subject of madness and literature. Lillian Feder and Sander L. Gilman cast literary representations of mental illness as manifestations of writers' psyches; thus, in different ways, Feder and Gilman acknowledge the impact of culture on a writer's imagination of mental illness. Yet, both scholars also subtly reiterate the psychoanalytic power dynamic of the analyst and patient, the latter always dependent on the former. While a psychoanalytic approach may be helpful in uncovering ways in which literary representations of mental illness are bound up in public and individual conceptualizations of mental illness, this approach is limited by an underlying rigid distinction between sane/self/subject and insane/other/object.

Lilian Feder's *Madness in Literature* (1980) examines "representative literary explorations of the deranged mind" in Western literature from the fifth century B.C. to the 20th century A.D., emphasizing "the psychological revelations inherent in the continuity, variation, and changes in the theme of madness" in order to reveal "some discoveries regarding mental functioning and aberration that imaginative writers have made in their depictions of madness" (xii). That is to say, Feder (psycho)analyzes literary representations of madness in an attempt to discover underlying patterns that reveal truths about the human mind, its cultural context, and the mutual interaction between them. Although Feder herself defines the concept of madness as dependent on its cultural context, her study, true to its theoretical milieu, seeks out universal patterns or structures within these cultural constructions. In Feder's view, writers reiterate these patterns but can also have the special gift of acting as mediators between madness and sanity: "Since the literary artist employs structures—myth, metaphor, symbol—which continually mediate between unconscious and conscious process, he is often a gifted explorer of what have been called the 'unlabeled metaphors' of the schizophrenic, an interpreter of the madman's apparently indecipherable 'messages'" (7).

Feder's method is to employ all areas of knowledge relevant to the comprehension of the types of symbolic transformation that characterize madness in literature (10). Contrary to Foucault, her approach chooses psychoanalytic formulations of mental processes as guides to the particular modes of thought and feeling expressed by mad characters. This point of reference underscores resemblances between the symbolic language and action of legendary or realistic mad characters of later literature of modern times (11).

An important element of Feder's analysis is the connection she establishes between myth, ritual, religion and literature and the mad. She studies ancient Greek mythology and its influence in all periods of Western literature from medieval, classic, modernism and surrealism to the most recent impact in late 20th-century exponents. Feder concludes that through the history of literature, the idea that madness can produce extraordinary insight is not a revolutionary one. It is "as old as human beings' interest in the mind and is reflected in the self-revelations of the mad protagonists of ancient myth and in Plato's prophetic and inspired madness" (283). This is true in recent novels in which madness is a release mechanism through the protagonist's struggle with a society that is fundamentally centered on the self (283).

Like Feder, Sander Gilman weaves elements of particularity and universality in his discussion of madness in *Disease and Representation* (1988). Gilman argues that art functions as humanity's way of controlling reality, so that portrayals of people with disease work to safely contain the feared disease itself within a boundary: "the frame of the painting, the finite limits of the stage, the covers of the book, the perspective of the photograph, or in the narrative form of the novel" (2). Looking at visual representations of madness from the Middle Ages through the 20th century, Gilman finds that the iconography of madness responds to an ongoing need to "localize and confine the mad, if only visually, in order to create separation between the sane and the insane" (48). While Gilman's approach presupposes a universally negative concept of mental and other illness and differences, it also emphasizes that such texts are always created and read within an interpretative community, and that readings of representations of mental illness affect its actual manifestations: "the idea of mental illness structures both the perception of the disease and its form" (19). Both Feder and Gilman rely on elements of essentialism and constructivism, thus manifesting a tension between reinforcing and destabilizing categories of power and difference. Their theoretical perspectives are helpful for the present analysis of madness and literature: Feder, in terms of the mythical representations of mad characters, and Gilman in the perception of insanity as a sign of difference and Otherness.

The Female Malady

The relationship of women and madness has been also widely studied from clinical, psychological, social, and literary perspectives. This discussion, which was influenced by the advent of feminism in the latter half of the 20th century, provides a necessary background for understanding the contexts in which some of the analyzed texts were written. Phyllis Chesler in *Women and Madness* demonstrates the inequality of the treatment of women in the field of psychiatry. First published in 1972, the book revealed the historical mistreatment of women in psychiatric institutions in the nineteenth and early twentieth centuries. It includes case histories of mentally ill patients, in-depth interviews, observations and analyses of treatment methods that disclosed abuses of female patients by doctors and institutions in North America.

The author brings to light the immense disparity between the treatment of women and men considered "insane." These include wrongful psychiatric diagnoses; the diagnostic pathologizing of women who reported harassment, discrimination, rape and abuse; class and race biases, sexual relations between patient and therapist, and unwarranted confinement of women to asylums. Chesler's study takes into account stories and biographies by notable North American women who experienced mental disturbances and were locked in asylums. Among them are Elizabeth Packard, Ellen West, Zelda Fitzgerald and Silvia Plath. The analysis of their writings reveals a great deal about the repressive conditions that have drawn talented women to suppress their creativity to fit social norms. In the definition of madness, Chesler emphasizes gender as a prime determinant:

> What we consider "madness," whether it appears in women or in men, is either the acting out of the devaluated female role or the total or partial rejection of one's sex-role stereotype. Women who fully act out the conditioned female role are clinically viewed as "neurotic" or "psychotic." [...] Men who act out the female role and who are "dependent," "passive," sexually and physically "fearful" or "inactive," or who choose men as sexual partners, are seen as "neurotic" or "psychotic" [94].

Introduction

These categorizations provide an insight that was not considered in previous studies of madness. Chesler's revelations in the seventies were pivotal for understanding the relationship between gender and madness in literature written in North America and Europe. Subsequently, these revelations influenced studies in Latin America, as we shall see in the texts selected for this book[3].

Sandra Gilbert and Susan Gubar in their study of 19th-century English and French women writers, *The Madwoman in the Attic* (1979), considered the literary text as the symbolic representation of the female author's anger against the rigidity of patriarchal tradition. For them, madness represented the price women artists had to pay to exercise their creativity in a male-dominated culture (81). Their study takes as a starting point the symbolic representation of the pen as a male tool, and therefore inappropriate and alien to women. Following this assumption, women who attempt to take up the pen cross boundaries dictated by nature (8). In this sense, all activities associated with writing, reading and thinking are not only alien but also inimical to "female" characteristics (8). Gilbert and Gubar's main proposal is that "a woman writer must examine, assimilate, and transcend the extreme images of 'angel' and 'monster' which male authors have generated for her" (17). Thus, they read madness in women's writing of the era as both a symptom and a protest of gender oppression, a strategy for killing the angel in the house, as Virginia Woolf proclaimed women must do in order to write (17). At the same time, as Gilbert and Gubar demonstrate, socially scripted roles for women promoted real-life experiences of illness as part of feminine identity. In the 19th century, complex social prescriptions did not merely urge women to act in ways which would cause them to become ill. Such training was actually intended to cause illness in women. Upper and middle-class women were defined as sickly, ill and frail, and consequently a "cult of female invalidism" developed in England and North America (54).[4]

Elaine Showalter, in turn, describes madness as what was considered the "female malady" (1987). She asserts that throughout Western history, the idea that there is a fundamental alliance between women and madness has been reflected in the construction of gender roles situating women "on the side of irrationality, silence, nature, and body, while men are situated on the side of reason, discourse, culture and mind" (3–4). Showalter focuses her study on the context of England for the cultural specificity of English madness. In her study, Showalter demonstrates that cultural ideas

Introduction

about femininity shaped the definition and treatment of mental disorders, arguing that what was considered madness in women was, rather, a deviation from the traditional female role. She draws from previous studies, such as Chesler, Gilbert and Gubar, and Felman to assert that "[a] serious study of the female malady should not romanticize madness as one of women's wrongs any more than it should accept an essentialist equation between femininity and insanity. Rather, it must investigate how, in a particular cultural context, notions of gender influence the definition and, consequently, the treatment of mental disorder" (5).

Showalter critiques psychiatric ideologies and clinical approaches that only contributed to stigmatizing behaviors that did not conform to the female gender role. Among these she mentions Darwinian psychiatry, psychoanalysis, and the antipsychiatry movement. The Darwinian theories viewed insanity as a product of organic defect, poor heredity, and an evil environment (18). Thus, women's psychology was linked to their reproductive organs, while male psychology was considered to be dictated by the mind. Accordingly, mental breakdown would come when women defied what was considered their nature, attempted to compete with men, or sought alternatives or even additions to their maternal functions. This Victorian psychology of women is apparent in the literature of the times. In the late 19th century, psychoanalysis introduced the concept of hysteria as the female malady. Showalter recognizes that Freud and his theories offered a considerable advance over the biological determinism and moralism of Darwinian psychiatry, but psychoanalysis still made essentializing distinctions between men's and women's mental disturbances that it linked to sexual differences. Lastly, Showalter explores R.D. Laing's antipsychiatry movement, which introduced the idea that mental illness had to be examined in terms of its social context. The view of madness as a social construct, says Showalter, seemed to offer new conceptual models for the relationship between madness and femininity. Madness became intelligible as a strategy in response to messages and demands about women's roles in a patriarchal society (122). However, Showalter argues that, like other psychiatric movements and approaches, in practice Laing's approach was "male-dominated and unaware of its own sexism" (19).

According to Showalter, changes in cultural fashion, psychiatric theory, and public policy have not transformed the gendered power imbalance that has kept madness a disproportionately female malady. Despite the wide acceptance of psychotherapy, modern psychiatry has not led to significant changes in the cultural construction of female insanity. Showalter contends, "Psychoanalysis with its emphasis on penis envy as the main determinant of female psychosexual development, has not offered much scope for a revolutionary discourse on women and madness" (19). Moreover, "even Laing's anti-psychiatry movement, which protested against shock treatment, and which promised to analyze women's situation in the family and the society, not only failed in its theoretical effort, but may well been the most sexist of all in its practice" (19). Showalter explains that while Laing's contribution to the understanding of women and madness is undeniable, "antipsychiatry had no coherent analysis to offer women" (246). She claims that the movement was male dominated and it also exploited women patients through questionable treatments comparable to the rape of asylum patients by the keepers (247). Showalter's debate has been central to understanding and advancing the exploration of women's representation of insanity as a subversive feminist mechanism and strategy.

New Approaches: The Madwoman Can't Speak

Marta Caminero-Santangelo, in *The Madwoman Can't Speak, Or Why Insanity Is Not Subversive* (1998), refutes the representation of madwomen in 19th-century literary texts as a way of resisting oppressive social structures. She exposes the hypocrisy inherent to such attempts to rehabilitate the concept of madness as a form of subversive speech, focusing particularly on the ubiquitous studies of the figure of the madwoman. Caminero-Santangelo observes that since Gilbert and Gubar's influential work, madness in women's writing has been read as a metaphorical rage against patriarchy, and even as a willful choice preferable to insanity (1). French feminism promoted a variation on this idea, proposing that since men have long claimed ownership of the language of rationality, women could subversively use the language of irrationality that had been relegated to them, appropriating it as a special feminine power (1). Caminero-Santangelo counters that in order for this idea of madness to be empowering, it must be understood completely figuratively, not as mental illness as actually experienced, and therefore the figure of the madwoman offers the illusion of power in a symbolic resolution of a problem that persists in reality (2, 3).

Caminero-Santangelo points to a body of post–World War II United

Introduction

States narrative texts that in fact, she argues, consider madness the ultimate surrender to dominant discourses because madness "is characterized by the (dis)ability to produce meaning—that is, to produce representations recognizable as meaningful within society" (11). Unlike Foucault or Felman, Caminero-Santangelo does not find any sort of potential for empowerment in the madwoman's speech. On the contrary, Caminero-Santangelo reads in her case studies a shared "interpretation of madness as an illusory self-representation of power that offers an *imaginary* solution to the impasse. As an illusion of power that masks powerlessness, madness is thus the final removal of the madwoman from any field of agency" (11–12). She further destroys this illusion by recognizing that, while through history women have indeed been pronounced mad because of what was considered "unfeminine" behavior, the texts she studies in fact represent the experience of madness "as something more than a label attached to difference," and while this experience "can be understood as a last protest against the world [...] it inevitably surpassed its causes, overshadowed them, and rendered helpless the women within its grasp" (50–51). Caminero-Santangelo observes that narrators who have recovered from mental illness never "long for the protest, the creativity, the rage of madness" as would be expected if madness really were a viable mode of expression and resistance for oppressed women (50–51).

Moreover, Caminero-Santangelo makes the case that "madness is not simply personally disabling; it is absolutely antithetical, at a fundamental level, to feminism" because the madwoman's inability to conceive of herself as a subject "preempts not just individual subjectivity but the building of collective resistance as well" (179). True collective action is complicated, Caminero-Santangelo notes, by the power imbalance inherent in feminist celebrations of the subversive power of madwoman: "Every time [feminist scholars] write another article or book about the emancipatory power of madness, they demonstrate just how fully they themselves can engage in public, rational forms of discourse" (180). The premise that the madwoman cannot speak rests on the essentializing definition of madness as an absolute inability to speak and be heard. People with mental illness can and do speak, however, and the ways that individuals speak and that society listens are intertwined with the literary representations of such exchanges. Strategies for speaking and for learning to listen to madness in Latin American women's writing are at the heart of the present study's focus on the poetics of madness.

Introduction

On Pain and Suffering

Literary imagery carries the potential both to mask and to reveal authentic experiences of mental illness and other disabilities, as the field of critical disability studies has argued. In identifying elements of a poetics of madness, we draw on the work of Susan Sontag and Elaine Scarry, who considered the power dynamics involved in representing illness and pain through metaphor.

Susan Sontag's *Illness as Metaphor* (1978) argues that, by repeatedly using certain "loaded" illnesses such as tuberculosis, cancer, AIDS and insanity as metaphors, and by drawing on metaphors to speak of these illnesses, not only do we avoid truly speaking of the human experience of being ill, but we perpetuate stigmatization and oppression of people who are ill. When such metaphors become a commonplace, a synecdochical substitution takes place, equating the person with the negative associations ascribed to the illness: "My point is that illness is *not* a metaphor, and that the most truthful way of regarding illness and the healthiest way of being ill—is one most purified of, most resistant to, metaphoric thinking" (3). Discussions of literary representations of illness and disability must bear this objection in mind. Critical disability scholars have shown, for example, that literature has almost exclusively used disability as a metaphor, rather than as a common human experience worthy of representation in its own right.

However, literary language also offers a capacity for expression of human experiences that evade denotative speech, as Elaine Scarry argues in *The Body in Pain* (1985). According to Scarry, physical pain cannot be directly expressed through referential language, but instead must be expressed figuratively, by comparing or relating the pain to something outside the body feeling the pain: "It is because it takes no object that [pain], more than any other phenomenon, resists objectification in language" (5). Thus, people have no choice but to describe internal feelings of pain as "burning," "crushing," "pounding," and so on, always implicitly referring to either the action of a weapon or the visible effects of bodily damage (15). A powerful component of Scarry's argument is the observation that "the act of verbally expressing pain is a necessary prelude to the collective task of diminishing pain," and that therefore developing a vocabulary for speaking about pain in medical, legal, testimonial, and literary and artistic contexts provides the means to verbally represent, and by

Introduction

extension, politically represent, physical suffering (9). Scarry finds that because pain resists representation through language, it is rarely represented in literature. She finds this absence troubling, because "the failure to express pain ... will always work to allow its appropriation and conflation with debased forms of power, conversely, the successful expression of pain will always work to expose and make impossible that appropriation and conflation" (14). According to Scarry, then, literary representations of pain can work to destabilize the power relationship bound up in conceptions and practices involving pain.

Although Scarry limits her argument to physical pain, her theoretical and ethical position is a promising approach to the study of literary representations of mental illness because many psychiatric disorders involve mental stress, emotional pain, and physical discomfort or distress. A large part of the stigma attached to these illnesses is related to the social taboo about discussing them. Scarry claims that emotional pain is not resistant to language, because unlike physical pain, emotional pain has an external referent: "we do not simply 'have feelings' but have feelings for somebody or something"; "love is love for x, fear is fear of y, ambivalence is ambivalence about z" (5). Scarry continues: "*psychological* suffering, though often difficult for any one person to express, *does* have referential content, is susceptible to verbal objectification" (10). Yet, since the mind-body relationship is a complex one, conditions such as severe anxiety or depression do often involve feelings of extreme mental and physical distress without clear referents outside the body. Scarry's argument, then, is relevant to our discussion of a poetics of madness, as we consider ways that women writers in Latin America have used literary language to give representation both to internal experiences of madness and to the sociocultural contexts in which they unfold.

Madness in Literature Through the Lens of Disability

A new approach to the relationship between individual bodies and sociocultural practices in literary representations of madness and mental illness comes from the field of critical disability studies, which emerged in the U.S. and UK in the 1990s. The introduction co-authored by the editors of the foundational *Disability Studies: Enabling the Humanities* explicitly includes psychological disorders in its definition of disability as "naturally occurring or acquired bodily variations that accrue as we move through history and across cultures," asserting that "many of us will become disabled if we live long enough," and that, indeed, disability can be considered "the fundamental aspect of human embodiment" (2). Although disabilities such as mental illness are in actuality a central image and concept in our lives, language and literature, they are perceived as a taboo subject, and when they are represented in literature, it is often as a marginal experience or as a metaphor for something else (1–2). The field of disability studies seeks to understand the many ways in which disability, including psychiatric disability, has been relegated to the margins of literary and critical activity, and is committed to opening up these areas to recognizing disabled people as active subjects with a shared culture or community identity, and whose life experiences are central, not marginal, to human experience.

Critical disability studies has been slow to develop as a discipline outside of Anglophone contexts. In Latin American literature, Susan Antebi's *Carnal Inscriptions: Spanish American Narratives of Corporeal Difference and Disability* (2009) is a monograph that pioneered this approach. A disability studies approach to madness or mental illness in Latin America considers the relationship between literary representations and social practices. The social context for the body of literature discussed in the present volume includes the potential for mental health care reform. Itzhak Levav and colleagues point to a relationship in Latin America between the return of democracy following late 20th-century dictatorships and a "renaissance of mental health issues in general and societal concern for human rights" (75). Sixteen Latin American countries participating in the groundbreaking 1990 Regional Conference for the Restructuring of Psychiatric Care held in Caracas agreed on the need to reform mental health legislation and move from centralized psychiatric hospitals to "community-based services as the chief means to attain accessible, decentralized, comprehensive, continuous and preventive care" (Levav et al. 71).

However, as Julio Arboleda-Flórez and David N. Weisstub observe, these changes were not consistently implemented; mental health care reform has been made a relatively low priority in Latin America because of more immediate concerns of violence and political instability (40). These political situations are linked in a very real way to trauma and stress that put a strain on the region's collective mental health. Literature registers and criticizes this relationship, as this volume demonstrates. In the case of Latin America, before the late 20th century, literature tended to reflect the sociocultural stigmatization of mental illness in an uncritical way.

Introduction

Latin American Literature of Madness

Madness has been a recurrent trope in master narratives of 20th-century Latin America. Several literary works from the Boom period depict mad characters such as Susana San Juan in Juan Rulfo's *Pedro Páramo,* the neurotic Pablo Castel in *El túnel (The Tunnel)* by Ernesto Sábato, José Arcadio, Macondo's patriarch, in *Cien años de soledad (One Hundred Years of Solitude)* by Gabriel García Márquez, and dictators mad with supreme power in *El otoño del patriarca (The Autumn of the Patriarch)* by García Márquez, *La fiesta del Chivo (The Feast of the Goat)* by Mario Vargas Llosa, and *Yo el supremo (I, the Supreme)* by Augusto Roa Bastos. These texts suggest that power inebriation brings on insanity. Madness also functions as a representation of society either as an allegory or as an alternate side of reality. Two novels by José Donoso fit this category, *El obsceno pájaro de la noche (The Obscene Bird of Night)* and *Coronación (Coronation)*. Other narratives deal with dislocated perceptions of the world such as *Informe sobre ciegos (Report on the Blind)* by Ernesto Sábato or *El reino de este mundo (The Kingdom of this World)* and *Los pasos perdidos (The Lost Steps)* by Alejo Carpentier. In *Rayuela (Hopscotch),* by Julio Cortázar, it is difficult to categorize Oliveira, the main character, as he is always in a liminal place between sanity and insanity.[5] In more recent postboom narratives, the figure of the madman/woman participates in the collective anxiety generated by the turn-of the-millennium delusion of the revolutionary wars, the rise of drug trafficking, sexual revolutions, and technological innovations. A myriad of new emergent literary movements including McOndo, Crack, *los enterradores,* and other trends such as the *sicaresca* and the so-called "narco-literature" express the anguish of the human condition toward contemporary challenges: *Insensatez (Senselessness)* and *La diabla en el espejo (The She-devil in the Mirror)* by Horacio Castellanos Moya, *El fin de la locura (The End of Madness)* by Jorge Volpi and *El anticuario (The Antiquarian)* by Gustavo Faverón are some examples of this trend. Other writers drew on personal experiences or encounters to inscribe in literature discourses associated with mental illness: Chilean Diamela Eltit, in *Lumpérica (E. Luminata,* 1983), *Por la patria (For the Fatherland,* 1986), *El padre mío (Father of Mine,* 1989), and *Vaca sagrada (Sacred Cow,* 1991); Argentinian Luisa Valenzuela in several works, especially *Cambio de armas (Other Weapons,* 1982); and Brazilians Hilda Hilst, *Com os meus olhos de cão (With My Dog Eyes,* 1986) and Rodrigo de Souza Leão, *Todos os cachorros são azuis* (*All Dogs Are Blue*, 2008).

Recent historical events of military regimes and state violence perpetrated in Latin America produced a significant number of narratives reflecting the chaos and madness of these critical periods in different countries. At the same time, the surge of the postmodern literary movement in Latin America brought new models and techniques based on fragmentation, decomposition, mixed genres, chronological and spatial ruptures, and especially the emergence of marginal non-traditional voices with new recourses and techniques such as disentangled discursive strategies associated with the language of madness and delirium. In this category, women writers made their incursion into the Latin American literary forum.

According to Debra Castillo, Mexican Rosario Castellanos was one of the first women writers "who confronted the rhetorical tradition that defines good prose as clear, straight forward, masculine and bad taste in prose as a fondness for the excessively ornamented, and therefore effeminate" (51). Castellanos called for women to stop being passive and submitting to the norms imposed on femininity. A massive response met this call. In Mexico, a number of writers including Elena Poniatowska, Ángeles Mastretta, Margo Glantz, and Carmen Boullosa entered the public forum with new approaches to representing women's roles intertwined with social and political issues. In Argentina, voices like Luisa Valenzuela and Alicia Partnoy denounced the maneuvers of repression. In Uruguay, Cristina Peri Rossi wrote from exile about political oppression in that country and explored women's sexuality. In Chile, Isabel Allende wrote about the country's dictatorship while Diamela Eltit generated controversy with an irreverent type of prose confronting Pinochet's regime. In Puerto Rico, Ana Lydia Vega and Rosario Ferré proposed new trends in Caribbean literature. All these writers strived for an appropriation of language, voices and bodies. Their common goal was to break the restrictions imposed by gender roles and political-historical challenges of the times.

Gilbert and Gubar's *Madwoman in the Attic* had a resounding impact on Latin American critics who recognized in it the concept of the traditional Latin American middle class housewife gone mad by social restrictions imposed on her. Helena Araújo in *La Sherezada criolla* (1989) draws from this iconic work to assert that the same behaviors of the European women studied in the book are replicated in Latin American societies: "Ausente de su cuerpo durante siglos, la mujer lo assume negativamente

Introduction

en compulsiones, fobias, y síntomas enfermizos" (128) [Absent from their bodies for centuries, women assume it [the body] negatively in compulsions, phobias and debilitating symptoms]. She blames the role of Catholic religion in the upbringing of women who are socially conditioned for the glorification of being virgins and mothers. "¿Qué mejor acondicionamiento para la neurosis?" (128) [What better conditioning for neurosis?], asks Araújo. She analyzes several works by Latin American women who wrote what she called "oppressed literature."

Sara Castro-Klarén in "Crítica literaria feminista y la escritora en América Latina" (1985) reapropriates the term "madwoman," turning it into "la loca criolla del ático" (the *criolla* madwoman in the attic) to stress that in Latin America such a concept carries a load of connotations related to class and gender issues. She calls for a critical work of parallel importance focusing on women's letters in the Americas (quoted by Castillo 6). Debra Castillo develops Castro-Klarén's claim and explains that "in Latin America la *loca* has a range of significations from those obtaining in either of the English-language books, as the juxtaposition 'loca en el ático'/ 'loca de la Plaza de Mayo' immediately underlines" (7). For Castillo, madness and sanity are differently coded and valued in Latin American societies (7). Such codes refer to the common appellative assigned to a woman who attempts to cross the boundaries: "*Una loca* represents the most common appellation for any woman who crosses the threshold of the home and who steps outside the traditional bounds of a proper, womanly *pudor* (decorum, but also modesty, humility, and purity) and *recato* (prudence, caution, shyness, also coyness)" (16). Castillo points to the case of Madres de la Plaza de Mayo in Argentina, who were officially considered "locas" for crossing traditional boundaries of domestic space into the public realm. Penalized and labeled insane, these women became models for a new kind of political struggle. Their actions resonated across the continent in fighting repressive regimes for gender equality and political agency (16).

In response to feminist uprising and activism, books by women authors in Latin America in the last decades of the 20th century denounced repression, both domestic and political. They were part of the liberation movements that fought against dictatorships and military regimes, while slowly acquiring recognition and a place in the literary realm. These books reflected diverse concerns, ranging from women's identity, place, sexuality, bodies and memory, to social and political issues in the region. In the process, they became part of the building of history and national identities through literature. Many of these writers used madness to deliver a message about women's role in society in the midst of political oppression. Some of them are Elena Poniatowska, Carmen Boullosa, Sabina Berman, Cristina Rivera Garza, Diamela Eltit, Luisa Valenzuela, Griselda Gambaro, Cristina Peri Rossi, Clarice Lispector, Gioconda Belli, Claribel Alegría, Helena Araújo, Albalucía Ángel, Marta Aponte Alsina, Laura Restrepo, Lya Luft, and Irene Vilar, among others. Most of these writers intertwine sociopolitical exclusion with women's struggles for rights and dignity.

Despite the predominance of this trend in Latin American literature, only a few studies have focused on the intersection of women and madness in the region. One example is the anthology edited by Gladys Ilarregui, *Femenino plural: la locura, la enfermedad, el cuerpo en las escritoras hispanoamericanas* (*Feminine Plural: Madness, Illness and the Body in Latin American Women Writers*, 2000). The essays in this collection examine a myriad of texts from Spanish America from the colonial period to the present with emphasis on representations of female illness as resistance and transgression of social restrictions. The articles examine issues of religious impositions, sexual violence, mother-daughter relationships, language liberation, performativity, and transgressions offered by contemporary representations in the works of Diamela Eltit, Alejandra Pizarnik, Luisa Valenzuela, Carmen Boullosa, Judith Ortiz Cofer, and Ana María Shua. The volume constitutes also a transatlantic dialogue with peninsular writers such as Nuria Amat. The anthology as a whole provides meaningful insights about the female body as the locus of violence and transgressions in the literature of Spanish America.

Ana Cruz García in her book *Re (de-) generando identidades: locura, feminidad y liberalización en Elena Garro, Susana Pagano, Ana Castillo y María Amparo Escandón* (*Re (de-) Generating Identities: Madness, Femininity, and Liberalization in Elena Garro, Susana Pagano, Ana Castillo and María Amparo Escandón*, 2009) provides a critical account of Mexicans and Chicanas writing on the madwoman (*la loca*) as a figure of rupture from traditional feminine roles, and her representation in the Mexican and Chicano narratives. Cruz García works with the concept of constructive insanity as a tool to provide a renovated power for agency. She concludes that in both Mexican and Chicano literature by women writers, the abject (Kristeva) and the *mestizo* (Anzaldúa) represent an intermediate state, and metaphorically, resistance to defining the feminine in absolute terms.

Introduction

A publication by Carmiña Navia Velasco, *Escritoras latinoamericanas: razón y locura* (*Latin American Women Writers: Reason and Unreason*, 2012), provides a panoramic view of narratives by Latin American women writers dealing with the subject of madness from the early 20th century to the first decade of the new millennium. Navia Velasco offers an overview of the existing bibliography on the subject that invites deeper textual analysis. An important contribution of this volume is that it reveals hidden voices and little known authors, pointing out connections between nations and periods through the analysis of common concerns and claims.

Another important study is Charlotte Rogers's *Jungle Fever: Exploring Madness and Medicine in Twentieth Century Tropical Narratives* (2012). Although this study deals with male authors, its in-depth analysis and argument are central to the debate on madness as a cultural construct in Latin America. Rogers explores five master narratives of Europe and Latin America: *Heart of Darkness* (1899) by Joseph Conrad, *La voie royale* (1930) by André Malraux, *La vorágine* (1924) by José Eustasio Rivera, *Canaima* (1935) by Rómulo Gallegos, and *Los pasos perdidos* (1953) by Alejo Carpentier. By comparing and contrasting the insanity of the protagonists derived from their experiences with the jungle and primitive world, the author concludes that "by erasing the neat, artificial barriers between reason and nonreason, these novels reveal that an uneasy coexistence between the rational and the irrational lies at the heart of existence" (28).

The particular historical, social and political circumstances of Latin America demand a careful reading of literary theories and cultural practices applied to its specificity. The present study aims to provide a balance of theories from the Anglo-European tradition and Latin American perspectives drawing attention to the region's own realities. Chilean theoretician Nelly Richard has defined the positionality of Latin America in the international scope as a "multi-temporal heterogeneity." The characteristics that best describe Latin America, according to Richard, are the "discontinuous state of a historic-social formation comprised of memories and segmented imaginaries, interwoven with tradition and progress, morality and telecommunication, folklore and commerce, myth and ideology, rite and simulacrum" ("Cultural Peripheries" 75).

Thus, the surge of postmodernism in Latin America allowed women access to the literary and artistic terrain, taking advantage of decentering cultural powers and recognition of the margins and "discourses of otherness." Richard argues:

Introduction

> Feminism and Latin America are categories relegitimized by the new movement towards the borders of the center. Both women and Third World are categories more spoken for by postmodernity, without obliging the cultural institution the right to speak, without ceding to them the much greater right to become autonomous subjects of enunciation, to assume a critical positionality itself capable of intervening in the rules of discourse that determine property and pertinence ["Cultural Peripheries" 160].

Following this line of thought, we have selected literary works by women authors who have written in the last decades of the 20th century and the beginning of the new millennium. The genres differ in nature and style, and it would be risky to categorize them under a single rubric. However, all of these works can be considered postmodern narratives dealing with women's roles in society, as well as sociopolitical issues inscribed in the historical period at the turn of the millennium. Therefore, women, madness, and Latin American literature will be addressed here in the context of the postmodern movement that characterized the late twentieth and early twenty-first centuries. The postmodern is understood as a period, as a movement and as a technique. We follow Nelly Richard's approach when she considers the crossovers between the postmodernism debate and feminism "not only as an exciting task, but as a necessary one for Latin America" (*Masculine and Feminine* 59). Among the fundamental themes addressed in the present volume are discussions of identity and power, historiographic discourse, metafictional narratives, self-referentiality and techniques such as pastiche, parody, irony, and mixing of genres and narrative devices.

The objective is to look at madness reflected in works of fiction by a selection of influential Latin American women writers. The selection covers a range of countries—Mexico, Chile, Colombia, Uruguay, Brazil, and Puerto Rico—thus providing a mapping of cultural production across the region. Most of the novels focus on historical events of political violence and repression that took place in their respective nations in the last three decades. Therefore, we study the spatial and temporal cartography of the region in which the topics of femininity and madness/insanity are constructed in the context of sociopolitical definitions.

Book Organization

This book is organized by the chronological order of the publications:

Introduction

The first chapter examines Cristina Peri Rossi's *La nave de los locos* (*Ship of Fools*, 1984). The novel establishes a dialogue between past and present in a postmodern narrative that denounces South American military regimes and challenges normative discourses and gender categories. *La nave de los locos* (1984) is a blank parody or a "pastiche" of the *Narrenshieff* (*Ship of Fools*), a poem by Sebastian Brant in 1494. The narration, divided into "journeys," tells a story focusing on topics that bring about a social or political commentary on a range of subjects. Peri Rossi plays with the constant reflection/re-inversion between reason and unreason to punctuate her critique. The analysis centers on the novel as a parable, which approaches the concept of madness in a symbolic form.

The second chapter considers Brazilian Lya Luft's 1987 novel *Exílio* (*The Red House*). Luft's lyrical novel portrays a space of physical and emotional crisis where the unnamed narrator/protagonist wrestles with the multiple interior, family, and societal pressures she must negotiate as a contemporary Brazilian woman. The Casa Vermelha (Red House) is a liminal place inhabited temporarily by a variety of marginal figures where the protagonist experiences emotional alienation as well as a life outside of the pressures of her contradictory female roles as selfless wife and mother, lover, and professional obstetrician. Luft asks readers to consider to what extent depression can be represented in literature by maintaining a tension between offering intimate access to the protagonist's ineffable emotional pain through spatial imagery (physical mutilation, decaying structures) on the one hand, and on the other, distancing the reader through fantastic uncertainty in a strategy that will be likened to Doris Sommer's particularist writing.

Chapter Three analyzes *El infarto del alma* (*Soul's Infarct*), a 1994 collaboration between two Chileans, writer Diamela Eltit and photographer Paz Errázuriz. Multiple, fragmented narrative voices accompany portraits of couples living within the marginal Philippe Pinel psychiatric hospital, alluding to a wider context of socioeconomic disparity and human rights violations in postdictatorial Chile. By juxtaposing clashing verbal and visual discourses of madness and love, the book creates a vantage point from which to contemplate the conflicting cultural meanings that play a role in how mental illnesses are understood, and forges a place in literature to highlight the voices and bonds between these silenced, isolated citizens.

In Chapter Four, Cristina Rivera Garza, a member of the new generation of Mexican writers, proposes an alternative view of madness in *Nadie me verá llorar* (*No One Will See Me Cry*, 1999). The chapter analyzes how the author uses the asylum to reveal another side of Mexican history at the turn of the 20th century. Parody, pastiche and fragmentation are presented through alternate narrative techniques that allow the reader to see into the complex dimensions of the so-called "mad," "criminal," and "excluded" in contemporary Latin American cities. A link between the photographic lens and madness is established in the novel as it opens with a question, "How does one come to be a photographer of crazy people?" Thereafter, repetitive questions of similar sort function as markers in spatial and temporal leaps throughout the narrative. Rivera Garza's novel conveys a compelling message corresponding with Foucault's concept of madness and confinement. In an era that witnessed the outbreak of a revolutionary struggle that took over one million lives, the demise of the 30-year-old dictatorship of Porfirio Díaz, and the rise of subsequent regimes that sought to rebuild the Mexican nation, the state saw the asylum as a strategic mechanism of segregation to protect society from the contagion of madness and vice. But without clear lines to distinguish madness and reason, such segregation was also an effective social control that facilitated the displacements of whomever was considered a threat to social order. Confinement was thus a way to exert control on potentially dangerous members of society.

Chapter Five focuses on *Delirio* (*Delirium*, 2004). In this novel, Laura Restrepo portrays a woman afflicted by mental illness whose power of sight allows allegorical representations of Colombia's multiple social and political realities. *Delirium* depicts the mental collapse of the main character, Augustina, triggered by the crisis of values of a country under siege by political violence, corruption, chaos and falsehoods at individual and collective levels. Laura Restrepo delivers a message that transcends the fine line of reason and unreason: the inscrutable chaos experienced by a country and a region living in a stage of hyperreality as a pathway to survive the horror of daily existence.

Chapter Six looks at how Puerto Rican American writer Irene Vilar explores the relationships between literary creation and consumption, mental illness, family relationships and gender roles, and politics in her memoirs *The Ladies' Gallery* (1996) and *Impossible Motherhood: Testimony of an Abortion Addict* (2009). Vilar's first memoir rewrites the clichés of the rebellious (but unintelligible) madwoman and of madness as a metaphor for sociopolitical oppression by appropriating literary discourse. She discusses the relationship between the neocolonial status of Puerto Rico and experiences of mental illness in her own life and the lives of her mother, Gladys Mirna Méndez Lebrón, and her maternal grandmother, Lolita Lebrón, an icon of Puerto Rican independence activism known for her participation in a 1954 attack on the U.S. House of Representatives. The second memoir refers constantly to the process of writing the first, highlighting its distortions and omissions as well as its usefulness in developing self-understanding and the ability to resist patterns of self-harm. *Impossible Motherhood* mixes the codes of Latin American testimonio and North American neoconfessional, disturbing genre expectations and defining a particularist (Sommer) space for representing the intersections of gender, mental health and illness, politics, and culture.

By examining women's narratives depicting madness in different regions in Latin America, we begin to map out the crossroads between the politics of power and gender relations that reflect women's positions at the turn of the millennium at the individual and collective levels. This is what we call a poetics of madness, the intersection of textual analyses to reflect the human condition through the dynamics of reason and unreason in a given historical period.

We hope that this book will contribute to the understanding of women writing in Latin America. Women have achieved recognition and a space beyond what many of their 19th- and 20th-century predecessors imagined. Today, in the midst of the third wave of feminism, the challenges are different but constant. The grounds provided by earlier feminists certainly contributed to the stage where women are writing now. As exponents of the turn-of-the-millennium intellectual community, we consider the influence of Western thought in the Latin American cultural scope to be especially relevant. Consequently, we intermingle theories from the North American and European traditions with Latin American perspectives. This is evident in the narratives and textual analysis that reflect the cultural *mestizaje* (mixed concepts and categories) from both sides of the cultural spectrum.

CHAPTER ONE

A Dialogical Journey

Cristina Peri Rossi's *La nave de los locos*

Elvira Sánchez-Blake

If to live is to navigate, the sea is the land of the sailor, and all beyond the sea is a shipwreck. (Cristina Peri Rossi, State of Exile, 2008)

La nave de los locos (*The Ship of Fools*, 1984) by Uruguayan writer and journalist Cristina Peri Rossi establishes a dialog between past and present in a compelling novel that denounces military regimes and challenges hegemonic discourses and gender categories. In this novel, the concept of madness is approached in symbolic form. The author uses a postmodern technique that parallels two discourses. The main text focuses on the story of the protagonist, Equis (named after the letter X, and thus known as Ecks in the English translation), in his erratic wandering around the world. The chapters are divided into journeys, dreams, journal entries and other discursive units characterized by disarticulation and discontinuity. The subtext is composed of descriptions of the 12th-century Tapestry of Creation interwoven into the main text, representing the symbolic order of the universe. Order and disorder thus are the powerful signifiers used by the author to illustrate and deconstruct relations of power and systems of domination. Peri Rossi uses madness as an allegory to denounce, critique and subvert the dominant social and political order that has ruled the world across time and space and to deconstruct rigid power relation structures. As a parable, *La nave* reenacts the variations of the "Ship of Fools" motif, playing with the constant reflection of reason and unreason in order to punctuate its critique.

The novel, written in 1984, has been widely analyzed by critics of all latitudes. It represented a rupture with the traditional narrative and feminist agenda focused on victimization. Peri Rossi's appropriation of postmodern techniques such as fragmentation, discontinuity, parody, language games, chronological jumps, pastiche, and ironic discourse complements a political strategy that deconstructs master narratives and renders multiple interpretations.

In this chapter I explore the concept of madness as a socio-political allegory to disarticulate the hermeneutics of the text: the intricate weaving of myths, parables, structures and enigmas posed by the author. I submit that Peri Rossi deconstructs dominating power relations, playing with the reflection between reason and unreason to expose the interstices of dictatorial political regimes, religious beliefs, and sexual norms centered on monolithic structures.

"How can we know where reason stops and madness begins, since both involve the pursuit of some form of reason?" asks Shoshana Felman (36). For Felman, madness as a symbol and an allegory is considered a phenomenon of thought, a philosophical sociological construct where "the question of madness is nothing less than the question of thought itself" (36). Felman's rhetorical approach takes the distinction between figures and tropes, metonymy and metaphor, literal and figural meaning, as its point of departure, only to deconstruct or subvert them at the end (27). According to Felman, madness as a signifier inquires not so much at the meaning of that signifier, as its power. "It asks not what it is (or what it signifies), but, what it does—what are the textual acts and speech events it activates and sets into motion" (32). In addition, Felman proposes a reading effect theory describing the role of the reader as an actor and lively participant in the reading process (31). This theory, according to Felman, "demonstrates the *transference effect* as the interpretant of the dynamic *place* of the addressee—the reader—insofar as the reader is himself 'sign of the sign,' sign of the text."

Madness works in *La nave* as the textual allegory to represent universal chaos. The author uses the tapestry of creation as a metaphor of the harmonic universe in opposition to Ecks's journeys symbolizing chaos, to reflect the tension between reason and unreason. Peri Rossi turns to schizophrenic textual[1] representations using ruptures, distortion and breakdowns in the chain of signifiers in a hermeneutic circle that transcends time and space. However, despite the apparent disconnection of meanings, in Peri Rossi every move has a purpose and every utterance creates new meanings, and even disconnected writing contains a powerful signification at the end. Following Felman, the concept of madness as a metaphor will be used in this analysis to connect and restore the chain of signifiers. In the process, the reader will be fully participative, as a player and contender in the dynamics of textual interpretation.

The Author

Born in Uruguay, Cristina Peri Rossi went into exile in 1972 after the military regime took over in her country. Since then, she has resided primarily in Barcelona, Spain, and a few other places in Europe. Her literary career can be divided roughly into two periods: work preceding exile and work following her life in Spain. Her obsession about politics and exile is present in most of her narratives and poetry, which reflects many of her own biographical experiences.[2]

Literary critics recognize Cristina Peri Rossi as a highly controversial writer with a non-linear, provocative, irreverent poetic and narrative discourse. *La nave de los locos*, the novel that made her work visible in academic circles and launched her as a canonical author, has been one of the most analyzed narratives in Latin American postmodern feminist criticism. The novel provides ample room for multiple interpretations by the challenges it poses to the reader. In addition, Peri Rossi's style is unique in its combination of the fantastic, the poetic, the political and the literary. She has both the political motivation and the inspiration to transform literary discourse from an irreverent and contestatary position. The fact that the author's writing poses a challenge to the reader and is considered somehow "inaccessible" to many people makes her literary work more appealing to critics and less recognized on the bestsellers lists.

Nevertheless, *La nave de los locos* has become a canonical postmodern novel that surfaces from time to time as the paradigmatic narrative containing political, feminist, psychoanalytical, allegorical, post-boom, exile and social issues, which makes it more provocative and contemporary for the 21st-century reader. When asked to identify her reading audience, Peri Rossi clearly expressed that she does not want just any reader, but rather, one who is competent enough to understand her work: "Cuando uno escribe se imagina un lector. El lector que yo imagino ha leído los mismos libros que yo, ha visto las mismas películas que yo, o sea, el lector es mi doble. Y a ese lector es al que me dirijo"³ [When I write I imagine a reader. The reader that I imagine has read the same books and has seen the same movies that I have. The reader is my double. And it is to this reader that I address my writing]. This declaration implies that her audience is not a large number of readers, but an intellectually select group. At the same time, she asserted that her writing poses an intellectual challenge in the form of a game inviting the reader to be a contender and participant in the reading process. The strategy to select her readers and to challenge them was also defined as part of her literary agenda: "La literatura es un juego. Si voy a transmitir alguna clase de conocimiento lo voy a transmitir jugando mejor que a través de un ensayo. Pero por otro lado, el juego es un placer y la literatura tiene la obligación de proporcionar placer al lector porque el lector que compra un libro lo hace para aprender gozando"⁴ [Literature is a game. If I am going to communicate some kind of knowledge I would rather transmit it by playing than through an essay. But on the other hand, playing is a pleasure and literature has the obligation to provide pleasure to the reader because the reader who buys a book expects to enjoy learning].

The Novel

La nave narrates the journey of Equis (Ecks) from an unknown place to a non-destination. The journey's metaphorical and real episodes include different periods and times through continuous references to the ship of fools motif and through the predominant visual and cinematic intertextuality. The most salient events focus on violence against women, presented first through the description of a paradigmatic scene from the film *Demon Seed*, in which the character played by actress Julie Christie is raped by an evil machine.⁵ This experience signals the beginning of Ecks's journey through the series of encounters with violence against women that will lead to his surrender of virility at the end. Ecks wanders around several places where he discovers multiple forms of oppression. In the process, he meets people fleeing military repression, social exclusion and political abuse. The main narrative alternates with a subtext that describes the tapestry of creation. The descriptions of each segment interact with the narrative sequence as a dialogic representation of harmony and chaos. At the end, Ecks is confronted by a perturbing recurrent dream that poses an enigma: "What is the greatest tribute a man can give to the woman he loves?" The climactic event of the novel, a sexual performance in which two strippers reenact scenes from various Nazi-theme films, reveals the answer to the enigma. The revelation is the surrender of virility, allegorized by the fall of the King. The enigma's answer discloses the novel's pivotal message, the dismantling of phallocentric power structures that have ruled the world for centuries, in which the dynamics of reason and unreason are at play.

The novel, defined by Jeanne Marie Vaughn as "the site of a playful intertextuality, a piecing together of opposing and contradictory elements, which the reader is invited to decipher" (371), can be read as a literary game. Indeed, *La nave de los locos* constitutes a chess game, where characters represent the pieces, the board is the tapestry of creation, each journey is a move, dreams pose strategic challenges, and the final enigma is nothing more than the climactic checkmate. The king who falls at the end couldn't be more illustrative of this parodic interplay of symbols and representations. In an attempt to decipher the clues posed by the narration, I will now play the role of the contender by analyzing the main elements of the novel: the intertextualities in connection with the ship of fools motif, the tapestry of creation, and the cinematic visual representations conveyed in the final scene.

The Game

The first journey opens up with a dream that unravels the first clue of the novel: "¿Cómo debo distinguir lo significante de lo insignificante?" (*La nave* 9) [How shall I know what is meaningful from what is not? (*The Ship* 1)]. How do you separate the grain from the chaff in a field of wheat? This question presents the first challenge to the reader: to winnow the wheat from the chaff as he/she navigates through the text. Having to discern between the significant and insignificant throughout the narration is equivalent to choosing the right pieces on the game board and planning the game moves. In the second journey, lost among the description of travel on a ship, the chess game makes its first appearance:

> La bella pasajera se acercó y mirándolo tranquilamente con sus grandes ojos verdes, le dijo:—Lo desafío a una partida de ajedrez. [...] Ella distribuyó las fichas con soltura. "He perdido," pensó él, enseguida. Todavía no había dispuesto las piezas en el tablero, pero ya no tenía posibilidades de triunfo. Con un sentimiento íntimo de derrota, colocó la hilera de desventurados peones que pronto iban a desertar. Ella tenía unos alfiles delicados, unos bronceados caballos que se movían con seguridad e

inteligencia en el tablero. "Perderé," pensó. "Ya he perdido" [*La nave* 15–16].

The Beautiful Passenger came towards him, fixing him coolly with her large green eyes. "Chess?" she said. [...] She distributed the pieces with assurance. Right away he knew, "I've lost." The game had not yet been set up, but already he seemed to have no chance. With a keen sense of impending failure, he set out his line of luckless pawns who would soon desert him. Hers were fine bishops and bronze knights who moved with strength and purpose over the board. "I shall lose," he thought. "I've already lost" [*The Ship* 8–9].

The scene represents the setting of a game board, the distribution of pieces, and the anticipation of defeat. In the next section, "El viaje leído" (The Already-Read Journey), the reader faces another challenge: the sunken city in the ocean. In this scene, a little boy demands his father take him to the street. The father looks through the ship into the vast ocean and tells his son that at the bottom of the ocean a city is submerged: "Pero hay que saber mirarla porque está escondida" (*La nave* 18) ["But you have to know how to look, for it's well hidden" (*The Ship* 11)], says the father. The boy searches in his pocket for a piece of blue glass given to him, and answers: "Me parece que con estos lentes voy a poder verla" (*La nave* 18) ["I think I will be able to see it with this" (*The Ship* 11)]. This passage reveals another fundamental clue in the novel: the importance of vision and the ability to look beneath surfaces. On another level, the submerged city anticipates the coexistence of two parallel worlds: the included and excluded, a theme developed across the narrative. These three elements—the first dream, the game and the visual component—set the tone of the novel as it unfolds in a convergence of signifiers and signifieds.

Intertextuality

Peri Rossi uses the articulation of intertextualities in the novel to shed and reveal multiples layers of interpretations. As the novel progresses, a mixture of visual, literary, religious, scientific, philosophical, psychoanalytic and mythical discourses creates an interconnected play of meanings (Vaughn 371). The array of intertextual references includes ancient texts and contemporary literary works. The references to works of art are also significant in a blend of classic, modern and postmodern universal works. The same is true for old and contemporary films, essential to understanding the novel. An interesting strategy is the mimicry the author makes in distorting titles and references of well known texts and works of art: "*El jardín de los anhelos que se bifurcan*, by George Lewis Borges, *El fuego fatuo* by Dieu la Rochelle, *Las hortensias*, by Felisberto Hernández, *La muerte de un jugador de ajedrez chino* by Akira Kusawatta, and *Mujeres y utopías* by César Moro" (*La nave* 40–42).[6] This deliberate distortion of names and titles is part of Peri Rossi's strategy to confuse readers and test their literary competence. For instance, the title of *Jorge Luis* Borges's short story, "El jardín de los *senderos* que se bifurcan" ("The Garden of Forking Paths," 1944), or the celebrated humanist work by Thomas More (Tomás Moro), *Utopia* (1516), are obvious plays on words recognizable by any moderately educated reader. In several instances, the narrator directly addresses the reader, asking him/her to play an entertaining game of identifying the cities, artistic pieces and other elements in the novel, a technique that evidences the intention of making the reader a participative player.

Through this playful game of meanings, the narrative discloses the enigma posed in the first dream: to distinguish the chaff from the wheat, the significant from the insignificant. In the process, the reader becomes a traveler as he/she navigates through the intertextual collection of references in a dialogical journey across time and space. Along with its role as contender in the narrative game, in this journey the ship of fools motif is, I would argue, the most significant intertextual reference that merits closer attention.

Ship of Fools

The ship of fools is a recurrent trope that travels throughout different periods and places to showcase the incongruity of human actions across history's critical periods. In its multiple versions, both motifs—the journey and madness—are interrelated subjects that play along in this dynamic of allegoric representations. Michel Foucault in the first chapter of *History of Madness* describes how in medieval times, the mad were segregated from society by sending them away in boats without a destination. Foucault explains how many writers and artists, including Sebastian Brant, Hieronymus Bosch and Brueghel, based artistic works on the imagery of these ships. For Foucault, the symbolic meaning of these voyages has been rooted in Western culture with motifs from the 15th century: the *Dance of Death* in the Innocents cemetery in Paris (1460), Guyot Marchand's

Dance Macabre (1485), Brant's *Das Narrenschiff* (1494), Bosch's paintings (1500) and Erasmus of Rotterdam's *Praise of Folly* (1509) (*History of Madness* 14). These literary and iconographic representations of madness seemed to reflect that "for many of the fifteenth century, the fearsome freedom of dreams and the fantasies born of madness held a power of attraction stronger than the pull of the desires of mortal flesh" (*History of Madness* 18).

At the core of the various ship of fools versions is the reflection of actions by individuals portraying socially accepted norms and behaviors that ultimately display society's madness. From Sebastian Brant's poem in 1494 through the 21st century, poems, paintings, musical pieces, theater, films and novels have depicted the insanity of society's cultural and political concerns of the times.[7] Curiously, most (or all) of these works do not reflect the insanity of excluded individuals but the foolishness of society as a whole of the so-called sane and rational. At the same time, these works (whether literary or artistic) operate as mirrors by allowing readers and audiences to reflect on the absurdity and ridiculousness of their actions. If Brant's satiric poem *Das Narrenshieff* depicted and criticized medieval European's political and religious practices, Bosch in his painting *The Ship of Fools* represented the Renaissance conflict between psyche and soul. In 20th-century representations, Katherine Anne Porter's novel and film denounce the political maneuvers that preceded World War II and the Holocaust. By the same token, Peri Rossi's *La nave de los locos* reflects political upheavals of the late 20th century: dictatorship, oppression, and ancient social practices that constrained the development of sane human beings. The analysis of different versions of the ship of fools through history allows us as readers to revisit the myth and development of the topos that inspired Peri Rossi's novel, and the dialogue she establishes with the theme and its multiple interpretations.

Brant's original poem, written in 1494, consists of the description of several shipments of fools[8] to Narragonia (Land of Fools). Each poem is devoted to a sin or vice, accompanied by a finely detailed woodcut that gives either a literal or allegorical interpretation of that particular behavior. Some of them are arrogance toward god, marrying for money, jealous husbands, gluttons and drunkards, false churchgoers and corrupt clerics and lawyers. Toward the end of Brant's poem, an entire chapter is devoted to the apocalyptic theme of the Antichrist; a terrible storm carries away the ship of fools on a senseless course identical to the end of the world.

Sebastian Brant was considered one of the greatest evangelists and reformers of medieval Europe. "He was a reformer from within, a biting unsparing exposer of every priestly abuse, but a loyal son of the church" (Brant, *The Ship of Fools* xii). The theme of the book expresses the awareness of the German Catholic humanist, who reflected the conflictive transition between the Middle Ages and the Renaissance in which the spirit of the Reform was taking place. In this context, *The Ship of Fools* acts as a metaphor for the European social and religious crises of the times.

The medieval depiction in Brant's satirical poem is replicated in Peri Rossi's *Ship of Fools* in many ways. She draws from 13th-century artistic inconography to recreate the "dreams and fantasies" associated with madness and to reflect their meanings in 20th-century imagery. The cosmological, sacred figures in dreams, voyages, and intertexts across the novel provide clues for interpretations associated with medieval symbolism. According to Stephen M. Hart, Peri Rossi shares with Brant the use of visual and textual metaphors to exemplify the follies of humankind. For instance, the woodcuts that illustrate each poem in Brant's work correspond to Peri Rossi's enactment of the Tapestry of Creation. For Hart, "Peri Rossi's allusion to Brant's self-professed aim of debunking the folly, blindness, error and stupidity of all stations and kinds of men, is thus refocused *feminocentrically* since her novel strives to deconstruct the patriarchal notion of Godhead, which itself is the 'madness' of the world" (emphasis added, Hart 126). The focus on feminine and gender-related issues certainly distinguishes Peri Rossi's work from the other versions of the subject and is its most prominent contribution to the ship of fools motif.

Katherine Anne Porter's novel *Ship of Fools* (1962) and the corresponding movie provided the setting that likely inspired Peri Rossi's narrative. In the novel and subsequent film (produced by Stanley Kramer, 1965) a German passenger vessel departs from Veracruz, Mexico, transporting a cargo of mainly German tourists to the city of Bremerhaven, Germany, in 1933. The characters, carefully detailed in the novel through dialogue and actions, reflect the class, racial, and sexual prejudices and conflicts that preceded the Nazi uprising and the Second World War. According to the *New York Times* review, "The movie is symbolic of the passage of the foolish humanity into the maw of Nazism [...] and it may even be symbolic of the eternal folly and helplessness of man" (Crowther n.p.). Both the prize-winning novel and the movie had significant repercussions for 1960s and 70s audiences and evidently for Peri Rossi, who establishes the connection to her text. In the first scene of the movie, Karl Glacoux, a dwarf who acts as the narrator, addresses the audience to introduce the ship, stating: "If you look carefully enough you may find yourselves in it." Correspondingly, Peri Rossi in the first journey invites the reader to distinguish what is meaningful from what is not by separating the wheat from the chaff. In addition, the protagonist of the movie, Karl Glacoux, finds his counterpart in the character Glaucus Torrender, described in Journey VIII: "Glaucus[9] no era un loco común. Extremadamente inteligente y despierto, agudo, muy observador" (*La nave* 50) ["Glaucus was not an ordinary madman. Intelligent, alert and perceptive" (*The Ship* 47)]. He befriends the ship master, Artemius Gudröm. They were good friends "como lo pueden ser un hombre medio loco que parece cuerdo y un hombre medio cuerdo que parece loco" (*La nave* 51) ["as much as a half-madman, seemingly sane, and a half-sane man, seemingly mad, can ever be" (*The Ship* 47)]. Glaucus is the only one of the supposedly insane passengers who follows the sailors when they are asked to leave the boat and swim to the coast. However, he drowns himself before reaching the shore. Glaucus's story illustrates the liminal border between the sane and insane that persists throughout the rest of the narration. In addition, some critics have compared the Ecks character with the role that Glaucus plays in the legend, adding another layer of signification.[10]

La nave also uses Porter's narrative to set the tone for the novel. In Journey II, "El viaje," Peri Rossi describes the ship's passengers and the pastimes on board. One of the characters, La bella pasajera, "the beautiful passenger of green eyes," for instance, could be a reference to Vivian Leigh's character who plays Mary Treadwell in the movie. Similarly, the description of the ship as "el viaje leído" or "the already-read-journey"[11] is probably directed towards Porter's book. The anaphora, "el viaje leído," acts as the clue directing the reader to Porter's novel with obvious references to scenes and events, including the description of the ship, the relationship among characters, the night dances, and the rituals and codes that rule life on board.

The Ship of Fools by Porter, according to Pilar Rotella, "is still the universal ship of generalized human folly with all of us as passengers, exiled and drifting, searching for a safe harbour nowhere to be found; on the other hand, it becomes a very particularized expression of our human tendency to establish distinctions based on control and submission, conformity and non-conformity, homogeneity and difference, victimizers and victims" (259). The objective of presenting passengers stripped of their pretenses to expose their true characters resonates in Peri Rossi's novel. In *La nave* the message is extended to expose and mirror individuals and society of the late 20th century for what they really were. In this regard, the novel follows the movie's final question expressed by Karl Glaucox, "What has all of this to do with us?"

Spanish versions of the ship of fools by Pío Baroja (1925) and Colombian Pedro Gómez Valderrama (1984) are not prominently referenced in Peri Rossi's novel but are worth mentioning. Pío Baroja's "La nave de los locos" is a novella among a collection entitled "Memorias de un hombre de acción" (Memories by a Man of Action), written with the objective of contesting José Ortega y Gasset's ideas about what the novel as a genre should be.[12] The story narrates the travels of a Spanish soldier returning to his homeland after the Carlist wars, describing it as a ruined land. An interesting element of Baroja's account is his feminization of "madness" when he describes Spain:

> La dama locura se paseaba por los rincones de España [...] pero no era una mujer fina y sonriente, graciosa y amable [...] sino una mujerona bestial que negra de humo y de pólvora, borracha de maldad y de lujuria, iba quemando casas, fusilando gente, violando y quemando [213].
>
> Lady madness was walking over all corners of Spain [...] but she was not a fine and smiling, gracious and kind woman [...] but a big bestial woman, black with smoke and gunpowder, drunk with evil and lust, who was going around burning houses, shooting people, raping and burning.

Peri Rossi fundamentally contrasts with Pío Baroja by turning madness into a masculine domain. As noted by Hart, "while Pío Baroja uses the life-as-a-madhouse theme to suggest that madness is female [...] Peri Rossi uses the same *topos* to undermine the phallocentric myth of creation" (126). The phallus as symbol of power and domination is in Peri Rossi's view the source of irrationality that dominates the world.

Gómez Valderrama's text is the title of a collection of short stories published in 1984, the same year as Peri Rossi's novel. The story that corresponds to the title *La nave de los locos* describes the trajectory of a ship that travels through the diverse geographies of Europe and America, and in different temporalities from the Middle Ages to contemporary times. The journey finally ends in Bogotá, where the ship is turned into an official vehicle from La Secretaría de Salud (Health Department) transporting "locos," the common term for homeless and beggars in Bogotá, to abandon them to their fate on a random street. The most remarkable issue in this story is that by the time it was written, it was common practice to collect homeless and *"loquitos"* from the streets of Bogotá and other populous cities in Colombia to abandon them in deserted places where they would probably die of starvation.[13] This practice was a way of "cleansing" the cities, especially in advance of big events and visits from foreign dignitaries. Gómez Valderrama delivers his critique by adapting the ship of fools theme to new forms of social exclusion in the 20th century. In this way, both authors, Peri Rossi and Gómez Valderrama, convey the ship of fools motif to deliver similar messages using madness as a contemporary allegory of power and exclusion.

Variations on the ship of fools converge in *La nave de los locos* by Peri Rossi through the use of different elements of previous versions and by contesting, parodying and establishing a dialogue with this motif across time and space. Iconographic symbolism taken from Brant, characters and setting from Porter, descriptions of artistic works from Bosch, Brueghel and Jan Balet, and the motif as a whole from the medieval tradition discussed by Foucault are essential to understanding the novel. *La nave de los locos* by Peri Rossi represents the practices of modern societies that exclude and exterminate those whose behavior is seen as deviant from the norm. As noted by Invernizzi Santa Cruz, "*La Nave* becomes the bus transporting pregnant women to have an abortion in London [...] and the load of four hundred pregnant Jewish women to the experimental laboratories of Boyer in Nazi Germany, or in the Cement factory, where the disappeared are transported to planes from where they would be dropped in the sea" (35). Ultimately, the ship reflects Peri Rossi's own experience when she left Uruguay in 1972, summarized in her poem entitled "The First Journey":

> My first journey
> was into exile
> fifteen days at sea
> without landing
> the constant sea
> the ancient sea
> the sea, sickness
>
> Fifteen days of sea
> and uncertainty
> not knowing where I was going
> not knowing destiny's port
> knowing only what I'd left...
>
> To depart
> is always to split apart [*State of Exile* 99–103].

State of Exile, the translated title of the poem collection that Peri Rossi wrote during her years of transit around cities in Europe until she finally settled down in Barcelona, reflects the author's interior process of feeling excluded, expatriated and out of place, embodied in the character of Ecks.

Madness and Exclusions

Exile has been a constant theme in Peri Rossi's prose and poetic production. In the prologue to *State of Exile*, she writes: "If exile were not a terrible human experience, it would be a literary genre" (xxiii). Indeed, Peri Rossi turned exile into a literary genre. By explaining the etymology of the word, she condensed the ulterior motivations that underlie her writing: "'ex' signifies precisely 'one who no longer is,' 'one who has stopped being'; that is to say: 'one who has lost all or part of her or his identity'" (*State of Exile* xxiii). Madness and exile intersect with the subject of exclusion and its variants in the character of Ecks and in the meaning of his name, the letter "X," "ex": *extranjero* (foreigner), excluded, expatriate, one who has lost his identity, "the absence of nomination" (Dejborn 142). As the protagonist of the novel *Exílio* analyzed in the second chapter demonstrates, the connection of madness and exile is a constant in the literature of late 20th-century Latin America. In *La nave* the first reference to being a "stranger" appears in Journey II: "Extranjero. Ex. Extrañamiento. Fuera de las entrañas de la tierra. Desentrañado: vuelto a parir. No angustiarás al extranjero" (*La nave* 10) ["A stranger. Ecks. Estranged. Expelled from the womb of earth. Eviscerated: once more to give birth. *Thou shalt not oppress a stranger*" (emphasis in the original, *The Ship* 2)]. Madness appears embedded in the condition of being a stranger/foreigner[14] in Journey IV when Ecks meets a woman in one of his travels. He invites her to have coffee under the pretext that she resembles someone he had met long ago. The woman immediately considers him a "crazy man" after she asks him if he is a foreigner (extranjero) and he answers, "Sólo en algunos países [...] y posiblemente no lo seré toda la vida" (*La nave* 29) ["Only in some countries [...] and hopefully, I will not be one forever" (*The Ship* 24)]. The association of madness with the condition of being an "extranjero" is then reinforced by Ecks's statement, "No nací extranjero [...]. Es una condición que he adquirido con el tiempo y no por voluntad propia. Usted misma podría llegar a serlo si se lo propusiera, aunque no se lo aconsejo. Por lo menos, no de una manera definitiva" (*La nave* 29) ["I was not born a foreigner [...]. It is a condition one acquires through force of circumstances. You could become one too, if you chose, though I don't advise it. Not on a permanent basis" (*The Ship* 24)]. As the dialogue in this scene progresses, the ambivalence of Ecks being mad and a foreigner is underlined by the confusion of the interlocutor. Her internal voice declares Ecks insane, and she realizes the peril of talking to him. His soliloquy about being a "foreigner" accentuates his apparent madness, finally leading the woman to flee from the scene.

Madness and exclusion are thus at the core of the ship of fools tradition. In Peri Rossi both themes are reflected in the allegory that transcends the storyline in multiple representations. Like a voyager on the ship of fools, Ecks wanders from place to place, some of which are dreams or readings, and tells what he encounters along the way. But Ecks is not the only passenger. Vercingetórix, a reference to the Gallic warrior and most recently, to the popular comic strip character, is an ex-convict and political exile. Morris, an "ex-céntrico" (eccentric), falls in love with a nine-year-old boy, Perceval. Perceval seems to have exiled himself from contemporary times since he wants to be the medieval knight after whom he was named. Gordon is "exiled from the moon," an astronaut adrift in the nostalgic obsession with his only journey to the moon. Female characters are also excluded in various ways, but their portrayal in the narrative is more related to exclusion due to violence and marginalization. All characters are travelers on the ship of fools, condemned to wander and be "excluded" by social norms. They accept their condition as Ecks confirms it: "Todos somos exiliados de algo o de alguien [...]. En realidad, ésa es la verdadera condición del hombre" (*La nave* 106) ["We are all exiled from something or from someone [...]. It is man's true condition" (*The Ship* 106)].

According to Carmen Domínguez, the novel's characters are in a state of perpetual escape because of the impossibility of landing at a destination: "They are both voluntary and involuntary travelers; involuntary, since they are forced by marginalization and expulsion into the ship of fools, but also, voluntary given that they are fleeing from exclusion, injustice and sexism in search of an harmony impossible to find" (161). Finally, on the ship of fools, the exiled and the mad are interconnected because both are physically isolated, both experience a rupture with language and a rupture with society. They are excluded and judged as estranged and "different." As Bridget Vera Franco notes, the line "*Vegno del loco ove tornar disio*" (*La nave* 115) plays with the double meaning of "loco" in Latin: physical place (locus-location) and "loco," the word for "mad" in Spanish (31). She explains, "the obsessive desire to return, impossible to achieve, ends up in madness for the exiled who does not find a way to renegotiate his identity" (31). In sum, the series of external and internal journeys and displacements along and across the narrative builds layers of discursive units in a chain of signifiers inscribing a fluid system of madness and exclusion.

The Tapestry

The segments of the 12th-century Tapestry of Creation from the Cathedral of Girona (Catalonia, Spain) act as a contrasting discourse to the sequence of journeys narrated in the main text. The meticulous description of each one of the figures in the tapestry is one of the powerful signifiers used by the author to illustrate and deconstruct dominant patriarchal order. The tapestry represents a religious hierarchy, which concentrically orders the elements of the world around the supreme Christian creator, the Pantocrator.[15] The tapestry is described as a metaphor of the universe:

> En el tapiz [...] todo en él está dispuesto para que el hombre se sienta en perfecta armonía, consustanciado, integrado al universo. [...] Todo en el tapiz responde a la intención de que el hombre que mira—espejo del hombre representado con hilos de colores—participe de la creación. [...] En telas así sería posible vivir toda la vida, en medio de un discurso perfectamente inteligible, de cuyo sentido no se podría dudar porque es una metáfora donde todo el universo está encerrado [*La nave* 20–21].
>
> Everything is so arranged that man can feel in harmony with the design, become part of its embroidered universe. [...] The observer—mirroring the man portrayed in threads of many colours—is invited to take his part in the creation. [...] Immersed in such art one could live one's life, engaged in a perfectly rational discourse whose meaning cannot be questioned because it resides in an image containing the whole universe [*The Ship* 13–14].

The tapestry as a metaphor for the universe functions as the ideal, harmonic utopia that mirrors the spectator. Indeed, as the narrative progresses, the mirror technique constitutes a powerful tool where the reader sees his/her own reflection by identifying with the elements presented by the text. According to Jeanne Vaughn, through the tapestry, the text demonstrates that violence is inherent in hierarchical oppositions, and the reader is told that "cualquier armonía supone la destrucción total de los elementos que se le oponen" (*La nave* 20). The comment is a stark contrast to the ordered, rational, reasonable world represented by the tapestry in the main body of the text—that of a totalizing metaphor that is also "a reality"—a one to one correspondence between signifier and signified [267].

The tapestry as the universal metaphor is at the center of the enigma posed by the text. As Vaughn notes, "the metaphor of the tapestry, which places God at the center of creation, is the same metaphor as the (male) subject of humanism, which is the same metaphor as the transcendental signifier of Lacan" (251).

The tapestry constitutes the textual strategy that mirrors the journeys' narratives.[16] In opposition to the tapestry's harmonic unity, the dreams and journeys represent the chaos and disorder of external reality. Ecks is caught between order and disorder, reason and unreason as he mirrors both discourses through the textual mirror. By the same token, the reader as player and textual participant must depart from the tapestry's metaphor in order to cross external reality—the journeys—to arrive at a greater metaphor that analyzes this reality by giving order to it (Olivera-Williams). This organization occurs in the "bastidor de la mente" (the framework of the imagination) where Ecks (and the reader) must find meaning among the chaotic universe.

The description of each segment of the tapestry parallels the series of events within the main text and can be read in opposition to or as a reflection of each one.[17] For instance, the birth of Eve from Adam's rib in the tapestry precedes the section called Eve, which discloses the multiple oppressions suffered by women in consecutive chapters. This is reflected through the sequence of Eve's confessions, newspaper excerpts and school children's homework describing Eve. The following chapters describe historical accounts of physical abuse of women such as the London abortion clinic, Boyer's experiments with pregnant Jews, Eastern infibulation practices and battered prostitutes.

Paradoxically, the descriptive segments of the harmonic unitary world represented in the tapestry are scattered and fragmented throughout the novel, while the narrative segments—the journeys—are organized in sections that can be read as whole units separated from each other. As the text progresses, while the tapestry gets its final dissolution in very fragmented sections, the journeys and dreams converge into a final scene integrating all elements presented in the narrative. At this point the reader—who has overcome the challenges of the game—is ready for the final move: the enigma, the point where all elements come together: signifier and signifieds, myths, parables, intertextualities and the final message of the novel.

The Enigma

At the end of the novel, Peri Rossi unravels the clue of the enigma posed by Ecks's recurrent dream:

> En el sueño, había una pregunta que flotaba como un enigma, como aquellos acertijos que los reyes enamorados de sus hijas proponían a los pretendientes. [...] En el sueño, Equis escuchaba la pregunta: *"¿Cuál es el mayor tributo, el homenaje que un hombre puede ofrecer a la mujer que ama?"* [emphasis in the original, *La nave* 183].
>
> In the dream there was a question. It hung like an enigma, like one of these riddles which kings in love with their daughters used to set for their suitors. [...] In the dream Ecks heard the question: *¿What is the greatest tribute and homage a man can give to the woman he loves?* [*The Ship* 188].

The enigma is accentuated by the suspense and hesitation experienced by Ecks in the process of solving the riddle. The narrative technique clearly emulates the chess game strategy posed to a player in the final move: "¡Qué proposición tan difícil! En el sueño estoy confundido, vacilo, atolondrado y torpe. Sólo me queda una oportunidad y no alcanzo a acertar la solución" (*La nave* 196) ["It is a difficult question; in the dream I am confused, bewildered, slow; I hesitate. I have only one chance to give my answer, and I can't find it" (*The Ship* 203)].

The climactic scene of the novel describes a performance by two strippers interpreting Marlene Dietrich and Dolores del Río. One of them is Lucía, a woman who Ecks had previously met in a journey to the abortion clinic in London. After tracing her steps, he finds her again engaged in the powerful spectacle.

> Lucía vestida de varón, con chistera sobre sus cortos cabellos rubios [...] imitando a Charlotte Rampling en *Portero de noche,* quien imitaba a Helmut Berger en *La caída de los Dioses,* quien imitaba a Marlene Dietrich en el *Ángel azul.* Siendo entonces Marlene Dietritch el origen y desenlace de toda simulación [*La nave* 191].

> Lucía was wearing a top hat over her short blond hair. [...] She looked like Charlotte Rampling in *The Night Porter*, imitating Helmut Berger in *Twilight of the Gods*,[18] who was imitating Marlene Dietrich in *The Blue Angel*. She was Marlene Dietrich, the beginning and the end of all imitations [*The Ship* 197].

The provocative dance between the cross-dressed women in front of a masculine audience prompts Ecks's solution to the enigma posed in his recurrent dream. This climactic scene reflects, in turn, the enigma posed by the author to the reader. However, this final scene cannot be deciphered to its full potential without first elucidating the cinematic intertextualities.

Cinematic Intertextuality

Peri Rossi uses several movies throughout the novel to represent erotic violence directed at the feminine body, to subvert gender roles, and to reverse the gaze to the spectator. The novel cites several films, such as the previously discussed *Demon Seed* directed by Donald Cammell (1977), *The Blue Angel* by Josef von Stenberg (1930), *The Damned* by Luchino Visconti (1969) and *Night Porter* by Liliana Cavani (1973).

The oldest film presented in the novel and the one that contains the first layer of signification is *The Blue Angel* (1930). In this movie, Marlene Dietrich plays Lola, the role that launched her career as a sexual icon. Lola is a performer for a cabaret dressed in provocative cross-gender attire. Her singing and dancing act drives both women and men crazy. The presence of the top hat, which symbolizes power and masculinity, is at the center of the performative act and the movie plot. The professor who falls madly in love with her, leaving his career and social position, also loses his hat when he falls from grace. He ends up committing suicide, defeated in his masculinity just as the king of the novel's enigma.

Marlene Dietrich's dancing scene in *The Blue Angel* is recreated in the film *The Night Porter*. The movie is about a sadomasochistic relationship taken up fifteen years after World War II by a former SS concentration camp officer, Roger, and the inmate, Lucia, whom he raped and dominated when she was a young girl. The movie revolves around the psychological implications of shared guilt and the identification of the slave with the master. In an iconic scene, Charlotte Rampling, who plays the role of Lucia, sings Marlene Dietrich's "Wenn ich mir was wünschen dürfte" to the concentration camp guards while wearing pieces of a Nazi uniform, including the same top hat worn by Lola in *The Blue Angel*. This scene connects with many of Peri Rossi's themes: Lucia is the name of the protagonist and might be the source of inspiration for Peri Rossi's emblematic character. The act displays the half-naked body of the female protagonist dressed in an SS military uniform and a top hat, just as Lucia's attire is described in the novel. Furthermore, the masculine gaze is at the center of the plot as the prisoners watch the cross-dressed female body clad in Nazi symbols.

In *La caída de los dioses* (*The Damned*), Lola's performance is once more depicted in a different fashion. The film is a parody of order/disorder, dismantling the idea of Nazis as supreme holders of the sublime cosmic race. In another parodic scene, the protagonist, Martin (Helmet Berger) emulates Marlene Dietrich in *The Blue Angel*. The performance of the central male character further erotizes Lola's act through exaggerated dressing, makeup and sensual movements. The top hat is once more a central piece in the transvestite scene and the song from the original *Blue Angel* movie is performed in a sensual masculine voice. By unveiling the multiple layers behind the central performative scene, in which several signifiers intersect—the dynamics of power relations, gender, violence and performance—the reader is prepared for the checkmate.

Checkmate

Ecks finds the answer to the riddle by watching the dancing act that parodies the series of films previously described. Ecks's voyeuristic approach allows the reader to see in detail the scene where two dancers impersonating Marlene Dietrich and Dolores del Río carry out their sexually charged performance. The act is extremely powerful as the performers are not who they represent, and neither one belongs to a gender per se: "alguien que se había decidido a ser quien quería ser y no quien estaba determinado a ser" (*La nave* 191) [someone who had decided to be what s/he wanted to be, and now what s/he was programmed to be (*The Ship* 198)]. After witnessing the performance, Ecks is able to solve the enigma when he watches Lucía's androgyn figure:

> Descubría y se desarrollaba ante él, en todo su esplendor, dos mundos simultáneos, dos llamadas distintas, dos mensajes, dos indumentarias, dos percepciones, dos discursos, pero indisolublemente ligados, de modo que el predominio de uno hubiera provocado la extinción de los dos [*La nave* 195].

> He saw the unfolding of two parallel worlds in all their splendor; two different calls, two messages, two appearances, two languages, yet inseparably connected in such a way that the triumph of one would cause the death of both [*The Ship* 202].

By observing the performance, Lucía's androgynous countenance, and the overpowering genderless ambiguity, Ecks finds the answer to the enigma: "El tributo mayor, el homenaje que un hombre puede hacer a la mujer que ama, es su virilidad" (*La nave* 196) ["The greatest tribute a man can give to a woman he loves is virility" (*The Ship* 204)].

> "La virilidad," repite Equis. Súbitamente disminuido, el rey como un caballito de juguete, el rey como un muñequito de pasta, el reyecito de chocolate cae de bruces, vencido el reyecito se hunde en el barro, el reyecito, derrotado, desaparece. Gime antes de morir [*La nave* 197].
>
> "Virility," repeats Ecks; and the king shrinks, is now no bigger that a toy, a paper maché puppet, a chocolate king; and he falls to the ground, blends with the mud; overcome, beaten, the poor little king disappears. He dies with a whimper [*The Ship* 204].

The revelation of the enigma is the text's final move—the checkmate—the fall of Western patriarchal order: the Christian Pantocrator, the psychoanalytical Oedipus Rex, the semiological Lacan's phallus as the main signifier. The revelation of the enigma deconstructs power structures and domination reflected in masculine power symbolisms. The fallen king refers to the absurdity of dictatorial political regimes (ruled by repression and torture). It also denotes religious beliefs based on monolithic structures, and systems of thought grounded on fixed gender categories. Ecks's revelation of the enigma is the novel's most analyzed passage, signaling dynamic reader participation as an active agent in the process of reading. Not only is Ecks pressed to decipher the riddle, but the reader, too, is forced to interpret it in order to understand the text.

From a gender perspective, critics such as Gema Pérez-Sánchez offer an interpretation following Judith Butler's deconstruction of gender categories and performance. She contends that "the repetition and layered citation of multiple gender positions—Lucía as Charlotte Rampling as Helmut Berger as Marlene Dietrich—empties gender difference of any signification, rendering it inoperable, exposing its discursive construction" (136). According to Pérez-Sánchez, the enigma riddle is solved by Ecks because the act of watching this parodic, theatrical impersonation of how sexual difference and heterosexuality are constructed through iterative, regulatory norms teaches Equis Peri Rossi's radical, feminist lesson. [...] In an ironic twist of the workings of the male gaze, through watching a pornographic routine, Equis will be liberated of the oppression of dictated gender roles [136].

Ecks learns the lesson initiated by watching Julie Christie's rape by a phallic machine in *The Demon Seed*. His voyeuristic and scopophilic tendencies change after learning about the different forms of violence against women. By renouncing the phallocentric concept of virility, Ecks proposes a new model of the masculine subject, one that renounces power and offers a new form of love, "de igual a igual" (equal to equal) (Dejbord 167). The reference to Adam's search for his "semejante" (likeness) in the tapestry comes true in this segment. Ecks's quest ends when he renounces the power of the phallus and learns that real power lies in erasing differences and exclusions.[19] As Mary Beth Tierney-Tello points out:

> Ecks's quest represents "a utopian search for difference without violence, difference without exclusion or suppression, difference without sacrificing the other. In short, a new dream of symmetry, contrary to the "old dream" of the patriarchal sexual economy documented by Freud, [...] and contrary to the "old dream" the military regimes of the world attempt to install, persecuting all those who might threaten the homogeneity of the sociopolitical and cultural orders [184].

In short, harmony as in the tapestry of creation can be achieved in a new universal order that erases power relations based on fixed categories that exclude, suppress and dismiss the Other. It means the reversal of the gaze, dismantling the violence against women and against humanity epitomized by the Nazi themes of the movies embedded in the performance. The image of Lucia as an *efebo* (androgyn) that inspires Ecks's clue reflects the agency and power of the new subject in a new order of symmetry.

By dismantling the phallus as the central signifier in the system of Western thought, the text empties its own signification rendering madness as the main metaphor. *La nave* is caught in the movement of its own metaphoric repetition by shedding layer after layer of signifiers and signifieds, unfolding the main motif of the novel: the parable of the ship of fools intersects with the performative in a palimpsest that reflects and refracts all the themes of exclusion and violence presented in the narrative.

The journey through cultural production across time and space reconfigures and reconstitutes the metaphor of the world by deconstructing it. This is achieved through the conversion of the tapestry as symbol of chaos and fragmentation, while the external reality—the journey—becomes a pluralistic and fluid unit not fixed by rigid categories. In the process, the role of the reader as actor, contender and full participant is essential for the fulfillment of the reading effect proposed by Felman.

How do you separate the grain from the straw in a field of wheat? This question is the first clue to distinguishing the "significant" from the "insignificant." As a contender in this game I have navigated through the text, deciphering the significant from the insignificant, following the clues and unfolding the intertextualities, unveiling the multiple layers beneath the ship of fools theme and decoding the multiple meanings of the final scene.

La nave de los locos is a text about people wandering around in a journey with no destination, reflecting on the irrationality of the ones considered rational. They are the observers, the "voyeurs," being both the excluded and the participants. Peri Rossi plays with mirrors of images of what people expect to see of themselves reflected in others, "distorting, fragmenting or 'equivocating' the codes through which these 'self-representations' are transmitted" (Kantaris, n.p.). While the reader watches the characters driven by their circumstances, they reflect themselves in the text as a mirror refracting the madness of their own world. The author plays with the constant reflection of reason and unreason to accentuate her critique. Madness, inscribed in the ship of fools motif and the tapestry of creation parody, is used as an allegory to deconstruct and subvert the so-called "rational discourses" reflected in repressive dictatorial political regimes, incongruous religious beliefs and binary gender structures. The final scene, the cross-dressed performance, unveils a powerful message that dismantles power-gender categories, reversing the masculine gaze and decentering monolithic cultural constructs. Ultimately, Peri Rossi deconstructs the layers of the ship of fools motif through its multiple artistic literary and cinematic representations. In doing so, she deconstructs the figure of the fool, the mad as Other, inscribing and proposing an alternative perspective in the name of this Other.

La nave de los locos is considered one of the canonical exponents of postmodernism and feminism in Latin America. Peri Rossi herself suffered political oppression and exile from her native Uruguay, an experience that is reflected in the novel through the alter ego protagonist Equis/Ecks in his wandering around the world. Life, travel and exile become one when Peri Rossi asserts, "If to live is to navigate [...] the sea is the land of the sailor, and all beyond the sea is a shipwreck" (*State of exile* xxv). We have chosen the analysis of *La nave de los locos* as the first chapter of this book to present madness in literature as an allegorical imprinting derived from cultural and social impositions. By understanding the universal claim of the collective reason-unreason dynamic, we set the tone for the rest of the book.

Chapter Two

Homesickness

Lya Luft's *Exílio*

Laura Kanost

> *Estou sempre nos limiares:*
> *sou sempre esta pausa antes*
> *do início de uma canção,*
> *sou um momento de espera,*
> *quase um fim de solidão.*
>
> I am always on the threshold:
> I am always that pause before
> The first notes of a tune,
> I am a moment of expectation,
> Nearly an end to solitude.
>
> (Lya Luft, *Mulher no palco*, 1984)

The once-grand Casa Vermelha (Red House) is surrounded by tropical forest on one side and, on the other, a sharp cliff overlooking an unnamed seaside city. It functions simultaneously as a boarding house, an asylum, a hospice, and a fairytale castle, and it is inhabited by a cast of dysfunctional yet very human characters who are living with a variety of severe mental and physical illnesses. In its own hybrid identity, and in the diversity of its human occupants, this house is a space of multiplicity. Through this setting, Lya Luft's 1987 novel *Exílio* (translated as *The Red House* by Giovanni Pontiero) explores the intricate workings of memory and the imagination, and projects a deeply ambivalent picture of the family and the role of women in contemporary Brazilian society. The memories and perceptions of the unnamed narrator/protagonist gradually reveal how she, an obstetrician, mother, and wife, has abandoned her former life to take up residence in this bleak place, but the novel's hermetic, lyrical closing leaves her future fate uncertain. Like Irene Vilar's personas in her memoirs, the protagonist of *Exílio* has been profoundly affected by her own mother's struggles with her socially prescribed role, mental illness, and ultimately, suicide. The novel belongs to the fantastic genre because neither psychology nor fairy-tale magic is ultimately confirmed as the explanation for the protagonist's interactions with a dwarf, a queen in a mirror, an evil voice, and the mysterious forest.

This chapter interrogates the complex relationship in *Exílio* between mental illness, gender, and liminality (social and physical in-betweenness).[1] After examining the concept of exile at work in this novel and exploring the Casa Vermelha as a liminal, asylum-like space, I analyze how *Exílio* manifests a dynamic subjectivity by maintaining tension between intimately expressing an experience of mental illness via spatial imagery and distancing the reader through fantastic uncertainty.

Doris Sommer identifies comparable distancing mechanisms in her studies of particularist or minority writing. In "Attitude, Its Rhetoric," she observes: "Particularist writing interrupts intimacy with unfriendly noises and identifies itself through announcements of limited intimacy and access, through gaps in communication that tell a reader where to stop" (205). Thus, Sommer outlines a variety of distancing rhetorical figures and tropes in particularist writing, which she considers imperative because "universalists who mistake their setting for the universe need obstacles to notice the boundaries, perhaps to stumble, and then to step more carefully" (209). I extend Sommer's framework to the specific case of mental illness as a disability, revealing that particularist textual maneuvers can work to remind readers that the perfect, self-sufficient universal subject is an inadequate and harmful model because all human beings interface with the world through imperfect, mutable bodies. While Sommer does not include the fantastic in her discussion of the distancing mechanisms of particularist writing, this genre indeed possesses an inherent ability to "detain [readers] at the boundary between contact and conquest" (201–02). According to Tzvetan Todorov's classic model, the fantastic effect arises when the reader is obliged to "hesitate between a natural and a supernatural explanation" for seemingly impossible events that occur in an otherwise possible fictional world (33). This chapter will argue that *Exílio* opens a space for a particularist representation of mental illness by suspending its readers in a position of uncertainty through liminal spatial imagery and narrative elements of the literary fantastic.

The Author

Born in 1938 to a family of German descent in the state of Rio Grande do Sul, Luft grew up in a bilingual environment and began her writing career as a translator of English and German works into Portuguese. She earned degrees in linguistics and English, German, and Brazilian literature, taught linguistics and literature, and branched out into writing poetry (*Canções de Limiar*, 1964; *Flauta Doce*, 1972; *Mulher no Palco*, 1984; *O Lado Fatal*, 1988; *Secreta Mirada*, 1997; *Pra Não Dizer Adeus*, 2005), essays (*O Rio do Meio*, 1996; *Perdas e Ganhos*, 2003; *Múltipla Escolha*, 2010; *A Riqueza do Mundo*, 2011), crônicas (*Matéria do Cotidiano*, 1978; *Pensar É Transgredir*, 2004; *Em Outras Palavras*, 2006), novels (*As Parceiras*, 1980; *A Asa Esquerda do Anjo*, 1981; *Reunião de Família*, 1982; *O Quarto Fechado*, 1984; *Exílio*, 1987; *A Sentinela*, 1994; *O Ponto Cego*, 1999; *Histórias do Tempo*, 2000; *Mar de Dentro*, 2002; *O Tigre Na Sombra*, 2012), children's literature (*Histórias de Bruxa Boa*, 2004; *A Volta da Bruxa Boa*, 2007; *Criança Pensa*, 2009), and short stories (*O Silêncio dos Amantes*, 2008).

Studies of Luft's novels have examined the relationship between grotesque, gothic, and ludic elements and the central role of women's subjective experiences under the pressures of patriarchal society. Maria Osana de Medeiros Costa, for example, examines these themes in Luft's novels from a psychoanalytic perspective, and her analysis of *Exílio* focuses on themes of repression and fantasy. Like *Exílio*, Luft's novels *O Quarto Fechado* (translated as *The Island of the Dead*) and *As Parceiras* (*The Partners*) also deal with the relationships of female characters with mental illnesses and other disabilities; experiences of pain and death; and confinement to or refuge in interior spaces within a patriarchal society governed by a repressive military dictatorship from 1964 to 1985 (see studies by Joyce Baugher and Cristina Ferreira Pinto). Eva Paulino Bueno includes *Exílio* in her study of the portrayal of motherhood as a problematic yet inescapable role for contemporary women in five novels by Luft. Through all five novels, this critic traces the problem of the "profunda contradição entre esta 'maternidade necessária' e os outros desejos e aspirações de uma mulher" [deep contradiction between this "necessary motherhood" and women's other desires and aspirations] and its relationship to the theme of death throughout Luft's work (604). Bueno observes that, for many of Luft's characters, "a loucura se transforma no substituto do papel de esposa e mãe" (606) [madness becomes a substitute for the role of wife and mother]. An important intertext for Luft, then, is the work of fellow Brazilian Clarice Lispector, who "strives to present madness as a productive locus from which her female protagonists can escape the double-bind and fight the impositions of an oppressive society" (Almeida 112).

Exile and Liminality: Spatial Imagery and Mental Illness

The topic of exile is clearly prominent in Luft's novel, with that single word representing the entire work as its title. It is, however, a peculiar sort of exile, when the novel takes place in a vague geographical and historical context, and the only physical displacement involved is the narrator's decision to leave her husband and move to her lover's city of residence. The word "exile" suggests that the states of liminality in this novel are imbued with political significance. The narrator's exile in the Casa Vermelha represents her separation from both her traditional feminine role as longsuffering wife and mother, as well as her less conventional roles as a lover and a successful professional. Unable to negotiate these contradictory roles and lacking any social or familial support, the narrator is stranded in a state of gender "rolelessness." At the same time, and not coincidentally, she is experiencing a state of profound emotional alienation that she identifies repeatedly as depression. In her inability to conform to a socially recognized gender role, and in her liminality related to psychiatric disability, the narrator's "exile" in the Casa Vermelha does carry a political charge. Carla Cristina Garcia identifies a similar dynamic in her 1995 study of women and mental illness in Brazil. Noting that more women than men seek psychiatric treatment, Garcia suggests:

> Esse fato pode ser interpretado como uma das conseqüências do peso de ter que arcar com múltiplas funções, muitas vezes incompatíveis. Os trabalhos fora do lar, os cuidados com a casa e a família e os inúmeros partos perigosos que consomem a saúde tanto física quanto mental, fazem que as mulheres estejam sob tensões de ordem muito diferente das masculinas [115].
>
> This fact can be interpreted as one of the consequences of the burden of having to cope with multiple functions that are often incompatible. Working outside the house, caring for a home and family, and countless danger-

ous births that put a strain on both physical and mental health mean that women are under very different kinds of stress than men.

Likewise, by linking the narrator's difficult negotiation of feminine roles with her experiences of social and emotional exile, Luft's novel implies a strong connection between gender and mental illness.

Amy K. Kaminsky expresses deep reservations about "the evacuation of meaning of the term 'exile'" due to its frequent use as a metaphor for other states of marginalization (*After Exile* xi). Kaminsky insists on a concept of exile that "contains as its principal elements forced separation and a politically construed place of origin whose governing institutions have the ability to impose that separation" (22). Any metaphorical use of such a concrete personal and political condition as exile carries ethical implications—just as the comparable overuse of mental illness and disability as metaphors tends to empty these human experiences of their contextualized specificity. *Exílio* is not beyond this risk, but it resists such "evacuation of meaning" through its focus on exploring the social and spatial liminality common to these diverse experiences. The narrator is an exile only because she cannot go home again in any sense, and this inability to return home is a result of politicized social structures that leave no place for her as an unconventional woman who has left her unfaithful husband as well as their son, intending to move in with her new lover. The narrator withdraws into depression, and a complete lack of social support turns this state into a disability. Her deep emotional distress prevents her from performing her professional role as an obstetrician, which, although untraditional in one sense, ultimately revolves around motherhood.

In her individual experiences negotiating socially scripted roles, the narrator is "exiled" into the lonely space of liminality epitomized by the Casa Vermelha, temporary home to a variety of people who are confined to liminal social spaces because of physical and mental disabilities. The narrator reflects on her exile-like experience:

> Talvez eu deva enfim compreender minha mãe. Mal equipada para a vida. O que são dois filhos quando o abismo nos convoca tão insistente? É possível que para ela a vida tenha sido como esta Casa Vermelha: um lugar onde se reúnem os errantes, os desgarrados, uma ligação fortuita e sem raízes. Tudo o que minha mãe queria era poder voltar, voltar como eu, hoje, quero voltar para minha casa. Duro exílio [108 109].
>
> Has the moment finally come to try and understand Mother's suicide? Ill-equipped for life. What are two children when one is relentlessly drawn

into the abyss? Perhaps her life was just like this Red House: a place where vagrants and castaways unite, a fortuitous gathering without any roots. All Mother wanted was to be able to turn the clock back. Just like me. To be able to turn the clock back and return home. Such cruel exile [95].

As the novel progresses, a complex parallel is established between the narrator's absent mother's long struggle with alcoholism and eventual suicide, the narrator's own abandonment of her feminine roles and experiences of alienation and depression, and the Casa Vermelha as a space populated by a shifting and disparate group of misfits. The lonely social space of liminality is common to them all, and as a vantage point it works in the novel both to isolate characters and to create empathy among them. As we will see later in this chapter, by extension, the reader, too, uneasily inhabits an exile-like position due to the novel's use of the fantastic.

In *Exílio*, gender identity, mental illness, and the act of reading defy objectification. The "exile" of liminality for the novel's characters is bleak if not unbearable, but their unstable positions of political or mental "asylum" in the Casa Vermelha also entail a capacity for agency to enact positive change. This capacity exists because the Casa Vermelha is an ambiguous, hybrid space, a space of multiple potentials. The experiences of its occupants range from that of the narrator's brother Gabriel, who is confined to his room indefinitely and is allowed almost no contact with other human beings, to that of the narrator, who moves about the house freely and also leaves the grounds to go to work or visit her boyfriend. All of the residents, however, have some sort of illness or disability.

If the Casa Vermelha is viewed as an asylum—and its occupants do refer to it as such on several occasions—it is a structure that allows for some degree of multiplicity, but this potential must exist within the confines of the liminal category of disability. The book *Saúde mental e cidadania* (*Mental Health and Citizenship*) published by São Paulo mental health workers the same year as *Exílio*, directly condemns the conditions in Brazilian psychiatric institutions and calls for a more socially integrated approach to mental health care. The economic, political and social difficulties that this reform project has faced are evident in the fact that Carla Cristina Garcia's book, published nearly a decade later, still observes that "a hospitalização, no Brasil, está mais voltada para o controle e o confinamento do paciente, sem quase nenhum compromisso com o tratamento e a cura" (98) [in Brazil, hospitalization is more focused on the control and confinement of patients, with almost no commitment to their treatment and cure]. The Casa Vermelha at once represents and interrogates both the traditional asylum and the more integrative approaches that were being considered in Brazil in the 1980s. The characters and the reader in *Exílio* occupy a variety of indeterminate spaces that correspond to their range of experiences as subjects whose agency and self-definition are always necessarily negotiated through their interactions with their environment. Although these inner experiences of subjectivity always remain separate—a fact underscored by the constant distancing mechanism of the fantastic—they do mirror one another in their liminality, perhaps stimulating a respectful solidarity.

A salient example of this impulse in the novel is its depiction of the narrator's experiences with depression. By creatively verbalizing what is often considered an ineffable emotional pain, the novel invites the reader to identify with the narrator as a fellow human subject rather than an alien other. Because of the persistent use of fantastic uncertainty, to be discussed later in this chapter, the narrator's inner life is never fully exposed. Following Sommer, I argue that this technique functions as a particularist writing strategy to prevent Luft's narrator from becoming an object to be known and controlled by the reader.

Exílio successfully evokes the intensely personal pain of depression through imagery involving the liminal spaces of the body, the Casa Vermelha, and the forest. Elaine Scarry argues convincingly in *The Body in Pain* (1985) that in order to express the deeply personal feeling of pain, it is rhetorically necessary to refer to some object outside of the body that acts to inflict the pain upon the body, precisely because the pain is experienced entirely from within. She advocates the development of a vocabulary for speaking about pain as a means to verbally represent, and by extension, politically represent, physical suffering, thereby destabilizing the power relationships so intricately bound up in concepts and practices involving pain. Scarry claims that emotional pain is not resistant to language, because unlike physical pain, emotional pain does have an external referent: "we do not simply 'have feelings' but have feelings for somebody or something"; "love is love of x, fear is fear of y, ambivalence is ambivalence about z" (5). Yet, a person who suffers from severe anxiety may feel extreme mental and physical distress that does not have a clear referent outside of the body, just as a person with major depression feels an overwhelming and generalized emotional pain that truly is not "sadness about x." Looking at examples such as depression that defy the mind/body distinction may open Scarry's theory to promising applications in the literary and political representation of mental illness.

Two. Homesickness (Kanost)

The spatial imagery at work in *Exílio* demonstrates that the pain of depression may be effectively verbalized by displacing the site of suffering metonymically onto a space beyond the body. The narrator expresses the pain, alienation, and liminality of depression by referring to her own body, as well as to the house and forest that surround her. The spaces of liminality thus become a means of empowerment, as the narrator uses them to communicate intensely personal and internal sensations that might otherwise be impossible to convey at all. Scarry insists on the profound political implications of verbalizing pain, and *Exílio* is particularly effective in this sense because it uses the position of liminality—so often assumed to be voiceless—as a tool for communication.

The emotional pain of depression is necessarily experienced through the body, and the narrator often verbalizes this overwhelming state by referring to extreme types of physical pain, a technique also used by Irene Vilar in her memoirs. The persistent sadness of losing her parents and brother is likened to an insidious infection: "Perdas antigas: quase esquecidas, mas agora reavivadas, e cheias de pus; o tempo as infeccionou, e eu nem sabia" (21) ["Past sufferings almost forgotten, but now revived and full of gore. Time has infected them without my noticing" (15)]. Similarly, "a saudade de meu filho, de minha casa, de meu trabalho, das coisas mais insignificantes da vida que levei, é como um grande tumor roendo meu coração, minha mente" (56) ["the longing for my child, my home, my work, for the most trivial things connected with my former life, eat away at my heart and mind like some great tumour" (47)]. Alternately, the relentless anguish of depression finds expression through metaphors of bodily mutilation: "As lágrimas correm livres; estou sensível como alguém a quem tivessem arrancado a pele, tudo dói imensamente" (31) ["My tears flow freely; I am as sensitive as someone who has just been wounded, everything hurts unbearably" (24)]; she describes a "sensação de ter as pernas amputadas, o coração um torrão grosso de sal numa ferida aberta" (80) ["feeling that my legs have been amputated and that my heart is a great lump of salt being rubbed into a gaping wound" (70)]. In a third strategy, external spaces stand in for the body. "Tive perdas demasiadas, estou de raízes expostas e barriga aberta" ["I have suffered so many privations, my roots are exposed and my guts cut open" (11)], the narrator says, comparing her feelings to a nearby tree that was blown down and had to be cut into pieces to be cleared away, "mutilada" (17) ["hacked beyond recognition" (11)]. Reminiscent of María Luisa Bombal's *La última niebla* (*House of Mist*, Chile, 1935), the forest floor is likened to the narrator's inner feelings of decay and uneasiness: "Contemplo a mata, que me fascina; rastejo dentro de mim num chão igual ao dela: ramos caídos, madeiras podres, silenciosos vermes, cogumelos; tudo tão longe das copas do sonho" (14) ["I contemplate the forest and I find it fascinating: I crawl within myself on similar terrain: fallen branches, rotten wood, silent worms, toadstools; all so remote from the pinnacles of my dream" (8)]. Architectural spaces also represent the narrator's body and mind: "O pânico disparando nos meus labirintos com a sua cauda interminável" (19) ["Panic shooting through my labyrinths trailing its endless tail" (my translation)]. "Sem ele [Lucas], fiquei uma casa abandonada, portas abertas, assoalho carcomido onde correm sinistras ratazanas" (112) ["Without him I was like a deserted house, doors wide open, the floorboards eaten away once the rats moved in" (99)]. This last comparison suggests a strong tie between the narrator's emotional state and the structure of the Casa Vermelha. The rat-infested, neglected old building is more than an unpleasant place of temporary shelter for the narrator—it is a metonymical extension of the narrator's inner life during her experience of isolation and distress.

The Casa Vermelha embodies crisis, housing a variety of people who are stranded in the process of difficult life transitions, but also exuding a sense of pain through its own decaying structures. Inhabited by an elderly woman who is both in mourning and awaiting death, a woman who is dying of cancer and her lesbian partner who must adjust to her absence, a young man who is considered too insane to be in contact with society, and the uprooted and depressed narrator, among others, this boarding house perfectly fits Foucault's definition of the crisis heterotopia. Like all heterotopias, these are well-defined, controlled areas that have a special ability to reflect and interrogate other spaces within a culture. More specifically, the crisis heterotopia is a place assigned to "adolescents, menstruating women, pregnant women, the elderly, etc." ("Of Other Spaces" 24). Given the examples, "liminality" seems to function as a synonym for this sort of crisis. Foucault points mainly to temporary states in which people are considered to be in-between roles, but the Casa Vermelha groups these experiences with the prolonged liminality experienced by the narrator and her brother due to disability. As a crisis heterotopia, the Casa Vermelha embodies the sociocultural structures that place people in temporary or permanent liminal positions. Its state of disrepair simultaneously signals the anguished experience of being held within these structures, as well as the potential for them to break down.

Two. Homesickness (Kanost)

Through its physical structures, the Casa Vermelha evokes liminality. The house itself is a liminal space, located at a point where the sea, the forest, and the city converge, but not belonging to any of these spaces. Thus, when the narrator describes feeling "fora do mundo" (56) ["excluded from the world" (48)], she simultaneously alludes to the multiple liminal positions of her emotional withdrawal, her physical withdrawal from her normal environment, and the remote and peculiar space of the Casa Vermelha. The narrator's alienation within the boardinghouse is underscored by the contrast between names of the characters who live within the house and of those on the outside. She refers to the people she knew before entering the Casa Vermelha by their names—Gabriel, Lucas, Irmã Cândida—but only uses labels—a Velha (the Old Woman), as Moças (the Girls), a Menina Gorda (the Fat Girl)—to identify those she has met on the inside. This subtle difference suggests detachment, and also contributes to the otherworldly ambience of the Casa Vermelha, mimicking the conventions of a fairytale or fable, in which the characters are often not named, but labeled.

A metonymical relationship is established between the Casa Vermelha and the narrator's painful liminality: the condition of the decaying old house worsens throughout the novel as the narrator's depression and alienation grow more excruciating. At several points, the dilapidated, rat-infested house is likened to an ailing body: "lascas de tinta saindo por toda parte como pele velha revelando feridas mais velhas ainda" (32) ["paint peeling off everywhere like old skin to expose even older scars" (25)]; "a parede vaza como se a velha Casa apodrecesse e largasse gosma e pus" (116); ["the wall is leaking as though the old House were rotting, oozing pus" (my translation)]. The entire house is compared to one large wound in the landscape: "De longe, a Casa Vermelha parece um ferimento no morro" (32) ["From afar, the Red House looks like a great gash in the hill" (25)]. This decaying structure of isolation can be read as a figure for the changes to come with deinstitutionalization, but also as a faithful representation of the living situation in many Brazilian psychiatric institutions. In his contribution to *Saúde mental e cidadania*, Jurandir Freire Costa expresses outrage that "as pessoas morrem feito ratos nesses locais malcheirosos e horrorosos" (55) [people die like rats in these horrible, stinking places]. As a heterotopia, the Casa Vermelha simultaneously criticizes these conditions and suggests the potential—however distant—for the collapse of the structures that perpetuate them.

The protected forest beyond the boardinghouse is a third space that works to express aspects of the narrator's experience. This forbidden space continually beckons to the narrator throughout the novel until she finally follows its call. Because of its close associations in the narrator's language with her suicidal mother, her psychologically disabled brother, and the possibly nonexistent Anão (Dwarf), the forest becomes a spatial embodiment of mental illness, which in turn is closely associated in the novel's language with death.

Gabriel is described as being suspended in a living death, devoured by the all-consuming forest (21–2; 15 in the translation). "Gabriel vegeta numa floresta sem saídas; e eu deparo com uma floresta para a qual não vejo entradas" (31) [Gabriel vegetates in a forest with no way out; and I find myself in a forest to which I see no way in (my translation)]. The narrator admired her alcoholic and suicidal mother "como a uma floresta de sonhos numa montanha" (59) ["like a magic forest set on a high mountain" (50)], and declares her a "floresta de enigmas" (194) [forest of enigmas (my translation)].

The narrator is drawn to the forest but is also afraid of it, at night, with its "bichos gritando, macacos, os gatos que vêm para os telhados" (64) ["animals crying out, screeching monkeys, cats prowling over the roof-tops" (55)]. The Anão (Dwarf) is the one who finally leads her through the boundary into the forest, and from that point on, the narration becomes more hermetic and lyrical, difficult to interpret logically. The frightening yet alluring space of the forest comes to represent severe psychological distress as well as suicide.

Exílio successfully appropriates liminal spaces in order to verbalize the painful experiences of occupying them. Thus, liminality is used as a rhetorical device to break down the very boundaries that perpetuate it. Scarry argues that "the act of verbally expressing pain is a necessary prelude to the collective task of diminishing pain" (9), and in the case of *Exílio*, this means that articulating an experience of depression works against the all-too-common silence on the subject, as well as the notion that people with mental illnesses are unable to communicate with others. This rhetoric of liminality is complemented by the novel's use of the fantastic genre, which works to confine the reader to a liminal interpretive space. As the next section demonstrates, the fantastic vacillation in *Exílio* arises from the constant tension between revealing and concealing in the novel's narration and character development.

The Fantastic

The first-person narration in *Exílio* presents the entire plot through the perspective of a character who considers herself mentally ill. A series of distancing mechanisms constantly remind the reader that access to the narrator's subjectivity is only partial. The style of the narration can be likened to a mental diary, given mostly in the present tense in short installments that document the narrator's experiences, moving forward in time. Since these experiences include remembering events from the past, the reader must struggle to remain oriented, fill in gaps, and reconstruct a sequence of events, while always aware of the incompleteness and indeterminacy of such guesswork.

This challenging role for the reader begins with the very first sentence in the novel. *Exílio* opens with the voice of the Anão (Dwarf) comparing the narrator to the Rainha (Queen), and it is not until several pages later that the reader learns that this Queen is the narrator's mother. More information is gradually revealed about the mother and the Anão, until finally the reader learns that the Anão first appeared to the narrator on the day she found out that her mother was an alcoholic (57). The account of the mother's suicide, another key event, is withheld until the end of the second chapter. Similarly, Gabriel is mentioned early in the first chapter as the narrator's brother, "a quem a mata que tudo engole já devorou" (22) ["whom the encroaching forest has already devoured" (15)], but only late in the second chapter, with the narration of the mother's suicide, does the narration make explicit the meaning of this reference to the forest and explain how Gabriel came to be in his present mental state. A comparable pattern holds for the revelation of information about the narrator, as well as other key characters such as the Velha (Old Woman) and the Moças (Girls).

Yet, although the novel does follow a pattern of gradually explaining its initial mysteries, *Exílio* ultimately refuses to give away all its secrets. The nature of the narrator's relationship with Irmã Cândida is one salient example of an element that remains ambiguous throughout the novel. Certain words used to describe their interaction hint that the relationship was of a sexual nature. The narrator remembers, for example, an earlier encounter when the nun's lap effused an "odor de panejamentos e *armários fechados*" [odor of altar cloths and unopened closets (my translation; *armário* can mean closet or cabinet)] and "nossas respirações se fundiam; minha alma soltava burbulhas de inquietação e prazer" (38, emphasis added) ["our breathing would merge, my soul emanating ripples of disquiet and pleasure" (30)]. Furthermore, the narrator recalls, "tive por ela essa paixão difusa e confusa das adolescentes por uma mulher idealizada" (137) [for her, I felt that vague and confused passion that teenage girls have for an idealized woman (my translation)] and remembers fantasizing about Irmã Cândida's possible love life. Irmã Cândida was subsequently transferred to another area because of their relationship, suggesting that the authorities considered it inappropriate. Although these hints point to a lesbian relationship, the narration never makes it clear whether this closeness went beyond that of a motherly spiritual mentor and her love-starved, orphaned, mystically devoted Christian protege.

In this way, *Exílio* toys with the conventions of the realist novel, teasing the reader with information on the narrator's personal history, promising to explain how she became the person she is and to allow the reader to predict how she will act in the future, when it ultimately becomes apparent that we can never know enough about her to understand her present state nor her future actions. The ambiguous ending represents one final blow to any desire to know the narrator completely. *Exílio* concludes not with the prose that has consistently communicated the narrator's thoughts in a seemingly straightforward way throughout the novel, but with fragmented and hermetic poetic language that further frustrates a reader's desire to understand and control the narrator's fate: "Ah solidão de exílio ah frios grotões / ah musgo de sustos ah trilha de nostalgia/ ah orfandade ah cálidas fezes / ah caudas inquietas / ah vida esquartejada / ah chão de passarinhos mortos / ah maldita / ah venerada / enfim" (201) ["Lonely exile, chilling grottoes / mosses of fear, paths of remembrance / orphanhood, human excrement / and restless footsteps. / Life destroyed. /Dead birds everywhere. / Cursed, / yet beloved. / One" (179)].

Even within this final poetic installment, the language breaks down further, as the narrator does not finish her thoughts; there are no clear referents for the adjectives "maldita" and "venerada." Thus, while the communication of liminality is an important effect of this novel, *Exílio* begins and ends by highlighting the narrator's complexity as a subject, defying any impulse on the reader's part to fully know or "diagnose" her—similar to the positions constructed in *Delirio* and *Nadie me verá llorar*. The uneven dynamic of powerful reading subject versus object of knowledge, which would parallel the social injustices faced by the narrator as a woman and as a person with a mental illness, is thus avoided. Although a reader's

Two. Homesickness (Kanost)

impulse to know the narrator is frustrated through ambiguity, the use of the fantastic creates a liminal position for the reader that parallels that of the narrator. The general uncertainty created for the reader by the narration supplements the fantastic uncertainty surrounding several of the characters, who are associated with phenomena that cannot be satisfactorily explained by a psychological cause or a supernatural force. The Anão, whose presence seems to be intimately connected to the narrator's psychological and emotional states and who does not seem to elicit the attention of any other character, is one such fantastic element. From the beginning, we know that "nem se percebe quando [o Anão] vai ou vem" (14) ["you never notice when he comes and goes" (8)] but he often appears right after the narrator thinks about him. The Anão can read the narrator's thoughts, and never shuts doors behind him, suggesting, perhaps, his immateriality (22–3). He always wears exactly the same clothes, and has not visibly aged over the course of several decades (30). When the narrator asks the Criadas (Maids) if they have seen the Anão, they respond in a way that suggests that he does not exist to them: "deram risadinhas, acotovelaram-se, me olharam como se eu fosse louca" (33) ["they started giggling and nudging each other, and looked at me as if I were mad" (26)]. The narrator's father also laughs when she mentions the Anão (61). Indeed, the Anão rarely speaks to the narrator in public (91). The narrator never knows for sure where exactly he lives in the Casa Vermelha, and similarly, she is unsure about the validity of her memory of finding the Anão's room in her childhood home (168). When he dies, she reflects on his being "parte de mim" (198) ["part of me" (175)], verbalizing what the reader may be suspecting, that the Anão is a projection of part of the narrator's own psyche; however, this reference does not confirm this suspicion, because it could also be understood as an expression of how close their long relationship was.

The Voz who periodically calls the narrator on the telephone and berates her is similarly mysterious. The narrator herself does not understand who the Voz is or why she calls to verbally abuse her, but can only question, "Por quê? Quem seria?" (24) ["Why? Who can she be?" (17)]. The fact that it is a "voz de bêbada" (24) ["slurring voice of a drunken woman" (17)] suggests a possible connection with the narrator's mother. At one point, however, the narrator notes that the Anão's voice closely resembles the Voz on the telephone (92). In similar fashion, the ghostly quality of the Madame, who supposedly runs the Casa Vermelha but whom no one ever sees, is never explained away. Nor does the reader figure out why the narrator's brother, Gabriel, seems able to read her mind. The narrator's mother haunts her dresser mirror, but it is unclear whether this Snow White image is a magical occurrence related to the fairytale elements in the novel, whether it has a psychological explanation as a hallucination, or whether it should simply be interpreted as figurative language expressing the daughter's physical resemblance to her mother or the lingering effects of their troubled relationship. None of these many mysteries in the novel is ever neutralized by a clear psychological or supernatural explanation, leaving the reader suspended in the limbo of the fantastic.

Related to these fantastic elements is the unanswerable question of the narrator's mental health. Because it is impossible to decide securely on either a psychological or a supernatural explanation for the strange qualities of the Anão, the Voz, the Madame, Gabriel, and the narrator's mother, it is also impossible for the reader to "diagnose" or categorize the narrator with any certainty. The novel does present an accumulating body of evidence that may lead the reader to conclude that the narrator suffers from depression—a condition which, alone, would not suffice as a psychological explanation for the narrator's unusual perceptions of those around her. Early in the novel she thinks "talvez eu só estivesse deprimida" (15) ["perhaps I was only depressed" (9)]. "Onde a energia de antes, o otimismo, a vontade de viver, a alegria de fazer nascer?" (21) ["Where is the energy I once possessed, the optimism, the will to live, the joy of helping others to give birth?" (15)]. She wonders, "terei sempre essa sensação de estar mutilada, fora do mundo, dos segredos e do afeto alheio?" (56) ["will I ... go on feeling worthless, excluded from the world, from the confidences and affections of others?" (48)]. The use of the word "deprimida" in conjunction with these symptoms of loss of energy, despair, and alienation, encourages the reader to conclude that the narrator does indeed suffer from major depression.

While she may be mentally ill, the narrator certainly does not consider herself to be crazy. She is, however, surrounded by a variety of people in the Casa Vermelha to whom she does refer throughout the novel as "louco" or "doido" (mad, crazy): Gabriel, the Velha, the Anão, the Voz, the upstairs neighbor, and the Menina Gorda. The boardinghouse itself is repeatedly compared to an asylum. The narrator calls the Casa Vermelha a "casa de lunáticos" (116) [house of lunatics (my translation)]. Soon after, the Moça Morena remarks, "Isto aquí é um hospício" ["This is a madhouse" (107)] to which the narrator replies, "O mundo é um hospício" (120) ["The world's a madhouse" (107)]. The house is even likened to a ship of fools, a motif discussed at greater length in the chapter on Peri Rossi:

> Chove forte sobre a Casa Vermelha, que carrega na noite seu fardo de sofrimento e loucura, vidas desconectadas, sem raiz... mas de certa forma unidas entre si pela falta de um destino, de um sentido. Precário barco: quem é o timoneiro? [153].
>
> The rain beats down on the Red House, bearing throughout the night its burden of suffering and madness, lives without connections, without roots... but in a way they are united by their common lack of destiny, of meaning. Precarious ship: who is at the helm?

In her grief over the death of the Anão, the narrator describes herself as "como louca" [like mad] and reflects on the "noite neste asilo de lunáticos, do qual faço parte" (197–98) [night in this lunatic asylum, which includes me (my translation)]. The extended comparison between the Casa Vermelha and an asylum points to a possible psychological explanation for the fantastic elements in the novel.

Reading the house as an asylum and some of the narrator's perceptions as hallucinations would certainly provide a coherent interpretation of the novel's inexplicable moments. Yet because a psychological explanation is not confirmed in the novel, fantastic uncertainty remains. Although the boardinghouse is directly compared to an asylum, and most of its occupants are referred to as insane, these comparisons make use of an ambiguous rhetoric that could just as easily be interpreted as common figures of speech. Other characters' perceptions of the house and its residents are all filtered through the narrator, so that there is ultimately no reliable evidence to confirm or deny that the Casa Vermelha is an asylum. This psychological interpretation of the novel remains only a wavering possibility, as would be any supernatural explanation.

Throughout the novel, then, this fantastic uncertainty becomes a particularist (Sommer) strategy, a constant reminder that the narrator and her experiences cannot be controlled or categorized, nor made the object of a powerful reader's knowledge. The distancing mechanism is heightened at the novel's conclusion, when the narrator's language becomes much more fragmentary and private. Although *Exílio* utilizes liminal spaces and a liminal genre to communicate to a certain extent the narrator's painful and alienating experiences of depression and social isolation, the fantastic uncertainty simultaneously forces the reader to maintain a respectful distance that recognizes the narrator's autonomy as a subject.

Given the context of Brazilian literature, it is difficult to read about the Casa Vermelha without recalling its 19th-century predecessor, the Casa Verde in *O Alienista* (1882, *The Alienist*) by Joaquim Maria Machado de Assis. This novella satirizes the exuberant contemporary faith in the nascent psychiatric science and the new doctors' enthusiastic drive to diagnose and categorize their objects of study. It portrays an alienist who builds an asylum to house and organize his quickly growing number of patients. As the asylum becomes crowded with his numerous diagnoses, the doctor concludes that being mentally unbalanced is the norm, and begins to "treat" only those townspeople who are untroubled, with such success that, in the end, he himself is the only incurable patient remaining in the Casa Verde. As a late 20th-century reincarnation of the Casa Verde, the Casa Vermelha reiterates the futility of the urge to observe, categorize and control human subjects. Much like the alienist, the reader of *Exílio* may attempt to "diagnose" the narrator and explain away her experiences and perceptions, but ultimately these efforts are doomed to failure. Instead of reinforcing a subject-object power dynamic mirroring the oppression of disability, *Exílio* compels its readers to temporarily inhabit the painful position of liminality, and thus to imagine or even pursue possible alternatives.

Readers might agree that *Exílio* is not a pleasant book to read. While brief in length, it seems to drag on and on as the narrator and other characters become increasingly mired in an unrelenting succession of traumas and crises. A reader who suffers along in this literary liminality may catch a glimpse of the experience of living with major depression. Ironically, a reader who has depression may find this novel unbearable. On one level, the novel presents a hopelessly bleak picture of life with a mental illness: the narrator never "returns home" from her exile in depression and social liminality. Only the reader has the potential to emerge from the position of liminality—limited and indirect as it may be—and to make positive use of the resulting change in perspective. Although *Exílio* relentlessly confines the narrator, the novel as a reading experience may actively work to open liminal social spaces.

Chapter Three

Dissonance on Display

Diamela Eltit and Paz Errázuriz's *El infarto del alma*

Laura Kanost

Estoy en el manicomio por mi amor a la palabra.
I am here in the insane asylum because
of my love of the word.
(Diamela Eltit and Paz Errázuriz,
El infarto del alma, 1994)

El infarto del alma (translated by Ronald Christ as *Soul's Infarct*) is a 1994 collaborative work of prose and photography by Chileans Diamela Eltit (1949–) and Paz Errázuriz (1944–) that documents clashing modes of seeing and talking about the residents of the Philippe Pinel psychiatric hospital in Putaendo, Chile. This remote, highly structured institution embodies and perpetuates the marginalization of people with mental illnesses, which is part of a larger picture of socioeconomic disparity and human rights violations in the aftermath of the oppressive Pinochet regime (1973–1990). Through portraits of couples and multiple fragmented voices, the book bears witness to the existence of and bonds between isolated, disenfranchised citizens, and examines the relationship between the concepts of madness, self, and other. For Jacqueline Loss, the unconventional use of repetition and fragmentation in the text "emphasizes the degree to which the psychotic voices penetrate the text's structure" (Loss 89). The "mad" discourse of the text is, according to Ana Forcinito's reading, a way of problematizing representation itself: "trabaja alrededor de las interrupciones y las suspensiones (de textos, de estéticas, de secciones, de irrupciones dentro de la misma sección), donde se propone la dificultad misma de la representación: cada forma representativa está siempre interrumpida" (68) [it works around the interruptions and suspensions (of texts, of aesthetics, of sections, of irruptions within a section), pointing to the very difficulty of representation itself: every form of representation is interrupted by another].[1] Even as the "madness" of the hospital residents becomes a vehicle for abstract discussions of political resistance, subjectivity, otherness, and representation, their visual presence as individual human beings anchors *El infarto del alma* in specific experiences within the Chilean mental health care system.

Context

In this ambivalence, *El infarto del alma* registers the climate regarding mental health in Chile in the 1990s, while reflecting the general tendency for disabilities to "carry an excess of meaning" in culture (Quayson 4). The Pinochet regime had reversed a recent trend toward decentralizing Chilean mental health care, reverting to a psychiatric hospital-based model. With the return to democracy, the Chilean government undertook a process of mental health care reform, implementing a new National Mental Health and Psychiatry Plan in 1993 that promoted deinstitutionalization through the creation of alternatives to hospitalization such as group homes, community mental health centers, and day hospitals (Alvarado et al.). Although the changes have been a significant step, they did not immediately eliminate regional inequities and persistent stigma. A national survey conducted in Chile in the 1990s revealed that a majority of mental disorders still went untreated, and despite improvements in the national mental health care system, rural communities and the working class still had markedly lower access to treatment for mental illness (Saldivia et al. 71–72). This study also indicated that, in addition to the lack of facilities, poor understanding of mental illness and a fear of being identified as mentally ill were major obstacles that prevented Chilean people from seeking mental health care (74–75). Nevertheless, Chile certainly has made progress since the first half of the 20th century, when for more than five decades its government repeatedly refused funding for a new national psychiatric hospital to replace the poor facilities in its seriously overcrowded, understaffed Casa de Orates (Medina 78–80). The Putaendo psychiatric hospital, visibly neglected in Errázuriz's photos, was damaged in the 2010 earthquake and is currently being remodeled ("Nuevas obras").

Eltit and Errázuriz have both borne witness to and challenged marginalization throughout their works. Elit's *El padre mío* (*Father of Mine*, 1989), for example, is the transcription of a recording of a homeless man said to be schizophrenic, and Errázuriz's collaboration with Claudia Donoso, *La manzana de Adán* (*Adam's Apple*, 1990), is a multigeneric work of text and photographs dealing with transvestites and the sex industry. Both artists explore the intersections of various forms of marginality within a Chilean political context; according to Michael J. Lazzara's reading of *El padre mío*, for instance, "the discourse of madness became a narrative lens through which to project a poetics of traumatic memory, a discourse that would incite her readers to question language's very possibilities for narrating the disaster" (107). Other works by Diamela Eltit, such as *Lumpérica* (*E. Luminata*, 1983), *Por la patria* (*For the Fatherland*, 1986), *El cuarto mundo* (*The Fourth World*, 1988) and *Vaca sagrada* (*Sacred Cow*, 1991), use linguistic rupture and fragmentary, disconnected narrative forms to unravel the oppressive collective feeling under the Pinochet regime. The isolated yet profoundly social hospital residents portrayed in *El infarto del alma* can be interpreted as a metonymy for postdictatorial Chilean oppression and resistance, but this book does more than merely use mental illness as a political metaphor. By juxtaposing multiple visual and verbal discourses of mental illness, *El infarto del alma* creates a vantage point from which to contemplate the conflicting cultural meanings that play a role in how mental illnesses are understood.

Viewing Mental Illness

In looking at the relationship between individual bodies and sociocultural practices in literary representations of mental illness such as *El infarto del alma*, I draw on the field of critical disability studies, which also emerged in the 1990s (see Introduction). Disability studies claims that bodily variations are a fundamentally human yet marginalized condition, and interrogates the relationship between disability experiences and their cultural representations with the aim of reversing this marginalization. Within a disability studies context, I read *El infarto del alma* as a collage of contradictory conventional discourses of madness and the asylum— conflations of madness and love, madness and resistance, and the asylum and sociopolitical control—in which individual experiences of difference are displaced by cliché abstract metaphors (Sontag). The photographs allude to and revise the ancient tradition of the insane asylum as a public spectacle (Foucault *History of Madness*, 145). Because of their relative privateness and fixity, photographs tend to exaggerate the objectification of people with disabilities; as disability scholar Rosemarie Garland-Thompson explains, photography authorizes, stylizes, and intensifies the stare typically directed at disability, thereby giving the viewer of a photograph a special "license" to view disability as "a state of absolute difference" (58). Similarly, Sander Gilman argues that paintings and photographs of the "mad" act rather like miniature asylums to contain mentally ill people within the limited space of the frame or shot, thereby keeping them comfortably separate from the sane subjects who view them and fear the illness and metaphorical death they are believed to represent (*Seeing* 225). Nineteenth-century psychiatrists utilized photography as a diagnostic and therapeutic tool, underlining the uneven power dynamic of the medical gaze. Elaine Showalter observes that 19th-century psychiatrists embraced photography as a method of objectively recording and diagnosing female patients, and also as a therapeutic tool for encouraging them to conform to norms for feminine appearance (86–97, 149–54). Just as asylum photography tends to authorize an objectifying mode of viewing, then, it also conventionally documents an uneven power relationship in which the photographer flaunts the agency to control the process of representation. A late 20th-century South American manifestation of these conventions cited by Gilman (*Disease* 47) is *Humanario* (1976), a collaboration of Sara Facio, Alicia D'Amicio, and Julio Cortázar that portrays Argentine psychiatric hospitals through photographs and text. *Humanario* depicts psychiatric patients who do not appear to be participating in their own visual representation—many cover their faces with their hands, or are sprawled out on the floor, apparently asleep. Rivera-Garza's *Nadie me verá llorar*, discussed in Chapter Four, challenges this power dynamic by imagining a complex negotiation of Matilda's image. As we will see, while the photographs in *El infarto del alma* allude to the conventional "sane" viewing subject/"mad" viewed object dynamic, specific visual and textual details suggest a more turbulent relationship.

El infarto del alma has been interpreted in nearly opposite ways by literary critics: as an affirmation of solidarity that lends a voice to its disenfranchised mentally ill subjects whose everyday resistance would otherwise go unrecognized by the outside world (Richard, Tierney-Tello, Medina Sancho, Forcinito), and as a visual othering and isolation (Williams) and a cultural product accessible only to the elite (Loss). Even as the text and photographs repeat and thus legitimize marginalizing discourses of madness, I argue, they also expose jarring inconsistencies amongst them and underline their culturally constructed nature.

El infarto del alma displays its internal conflicts boldly on its cover. Readers are likely to feel unsettled before even opening the book, as their gaze is returned by a slightly larger-than-life photograph of a face that exceeds the space of the cover, or, as Nelly Richard puts it, "desborda sus límites confinatorios" (*Residuos y metáforas* 245) [overflows its boundaries]. In this respect, the person on the cover—who is a female hospital resident pictured again later in the book—projects a strong sense of agency: she is too complex to be easily contained within the neat box of a photograph, and her gaze meets the photographer's as if to assert her own authority and her willing participation in the portrait. Yet, the woman on the cover also wears the title of the book and the names of the authors and publisher stamped on her face, as though she were a blank slate on which members of the intellectual elite could write. The clashing impulses encapsulated in the cover announce a persistent tension in *El infarto del alma* regarding the degree of agency attributable to the residents of the Putaendo psychiatric hospital in their roles as patients and as photographic and textual subjects.

Opening the book to the first page, we see an image of a serious couple arm in arm, looking straight at the camera, standing in front of a dilapidated building. The accompanying page of text is nearly blank, with a single sentence at the very bottom of the page: "Te escribo: ¿Has visto mi rostro en algunos de tus sueños?" ["I write to you: Have you seen my face in any of your dreams?" (6)].[2] The black-and-white photographs on every left-hand page send mixed visual signals, combining the familiar codes of posed photographs with details pointing to the socioeconomic marginalization of the couples and the shabby institutional setting that confines them. The text on each right-hand page—printed, as Richard observes, in a typewriter-like font reminiscent of "la redacción del informe médico" (*Residuos y metáforas* 259) ["the composition of a medical report"]—wanders through a dizzying array of discourses and narrative voices: hermetic letters from a woman to an absent male beloved, an apparent travel diary narrating Eltit's trip with Errázuriz to the hospital in Putaendo, poetic fragments expressing drawn-out hunger and longing, intellectual essays on the history of the hospital in a greater Chilean context and on the relationship between selfhood and otherness, and an apparent transcription of a patient's narration of a dream.

For the most part, Errázuriz's photographs veer sharply from traditional asylum imagery by depicting a collaborative relationship. The majority of the photographs portray affectionate couples who apparently choose to participate in the photograph by posing, often looking back at the photographer/viewer. Rather than isolating individual "madmen" as voiceless Others subjected to a medical gaze, Errázuriz's photographs show people diagnosed with mental illnesses engaging in human interactions in spite of their exclusion from society. Richard considers this view as highly subversive, because it replaces cliché expectations with a vision of "algo muy personal (el amor) con lo cual los reclusos burlan el castigo de la despersonificación que hace pesar sobre ellos la institución social" [something very personal (love) with which the inmates defy the burden of depersonification to which the social institution has condemned them] to affirm that "no hay sujeto definitivamente cautivo de las prisiones del orden" [no subject is fully held by the prisons of order] (*Residuos y metáforas* 248, 246).

Occasionally, however, the photographs suddenly fall back in line with a more objectifying mode resembling conventional asylum photography. A sequence of photographs depicting a nude woman and her fully-clothed male companion alone in an outdoor setting is striking because, unlike all the other images of posed couples, these photographs seem to intrude on what might have been a private moment. The woman does not appear to be aware of the camera and the very public gaze to which her body is exposed, but perhaps she is asserting her freedom from the constraints of the asylum walls, her own clothing, and sociocultural norms. Eltit and Errázuriz offer no explanations to relieve readers of the discomfort of this ambivalence, and the degree to which this series of photographs differs from the others only intensifies its impact. Megan Corbin considers these images at length in her discussion of consent and the maternal gaze in this work: "the theme of consent—the consent of the *aislados* to be in the Phillipe Pinel mental institute, the consent of the woman to be sterilized, and the consent of the inpatients that appear in the text of *El infarto del alma*—remains constantly at play in these images" (71).

A second notable rupture in the photographic narrative comes at the very end of the book, where the photographs foreground the space of the hospital itself. The gardens surrounding the hospital and the neglected building interior figure in the background of all the other photographs, but the book ends with images of the hospital interior, for the first time devoid of people: light shining through windows, straight lines, peeling paint, decay.[3] The final image includes two distant human figures spatially isolated in two different corridors. Rather than intentionally posing and looking at the camera, both have their backs turned to the viewer. One of them is slumped over on the hard floor. Like the series of nude photographs, this final image is reminiscent of conventional asylum photography that treats patients as voiceless objects. For Ana Forcinito, these final images complicate the testimonial function of the book, since rather than leaving us with an affirmation of love as a resistance strategy, these photographs "nos interpelan a través de otra mirada testimonial y la denuncia que esta mirada implica" (67) [interpellate us through another testimonial gaze and the denunciation that this gaze implies].

The Text

The text of *El infarto del alma* juxtaposes disparate discourses linking madness to other forms of marginalization and foregrounds its own ambiguous position within literary and intellectual tradition. The "Diario de viaje" text highlights the photographer's agency by placing her as the active subject: "Cuando captura sus poses, les confirma la relevancia de sus figuras"; "les toma fotografías que prueban, aún a ellos mismos, que están vivos" ["When she captures their poses, she confirms the importance of their features" (18); takes their pictures, which prove, even to them, that they are alive (7)]. In contrast to the photographs themselves, which primarily emphasize the asylum residents' active role in their portraiture, the text downplays the patients' agency in contrast to Errázuriz's authority: "Paz, con extrema delicadeza, va de grupo en grupo, responde a las más diversas solicitudes, permite el flujo de las múltiples inesperadas poses" ["Paz Errázuriz, with extreme delicacy, goes from group to group, answers the most varied requests, allows the flux of multiple unexpected poses" (18)]. Here and throughout much of the text, the primary focus seems to be not what the hospital residents say or do, but how the photographer and writer respond to and reflect upon them.

By alluding to the genres of travel narrative and testimonio, Eltit's text situates itself within a broad Latin American intellectual tradition concerned with issues of subjectivity and power in representations of marginalized others. The incorporation of these genres fosters an acute awareness of such problems, as the text explores the imbalance of power in Eltit's and Errázuriz's interactions with and representations of the patients.

The text segment titled "Diario de viaje" (Travel Diary) portrays the writer as an intermediary with a special ability to interpret and represent childlike patients' reality on their behalf. The narrator, identified as Eltit, tells of their voyage into a markedly different space full of a markedly different group of people who nonetheless claim the travelers as part of their family:

> Cuando atravesamos la reja veo a los asilados. No me resultan inesperados sus cuerpos ni sus rostros (no me resultan inesperados pues ya dije que días antes he visto las fotografías), sólo me desconcierta la alegría que los recorre cuando gritan: "Tía Paz." "Llegó la tía Paz." Una y otra vez como si ellos mismos no lo pudieran creer y más la besan y más la abrazan y a mí también me besan y me abrazan hombres y mujeres ante los cuales debo disimular la profunda conmoción que me provoca la precariedad de sus destinos. [...] Estamos rodeadas de locos en un desfile que podría resultar cómico, pero, claro, es inexcusablemente dramático, es dramático de veras más allá de las risas, de los abrazos, de los besos, pese a que una mujer me tome por la cintura, ponga su boca en mi oído y me diga por primera vez: "Mamita." Ahora yo también formo parte de la familia; madre de locos.
>
> When we pass through the gate, I see the inmates. They don't strike me as unexpected, neither their bodies nor their faces (they don't strike me as unexpected because, as I said, days before I had seen the photographs); I'm only disconcerted by the joy coursing through them as they shout: "Auntie Paz," "Auntie Paz's here." Again and again, as if they can't believe it themselves, and they kiss her again, and they hug her again, and they kiss me and hug me too—men and women from whom I must conceal how deeply I'm distressed by the precariousness of their destinies. [...] We are surrounded by lunatics in a parade that might appear comical, but, of course, is inexcusably dramatic, is truly dramatic beyond the laughter, the hugs, the kisses, despite a woman's taking me by the waist, putting her mouth to my ear, and saying to me for the first time: "Mommy." Now I too form part of the family: mother of lunatics [10, 12].

This travel narrative particularly resembles the *crónica* genre in the overwhelming exuberance conveyed by the accumulation of details strung together in this last sentence, and also in Eltit-narrator's struggle for words to describe the alien bodies of the hospital patients: "¿Qué sería describir con palabras la visualidad muda de esas figuras deformadas por los fármacos, sus difíciles manías corporales, el brillo ávido de esos ojos que nos miran, nos traspasan y dejan entrever unas pupilas cuyo horizonte está bifurcado?" ["What would it be, putting into words the mute visuality of these figures deformed by medication, their bodies' difficult manias, the eager gleam of those eyes looking at us, piercing us, and permitting the glimpse of pupils whose horizon forks off?" (10).] Eltit-narrator recovers from her initial culture shock to accept the parental role that the asylum residents apparently expect her to play: "el 'mamita' se me vuelve cada vez más cotidiano, cada vez más natural" ["'mommy' becomes more and more routine to me, more and more natural" (22)]. This narration casts the patients as radically different from the verbally and visually articulate subjects, Eltit and Errázuriz, and yet the patients' claim to the two women as mother and aunt complicates this self/other subject/object dynamic. Even as Eltit describes the hospital residents' bodies and behavior as utterly different, the residents recognize her as one of their own. The narrator's identification with the patients becomes troubling, however, when in contrast to them, she freely leaves at the end of the visit and remarks, "volveré a la ciudad atrapada en el manicomio de mi propia mente" ["I will go back to the city trapped in the madhouse of my own mind" (23)].

The roles of Eltit and Errázuriz as mediators are further problematized by the text's connection to the *testimonio* genre. While various critics have read *El infarto del alma* as a *testimonio* (Tierney-Tello, Medina-Sancho, Forcinito), Richard calls the work a "perversión simbólico-literaria [que] desfigura el habla referencial del testimonio" (*Residuos y metáforas* 257–58) [literary-symbolic perversion [that] disfigures the referential language of testimonio], and Loss identifies it as an *antitestimonio*, inaccessible to the masses (99). Indeed, *El infarto del alma* might best be considered a "*metatestimonio*," since it exaggerates the dilemmas of representation and subjectivity central to *testimonio* by limiting the direct participation of the hospital residents to their portraits, while combining fictitious first-person narratives, the mediator's "travel journal," and one authentic first-person narrative. The hermetic letters that begin and end the book and the brief fragments titled "La falta" ("Want") could be read as voices of fictitious hospital residents, a "pseudotestimonial" gesture. Since Eltit, the mediator, is apparently the source of the words, these fragments merely create an illusion of affirming the literary voice of a hospital resident, while underscoring the authority of Eltit to assume a "mad" rhetoric as an aesthetic and political tool (recalling Caminero-Santangelo's critique in

The Madwoman Can't Speak, discussed in the introduction). Only the brief text titled "El sueño imposible" ("Impossible Dream") is identified as the direct words of a patient, Juana, recorded by Errázuriz in 1990. The dream is impossible because it is about social roles and material belongings that are denied to her and her partner: becoming a mother with her husband, José, rejecting her own mother who abandoned her, and living happily along with her sister in their own house given to them by a doctor. "El sueño imposible" does stand as a miniature testimonio, bearing witness to the collective marginalization of the Putaendo residents, and others like them. The combination of a truly testimonial text, a mediator's reflection, and participatory photography with apparently pseudotestimonial texts calls attention to the roles of the hospital residents and the artists. The power dynamic underlying the creation and consumption of *El infarto del alma* is exposed. By extension, so is the disempowerment of people diagnosed with mental illnesses within a centralized psychiatric hospital model.

This issue is further explored in *El infarto del alma* through allusions to Foucault's *History of Madness* and Sontag's *Illness as Metaphor*. Echoing *History of Madness*, Eltit presents the Putaendo asylum as a structure meant to impose social and economic control on the rogue citizens who threaten the public order by not participating in the work force: the hospital functions as "una maniobra fiscal para alcanzar la propiedad sobre los otros cuerpos ya del todo públicos por su falla mayor ante el salario, por su indigencia ante el consumo." The passage titled "Juana la Loca" further literalizes this interpretation of the function of the asylum by suggesting that at least one of the patients was swallowed up by the hospital in childhood, never to emerge, for no other reason than extreme poverty: "tal vez Juana esté loca. Quizás su padre y ella enloquecieron de indigencia juntos. [...] Se trata de un cuerpo político" ["perhaps Juana is crazy. Perhaps her father and she went crazy together from their poverty. [...] It is a question of a political body" (56).] The fact that *El infarto del alma* does not depict any sort of rehabilitative or therapeutic activity in this hospital gives even more force to a Foucauldian vision of the asylum as a structure of socioeconomic control. The constantly alternating discourses juxtapose individual experiences of living with a mental illness in a psychiatric hospital with meditations that use these experiences to explore abstract concepts of poverty, social control, and love.

By interweaving testimonial and pseudotestimonial texts with metaphorizing texts, *El infarto del alma* foregrounds and resists the sort of substitution that Sontag critiques in *Illness as Metaphor*. Just as Foucault's cultural theory of the asylum plays out literally in one part of Eltit's text, another segment portrays the hospital at Putaendo as the embodiment of Sontag's discussion of the meanings ascribed to illnesses through metaphorical language. Whereas Sontag examines the ways in which 20th-century insanity has replaced 19th-century tuberculosis as the illness associated with superior sensitivity, Eltit discusses how psychiatric patients literally replaced tuberculosis patients in the history of the Putaendo sanitarium. Eltit's text reads this substitution within its Chilean political context to expose and denounce the continuous socioeconomic injustice of which the Putaendo hospital is emblematic. Its tuberculosis patients, according to the text, were bodies at leisure, passionate and privileged. In the late 20th century, however, sickness is seen as a stigma, and incompatible with love or sex. The leisure class has been displaced by the opposite end of the class spectrum, since the sanitarium now contains people who are mentally unable to work and therefore are a threat to the social order.

In addition to the conflation of mental illness and socioeconomic control, *El infarto del alma* literalizes the cliché of "mad love." The narrator remarks in "Diario de viaje," "después de todo los seres humanos se enamoran como locos" ["when all's said and done, human beings fall in love like lunatics" (19)]: they disregard cultural norms to form unconventional pairings, "la belleza aliada a la fealdad, la vejez anexada a la juventud, la relación paradójica del cojo con la tuerta, de la letrada con el iletrado" ["beauty allied with ugliness, age annexed to youth, the paradoxical relationship of the lamed with the one-eyed, of the literate with the illiterate" (19)]. The idea is discussed at length in the strand titled "El otro, mi otro" ("The Other, My Other"), in which an unidentified intellectual narrator contemplates the relationship between Self and Other by considering cases in which this distinction is obscured or lost: motherhood ("es otro el cuerpo" ["the body is an other" (34)]), love ("donarse como cuerpo y como mente para el otro" ["giving itself as body and as mind for the other" (36)]), and insanity ("la forma de la locura es su tendencia a fundirse, a confundirse con el otro" ["the form of lunacy is its tendency to fuse, to confuse itself with the other" (36)]). These fundamentally human experiences point to the inextricability of Self and Other, or as disability scholar Lennard Davis proposes, "the partial, incomplete subject whose realization is not autonomy and independence but dependency and interdependence" (30).

Juxtaposed with this reframing of subjectivity through a meditation on "mad love" is the just as common metaphorical cliché equating mental illness with political resistance, implying that mentally ill people occupy a uniquely subversive subject position related to their unconventional speech, thoughts, and behavior, or that "madness" is a subversive rejection of imposed rationality. *El infarto del alma* pushes the metaphor to its limits by suggesting, in a section titled "El amor a la enfermedad" ("Love of Illness"), that the psychiatric hospital is literally a political apparatus: the Putaendo inmates are the poorest of the poor, unable to participate in Chile's neoliberal economic policies because of their disabilities, and in order to prevent this disruptive tendency from spreading, the State has confined them in a rural location and has prevented them from reproducing. Gisela Norat also sees a linkage to the dictatorship: "as wards of the state, the patients in Putaendo [...] metaphorically elicit memory of forced incarceration by a military regime that stripped detainees of all rights and through abusive practices catapulted many into madness" (60).[4] Eltit's text suggests that the patients in the hospital at Putaendo subvert the State-imposed control exerted by the asylum on their bodies in the form of forced sterilization and isolation from society by forming loving and sexual couples anyway. The cliché of resistance through madness only creates an illusion of a uniquely subversive subjectivity, since their love is effective as political resistance only symbolically (Caminero-Santangelo) and through the intervention of powerful intermediaries, Eltit and Errázuriz. *El infarto del alma* collects the variety of approaches to representing the psychiatric hospital residents—from testimony and participatory photography to stigmatizing metaphorization and the medical gaze—and intertwines them, foregrounding dissonance.

Perhaps readers have responded in such disparate ways to this work because, in a tendency to resolve dissonance, they look for patterns and focus more on some aspects than others. Ultimately, this portrait of clashing discourses deconstructs the concept of madness, emphasizing the role of culture and politics in how the psychiatric hospital and its residents are viewed and conceptualized. The juxtaposition lays bare the logical and ethical shortcomings of conventional representations of mentally ill subjects and intellectual discussions of "madness," but falls far short of promoting an alternative conceptualization. The book has certainly had the effect of bearing witness to the hospital and its residents and keeping them present in the public imagination, both in Chile and beyond. Twenty years later, it has been translated into English, has appeared in two additional Spanish editions, is available for free online at the National Library's Memoria Chilena website, and has become the basis for an internationally performed theatrical adaptation by Teatro Niño Proletario titled *El otro* (2012). Niño Proletario theater company members who visited the Putaendo psychiatric hospital in preparation for their roles met many of the same couples pictured in the book decades earlier.

Chapter Four

See the World Through My Lens

Cristina Rivera Garza's *Nadie me verá llorar*

Elvira Sánchez-Blake

> *¿Son éstos los ojos, por fin, los ojos de la locura?*
> Are these the eyes, finally, the eyes of madness?
> (Cristina Rivera Garza, La Castañeda, 2010)

Cristina Rivera Garza proposes an alternative view of madness in her 1999 novel *Nadie me verá llorar* (*No One Will See Me Cry*). She suggests a way of rewriting History from a different period perspective, using a dialogical, atemporal approach that allows the reader to imprint a relationship with the subject of the story. Rivera Garza's goal is not to portray the past or to take the reader on a historical journey, but to make the past contemporary. The author first explored the subject in her doctoral thesis, "The Masters of the Streets. Bodies, Power and Modernity in Mexico, 1867–1930," later publishing academic articles on the subject. "She Neither Respected Nor Obeyed Anyone: Inmates and Psychiatrists Debate Gender and Class at the General Insane Asylum La Castañeda, Mexico, 1910–1930," *Hispanic American Historical Review* (2001) summarized most of her proposals. More recently she extended her inquiry in the book *La Castañeda: Narrativas dolientes desde el Manicomio General. México, 1910–1930* (2010). This publication constitutes, in her own words, "a restitution" and a "border crossing" between academic and fictional writing on the same subject.[1]

The Author

Cristina Rivera Garza belongs to the new generation of young writers educated in the academic environment of theoretical readings applied later in their fictional works. Rivera Garza is a prolific author who attracts the young intellectuals of the new millennium. Her publications include novels, academic books, short stories, poetry, essays and a blog ("No hay tal lugar"/ There is no such place). Her first novel, *Nadie me verá llorar* (1999), received high recognition, including the prestigious Sor Juana Inés de la Cruz and José Rubén Romero National Book literary prizes. After this success, she has published several novels, *La cresta de Ilión* (*Ilion's Crest*, 2002), *Lo anterior* (*What Lies Before*, 2004), *La muerte me da* (*Death Hits Me*, 2008), *Verde Shanghai* (Shanghai Green, 2011) and *El mal de la taiga* (*Taiga's Syndrome*, 2012). Carlos Fuentes described *Nadie me verá llorar* as "one of the most notable works of fiction not only in Mexican literature but in literature of the Spanish-speaking world at the start of the twentieth-first century."[2] Her writing complements an academic career in the United States and Mexico.

In this chapter, madness is used as an artifice to redefine the writing of history. I contend that Cristina Rivera Garza's novel explores a new way of looking at the history of Mexico at the turn of the 20th century by focusing on the mad and the marginalized from society. By comparing and contrasting Rivera Garza's academic publications and the novel, I explore correlations between madness and literature in the definitions of gender, class and nation. The two artifices used in the novel, language in the form of "heteroglossia" and photography as a "space-off" technique, allow the intersection of these opposing discourses. Therefore, photography and language in the novel are used to stress the ambiguity and contradiction that shape the writing of history. While photography fixes and manipulates the image to create, visualize and imprint the idea of the insane, language dictates and justifies the control mechanisms of the excluded and marginalized from society.

The "space-off" is a term used by Teresa de Lauretis in film studies to define "the space not visible in the frame but inferable from what the frame makes visible" (26). According to de Lauretis, the "space-off" makes the invisible visible by signaling the absence in the frame or in the succession of frames. De Lauretis makes the analogy with the discourses of gender, defined as "a movement between the (represented) discursive space of the positions made available by hegemonic discourses and the space-off, the elsewhere, of those discourses: those other spaces [...] that exist in the margins or 'between the lines,' or 'against the grain' of hegemonic discourses and in the interstices of institutions, in counter-practices and new forms of community" (26). These spaces, which in the words of de Lauretis are "neither in opposition to one another nor strung along a chain of signification but coexist concurrently and in contradiction" (26), will be applied to photography as a discursive technique in *Nadie me verá llorar*. This strategy complements Bakhtin's concept of heteroglossia used throughout the novel as a mechanism that imprints and reflects madness as a discursive technique. According to Bakhtin, "The novel can be defined as a diversity of social speech types (sometimes even diversity of languages) and diversity of individual voices, artistically organized." "These distinctive links and interrelationships between utterances and languages, the movement of theme through different languages and speech types, its dispersion into the rivulets and droplets of social heteroglossia, its dialogization—this is the basic distinguishing feature of the stylistics of the novel" (484). In *Nadie*, the dialogic and heteroglossia operate as one of the predominant textual strategies of the novel.

I will examine the historical discourses, clinical cases and diagnostics as cartographies of the novel formed through photographic visual and language strategies. In the process I will refer to Rivera Garza's own reflections in her correlated publications.

The Writing of History

In an interview with Cheyla Samuelson, Rivera Garza posed the question that guided the writing of the novel *Nadie me verá llorar*: "How can we create a novel based on these historical documents that is not trying to portray the past, that is not trying to take the present day reader to the past, but that is trying to do just the opposite, to make the past contemporary?" (140). In all the publications related to the La Castañeda Psychiatric Hospital, her thesis, the novel, and the book, *La Castañeda*, Rivera Garza explores the discursive strategies used by psychiatrists and inmates to produce what she called "historical and clinical meaningful advances on mental illness." One of the main arguments focuses on the definitions of gender, class and nation through the analysis of medical cases in the early years of the Psychiatric Hospital and the Revolutionary period (1910–1930). Rivera Garza explains that the book *La Castañeda* "emphasizes the various ways in which patients' perceptions of their own afflictions have shaped medical understanding of mental illness, as well as gender and class interpretations in the context of nation-building" (*La Castañeda* 24).[3]

The author clarifies that she does not intend to "give a voice" to the historical subjects but rather, she relies on precepts of medical anthropology, especially those informed by ethnography to explore "the lines of the script, the main metaphorical elements that structured the illness, which are derived from cultural and personal ways of organizing experiences in meaningful ways and expressing those meanings effectively" (*La Castañeda* 15).[4]

In her thesis, articles and book, Rivera Garza uses Mikhail Bakhtin's theory on discourse analysis as a research method to study the case histories found at the Psychiatric Hospital *La Castañeda*. At the same time, she describes the narratives of both mental patients and doctors' diagnoses, as examples of heteroglossia:

> In the midst of the historiographical debates that usually emphasize the processes of construction, reconstruction or centralization of the State, polysemic narratives of mental sufferings vividly recall destruction, dismantling and dispersion; in short, the centrifugal forces that Bakhtin associated with the heteroglossia.[5]

By connecting the concept of madness with a discursive technique, the author maps the strategy that she uses in *Nadie me verá llorar* as the textual cartography: the multilayered polyphony of voices, linguistic techniques and layers of textual discourses. The use of heteroglossia is evident in the variety of registers, genres, focalizations, intertextual relations and palimpsests found across the narrative. Indeed, Rivera Garza uses a plethora of narrative techniques, allegories, and discourses to signal, reflect and represent the polysemic nature of mental illness to propose a new way of looking at the history of early 20th-century Mexico. She applies research methods and theories used in her dissertation from theorists such as Hayden White, Roland Barthes, Foucault, Walter Benjamin and Bakhtin.

Following Bakhtin's dialogic approach, Rivera Garza confronts the reflection of history at the micro level—the asylum—with History[6] at the macro level—the state—through the exploration of an individual life story, that of Matilda Burgos (based on the case of La Castañeda inmate, Modesta Burgos).

In the novel, Matilda lives a transformation as a poor country girl who migrates to Mexico City, where she becomes first a disciplined housekeeper, then a prostitute and finally, an inmate at the asylum, La Castañeda. Matilda's story takes the reader across the radical transformation of Mexico during the Porfiriato, modernization, and the critical period of the Mexican Revolution.

Laura Kanost has expressed in an earlier study that the title of *Nadie me verá llorar*, translated as *No One Will See Me Cry* in English, refers to Matilda Burgos's determination to remain strong and stoic in the face of the most difficult hardships in her life (302). The words also reference a song by Miriam Britos by the same tittle, *Nadie me verá llorar* (Navia Velasco 113). Born and raised in the countryside of Veracruz, Matilda is sent to Mexico City to live with her uncle, a progressive physician who is obsessed with theories of hygiene as the pathway to modernization. Matilda becomes his social project. Later, when Matilda meets political activist Cástulo Rodríguez, she gets involved in the political resistance movement that preceded the Mexican Revolution. The uncle's efforts to transform her fail when instead of becoming the model individual, she chooses to be the opposite: an anarchist, a prostitute and a performer.

The drastic turn from being a model individual to a prostitute and performer marks the onset of who Matilda will become later as an inmate at the asylum. As a prostitute, she is well known for her performances mocking Federico Gamboa's popular novel, *Santa*. In a parody of the popular early 20th-century Mexican novel, the performance ridicules Gamboa's masterpiece by explicitly subverting the passage where two women take part in a sexual act:

> Cuando "la Diablesa" (Matilda) y "la Diamantina" (Ligia) leyeron el pasaje juntas, no solo no pudieron evitar las carcajadas sino que además hicieron el amor sobre las páginas del libro. ¡Ay, pobre embajador Gamboa, tan cosmopolita y tan falto de imaginación! [*Nadie* 145].
>
> When the "Devil" and La Diamantina read this passage together, they not only howled with laughter but also made love on the pages of the book. Poor ambassador Gamboa, so cosmopolitan and so lacking in imagination! [*No One* 156].

Parallel to the cross-gender performance at the end of Cristina Peri Rossi's *La nave de los locos*, discussed in the first chapter, Matilda and her partner Ligia cross-dress as multiple characters performing Gamboa's polemic passage:

> Mientras ella misma [Ligia] se hizo cargo de transformar a la provinciana estúpida en una dama con alas de dragón, Matilda se convirtió en un hombre de frac cuya inocencia e ignorancia del bajo mundo le ganaron el

apelativo de "el Menso." Ninguna de sus piezas produjo más risas y más aplausos entre la concurrencia y fue gracias a ella que consiguieron trabajo en la Modernidad [*Nadie* 149].

While she herself went about transforming the stupid, provincial heroine into a fine lady with dragon's wings, Matilda became a man in a tuxedo, whose naivete and ignorance of the demimonde earned him the nickname "The Idiot." None of their pieces produced more laughter and applause among spectators, and it was thanks to this one that they found work in la Modernidad [*No One* 161].

The brothel, paradoxically called La Modernidad (Modernity), is described as the place where no desire is prohibited and where Matilda alternates her own sexual preferences. She acts as a woman, as a transvestite, as a lesbian and as an androgynous character. As a prostitute she finds freedom and the possibility of being whoever she wants to be, free of formalisms, gender determinism and nation and class categorization, as summarized in this passage:

> A Matilda le gustaba tener una compinche, pero más le gustaba su nueva libertad. Fuera de la cárcel de los Burgos y fuera también de la salita de Mesones [...] las calles se convirtieron en su única casa y el cielo azul de la Ciudad de México en su único techo. Así descubrió su verdadera patria [*Nadie* 147].
>
> Matilda enjoyed having a companion, a "buddy," but she enjoyed her new freedom even more. Freed from the prison of the Burgoses, the little parlor on Mesones [...] she found that the streets had become her only home. The blue sky of Mexico City the only roof she liked over her head. It was in this way that she discovered her true homeland [*No One* 159].

The various characters Matilda performs offer her access to alternative gender, social class, and national identities, contrasting with the previous rigid experience at her uncle's house. Exercising such freedom, however, ultimately determines Matilda's destiny in the Castañeda asylum.

When Matilda marries a client, Paul Kamack, she leaves her life of prostitution. After a short period, her husband dies and Matilda returns to the capital where she briefly joins a theater company. One day after a performance, she is arrested for refusing sexual favors to a group of soldiers. Accused of mental derangement, she is taken to La Castañeda, where she spends the remainder of her life. In the psychiatric institution, she meets the asylum photographer Joaquín Buitrago who, after having seen and photographed her previously at the brothel, La Modernidad, becomes obsessed with her.

Joaquin Buitrago is an upper class individual who has given up his family's comfort and inheritance for his addiction to morphine. His addiction leads him to become the resident photographer and a patient at La Castañeda asylum, where he decides to investigate Matilda's life story. He uses the archives and documents of La Castañeda, just as Rivera Garza did for her dissertation. In the process, he inquires about Matilda's diagnosis with the resident physician, Eduardo Oligochea, who learns about his romantic obsession and ends up manipulating him for his own benefit. As Joaquin reads and summarizes Matilda's archives, the narration unfolds her life through a storyline full of temporal jumps and diverse voices that form a textual puzzle.

Near the end, Matilda and Joaquin leave the asylum for a brief period of time and live together in his inherited family home, after he is supposedly cured of his morphine addiction. This period is an interesting segment of the story, as the reader hopes for a romantic happy ending. However, in an unexpected twist, Matilda chooses to return to the asylum, where she is "free" to be the person she has decided to be: free from society's demands, impositions and regulations. Liberated even from Joaquin, his love, his gaze, his imposing protection and his photographic obsession. This denouement reveals the contradiction of the novel: the opposition between language and silence, darkness and light, reason and unreason. Matilda conveys all these contradictions in this line: "Pronto podrá regresar a su refugio, a ese lugar sin puertas que Eduardo Oligochea denomina locura" (*Nadie* 198) ["Soon she will be able to return to her refuge, to that place without doors that Eduardo Oligochea calls madness" (*No One* 218)]. The refuge is that place, where there are no eyes, no sense in language and no plot. Instead, as Emily Hind declared, "it is the sum of irrationality" (155).

Nadie me verá llorar as a whole is a kaleidoscope of historical events, celebrities, and locations revealing Mexico at the turn of century and its insertion into modernity. By comparing and contrasting micro history—the lives of Matilda and Joaquín—with macro History—the events that configured the state at the onset of the 20th century—the author is proposing a new way to look at history. In the words of Rivera Garza explaining her thesis, later adapted for her novel: "This is a work intentionally full of rough edges, angles, sudden interruptions and arrests. This text does not tell a story the *way it really was* but tries to capture a few moments of danger in a kaleidoscopic montage that welcomes contradictions and challenges order" (quoted in Rufinnelli 35).

In the deliberate disconnection of discourses, Rivera Garza challenges conventional historiography by committing to what Linda Hutcheon called the poetics of Postmodernism. According to Hutcheon, "what postmodern writing of both history and literature has taught us is that both discourses constitute systems of signification by which we make sense of the past: the meaning and shape are not in the events, but in the systems which make those past 'events' into present historical facts" (89).

Rivera Garza uses a variety of postmodern techniques in order to challenge fixed categories in which Mexican history has been told. Using the dialogical and heteroglossia as her approach, the author problematizes and reinstalls contextual values of the past and makes them present. *Nadie me verá llorar* deliberately uses the discourse of madness to challenge the historical assumptions of objectivity, neutrality, impersonality and transparence of representation into a critical confrontation of the contradictions embedded into the writing of history. Indeed, as noted by Elizabeth Cummins Múñoz, the novel "exploits the multilayered discursive tension by juxtaposing the incongruous languages of psychiatry, insanity, positivism, social liberalism, nostalgia and others without any organizing ideological paradigm other than the deconstruction of their relative nature. The result is an epistemological stage on which all players contribute to the construction of its own organizing paradigm: the dramatization of signification on a textual level" (143). Therefore, the heteroglossic nature of mental illness is reflected in the text as a narrative technique that resembles other strategies used by Cristina Peri Rossi in *La nave de los locos*, or by Laura Restrepo in *Delirio*, and even by Diamela Eltit and Paz Errázuriz in *Infarto del alma*. At the same time, this strategy is used to disarticulate notions of class, gender and nation by recontextualizing new layers of signification at all levels. Main characters Matilda and Joaquín are always at the edge, testing the boundaries of social classes, gender categories and the configuration of spaces in what the author describes as "the inside and the outside."

The Inside

Nadie me verá llorar delivers a compelling message that corresponds to Foucault's concept of madness and confinement. As Rivera Garza explains, "in an era that witnessed the demise of a 30-year-old dictatorship of Porfirio Díaz, the outbreak of a revolutionary war that cost more than one million lives and the rise of regimes that sought to rebuild the Mexican nation [...] the State saw the asylum as a segregation strategy to protect society from contagion" ("She Neither Respected" 656). But without clear lines to distinguish madness from reason, such segregation was touted as an effective social control practice that displaced whomever was considered detrimental to society. Indeed, Rivera Garza states that the walls surrounding the asylum were meant to define a border separating "the strong and the competent" from the "weak and the corrupted" in an industrializing society increasingly concerned with the threat of the poor ("She Neither Respected" 659). Confinement was thus a way to exert control over potentially disruptive members of society just as Michel Foucault documented in *History of Madness*.

According to Foucault, life in the asylum reproduced in a microcosm the massive structures of society and its values: family, justice and social order. As discussed in the introduction, confinement was a convenient resource for social cleansing and control of moral issues and it extended to the world as a progressive idea for modernization (*History of Madness* 491). In *Nadie me verá llorar*, confinement complies with the role of preservation of social order and control for the sake of the nation's growth and progress. By the same token, social morality and order were intermingled with mental illness diagnoses. As Rivera Garza explicitly contends in her article and book, "the case of La Castañeda is particularly important to both the historiography of confinement and the historiography of modern Mexico because it emerged at a juncture in which diverse social projects collided and clashed" ("She Neither Respected" 656, *La Castañeda* 40–41).

As an institution, La Castañeda evolved according to the times, from the Modernization period of the Porfiriato—in which the hospital was built as a magnificent place[7] with all the opulence of the beginning of the century in Mexico—to the decline of the Revolution. Thus, the Hospital reproduced historical periods of prosperity and decadence. In terms of its mission, the Hospital contributed to reinforcing the dominant ideas of order and social control of the Porfirian and Revolutionary periods. During both eras, the institution offered assistance and "refuge" to dispossessed people and those whose families considered them mentally ill. However, by the time of the Mexican Revolution, the conditions at the psychiatric Hospital worsened and the institution could not replicate or reinforce the ideas of social order and control (*La Castañeda* 72).

Rivera Garza proposes that "in different formats and with diverse degrees of articulation, some inmates—especially those who did not suffer from severe mental conditions—participated in the elaboration of what Arthur Kleinman called illness narratives, stories in which the plot lines, core metaphors, and rhetorical devices that structure illness are drawn from cultural and personal modes for arranging experiences in meaningful ways and for effectively expressing those meanings" ("She Neither Respected" 654, *La Castañeda* 16). Asylum narratives, however, were hardly free-flowing constructions of life history. As Rivera Garza explains, "constrained by an institutional setting that emphasized doctors' authority and a medical questionnaire that provided limited space for inmates' answers, these narratives brought together state health authorities and inmates as they engaged in a contested dialogue over the medical and social meanings of mental illness in Mexico" ("She Neither Respected" 654, *La Castañeda* 16).

One of the issues at the core of the novel is the definition of madness and who determines the condition of insanity. The novel clearly reflects the academic proposal of the author: mental illness is associated with deviant behaviors, but in the case of women, insanity is diagnosed when normative models of femininity are at stake, as in the case of Matilda Burgos, whose mental state is questionable. Matilda's diagnosis is based on her sexual history, considered the true source of deviance and mental derangement, along with her "verborrea" (language excess). By disclosing real women's clinical histories from the archives of the Castañeda, Rivera Garza posits, was insanity declared merely based on deviant female sexual behavior? The detailed descriptions registered in the third chapter of the novel reveal the range of terminology used to diagnose women's disturbances: from evil impulses to religious delirium and irrational jealousy, and from indigence to violence, the most persistent diagnosis being the ambiguous claim of "moral insanity."

Moral Insanity

In her academic publications, Rivera Garza examines the prominent use of "moral insanity" to conclude that it was the main diagnosis and a marker of mental illness for women who did not fit the social and religious standards of the times. The argument is that the discussion on the proper place of poor women in society played a fundamental role in the definition of normal and abnormal behaviors ("She Neither Respected" 655). She explains that while most European and American psychiatrists were no longer using the term "moral insanity" to classify patients, it was one of the most frequently used diagnoses to describe women's mental illness in early 20th-century Mexico.

The concept of moral insanity as a medical category was formulated by English physician James Prichard in his 1835 book *A Treatise on Insanity and Other Disorders Affecting the Mind*. Prichard described moral insanity as "a form of monomania in which people recognized the difference between right and wrong, yet lacked the will power to resist evil impulses" ("She Neither Respected" 657, *La Castañeda* 290). Because this diagnosis openly called for definitions of "good" and "evil," Rivera Garza argues, "it induced the conspicuous incorporation of nonmedical factors in interpretations of mental derangement—an opportunity that female patients used to elaborate stories of their basic human experience with illness" ("She Neither Respected" 657). According to Rivera Garza, "The narratives that women constructed as they interacted with asylum doctors revealed their ability to interpret and rename the domestic and social worlds they inhabited, forcing doctors and readers alike to see those worlds through their eyes" ("She Neither Respected" 657). She contends that "these powerfully unnerving narratives also revealed the emphatic ways in which inmates articulated physical and spiritual pain to develop—whether implicitly or abruptly, cogently or frantically—moral and political commentaries on the causes of their misfortune. Thus at a fundamental level, the mad narratives constitute vivid reminders of the fragility of the hegemonic framework in which modern Mexico took shape" ("She Neither Respected" 658). Matilda's diagnosis, reflecting the real-life documents that inspired the novel, reveals her sexual past as the source of her mental disturbance:

> Se describe a sí misma como una mujer hermosa y educada, la reina de ciertos congales y numerosas orgías. Dice que trabajaba como artista en la compañía del Teatro Fábregas y en la ópera de Bonesi. Sufre de una imaginación excéntrica y tiene una tendencia clara a inventar historias que nunca se cansa de contar. Pasa de un asunto a otro sin parar. Proclividad a usar términos rebuscados a los cuales pretende dar otro significado.
> Explica su encierro como consecuencia de la venganza de un grupo de soldados que pidieron sus favores sexuales en la calle. Debido al odio que siente por los soldados se negó y así fue como la mandaron a la cárcel. Logorrea. Muestra exceso de movilidad. Sentido afectivo disminuido. Anomalía de sentido moral. Locura moral [*Nadie* 108].

> She describes herself as beautiful, well-brought woman, the queen of certain bordellos and countless orgies. She says she worked as an artist in the Fábregas Theater and in the Bonesi Opera. She suffers from an eccentric imagination and has a clear tendency to invent stories, which she never tires of telling. She goes from one subject to another without pause. Proclivity for using erudite terms, to which she attempts another meaning. She explains her confinement here as a consequence of the revenge of a group of soldiers who came up to her in the street and demanded sexual favors. Because of the hatred she had for soldiers, she refused, and had her sent to jail. Logorrhea. Displays excessive mobility. Diminished affection. Diagnosis: moral insanity [*No One* 94–95].

Matilda's diagnosis summarizes Rivera Garza's proposition on language as a powerful medium to control women's bodies. The clinical story emphasizes the use of terms associated with the production of language as a sign of mental anomaly: "She invents stories," "Proclivity for using erudite terms," "Logorrhea." Also, the references to her sexual past, "the queen of certain bordellos," reveal the link made between mental illness and her deviant behavior.

In the academic texts, Rivera Garza explains that doctors took interest in Modesta Burgos's case because of her intellectual skills, which they interpreted as a sign of mental degeneration. Diagnosed by Doctor Méndez, her case was considered one of the clearest examples of moral insanity: "Modesta B.'s lack of modesty, her use of affected terms, the pretense to pass herself as an educated woman and, above all, her willingness to talk about sex, endlessly and shamelessly describing orgies and other sexual practices deemed as deviant, made the diagnosis seem right" ("She Neither Respected" 675–76).

The clinical file of Modesta Burgos as an example of "moral insanity" was crucial for Rivera Garza to examine the contradictions of psychiatric practices. Rivera Garza asserts, "as women diagnosed with moral insanity intently presented themselves as active players in both the domestic and social arenas, they struggled to tell the story of their lives and, in doing so, they implicitly questioned medical diagnoses of alleged scientific status" ("She Neither Respected" 684). By 1930, the moral insanity diagnosis was discarded. Rivera Garza considered this a victory of female patients over Porfirian psychiatry. By introducing a discourse in which women appeared as mothers and wives, workers and neighbors, the inmates forced doctors to reconsider and eventually discard Porfirian medical tenets. The author concludes, "thus, even behind asylum walls, they [female patients] became players in the construction of the fragile hegemony in which modern Mexico took shape" ("She Neither Respected" 684).

Doctor-Patient Relationship

Clinical histories from the asylum presented in the novel also reveal the tension in doctor-patient relationships. According to Rivera Garza, "this process involved more than a static opposition between the 'dominant' doctor and the 'subordinate' inmate. Instead, exchanging sideways glances in the unequal relation of power created by the psychiatric interview, both actors addressed one another in continuous, and contesting, motion" ("She Neither Respected" 685). In the novel, this tension and contention is achieved through the dialogue exchanges between the patient Joaquin Buitrago, and the asylum director, Eduardo Oligochea. They address each other in a contesting and continuous motion, subverting doctor-patient power relations, and questioning who is in greater need of treatment.

Eduardo and Joaquin's interaction demonstrates how asylum inmates and their doctors developed tense, mad narratives of mental illness—texts of multiple voices in which both actors waged their own understandings of body, mind, and society, shaping strategies of negotiation that informed and contributed to the construction of mental illness. The asylum became the site of encounter. As Cummins Muñoz has remarked, "It is the site at which different discourses with seemingly self-contained meaning systems and varying degrees of power come into contact and new meaning is created" (263). Here, the dispute between reason and unreason posed by Foucault stands once more. According to Foucault, the division between reason and unreason constitutes the cycle of knowledge: "For unreason is both the reason for the division and the reason for unity that is to be found on both sides of the divide. Unreason is the explanation for the presence of the same forms of experience, but also for the fact that they are found on one side and on the other" (*History of Madness* 173). Therefore, when the physician is presented with distinguishing between reason, nature and illness, madness presents the full depth of its contradictions. This is also at the core of Rivera Garza's proposition: the interaction between physician and patient clearly illustrates the dynamic opposition between reason and unreason presented by Foucault:

This maximal and minimal risk accepted by classical culture in madness is precisely what the word "unreason" expresses: the simple immediate conversion of reason, encountered at once; and this empty form, without content or value, purely negative, where all that figures is the imprint of a reason that has taken to its heels, but which will always remain, for unreason, its *raison d'etre* [*History of Madness* 174].

Rivera Garza achieves this contradiction through the array of discursive resources in the novel and the confluence of the heteroglossia dialogic technique. However, I would argue, it is in the artifice of photography that the contradictions and opposition of elements expressed above achieve their maximum representation.

The Photographic Artifice

Parallel to *Infarto del alma*, in *Nadie me verá llorar* the reader-observer becomes an active participant through photography. In this novel, however, the visual photographs are not present in the text. Through the lens of photography, the narrative plays with light and darkness, the visible and the invisible and the *scopic* at the center of the storyline.

Rivera Garza explains that the use of photography in the novel originated in the collection of photographs she found in psychiatric hospital records while conducting her thesis research. According to the author, inmate photographs imprinted the physical and social characteristics of madness with the accuracy and objectivity inherent to the camera. However, in a social environment concerned about the danger posed by the urban poor, images of the insane contributed to the creation of a typology of illness based on definitions of class and gender (*La Castañeda* 187–188). The author wondered whether the faces portraying madness were indeed the faces of madness. Hence, she decided to use a dialogical technique confronting the reader with the photographic image as a way to unite the past and present in an attempt to achieve simultaneous temporalities. Rivera Garza explains,

> Si el husmeador de archivos supiera que anda en busca de la cara del loco, no le quedaría más remedio que [...] abrir la boca y preguntarse cosas. ¿Es este rostro sonriente, incluso retador y coqueto, la personificación misma de la locura? ¿Son estos ojos, por fin, los ojos de la locura? Esa pregunta, o preguntas muy similares, [...] me llevó a escribir una novela. [...] Ahí estaba, dentro del óvalo de una fotografía, esa mujer que

miraba hacia el futuro. [...] Me hizo escribirla tras volver la vista hacia atrás y hacia el presente de manera simultánea [*La Castañeda* 219].

If the file seeker knew that he was looking for the face of the madman, he would have no choice but to [...] open his mouth and ask himself some questions. Is this smiling face, daring and flirtatious, the very embodiment of madness? Are these eyes, really, the eyes of madness? That question, or very similar questions, [...] led me to write a novel. [...] There she was, within the oval of a photograph, that woman who looked toward the future. [...] I did write it after turning to face the past and the present simultaneously.

Rivera Garza's technique turns the questions to the reader, using as a medium the invisible sign of photography alluded to but not present in the text. Therefore, the space-off—the space not visible in the frame but inferable from what the frame makes visible—allows the author to establish a dialogue with the reader. This dialogical technique is achieved from the start of the novel, as it opens with a question, "How does one come to be a photographer of crazy people?" Madness and photography are joined from this first line. The strategy establishes a constant dialogue between these two premises through a series of questions, thus conforming to Bakhtin's dialogical approach. Repetitive questions such as "How do you become a photographer of prostitutes?" and "How do you become a crazy woman?" and others of that sort will function as markers in spatial and temporal jumps throughout the narrative. The role of the Joaquin as the photographer in the novel is to capture and preserve memory from the obscure and invisible side of reality.

The invisible side is evident when the reader learns that Joaquín's photography originates in his obsession with pain. But how do you register pain? Joaquín's first experience of this sort was through a dead woman found in the street. The woman's expression of pain was registered in his memory, becoming his first invisible photo and his introduction to pain and death:

> Joaquín buscaba captar el dolor en el instante en que se transformaba en su propia ausencia, en nada. Ésa era la única posibilidad que vislumbraba: todo era dolor y el resto era el remanso brutal de la muerte. La fotografía era la manera de detener la rueda del dolor del mundo [*Nadie* 29].
>
> Joaquin sought to capture the pain at the instant it turned into its own absence, turned into nothing, nothingness. That was the only possibility he envisioned: everything was pain, and the rest was the brutal rest, the

brutal peace of death. Photography was a way, his way, of stopping the wheel of the word's pain [*No One* 21].

Joaquín's photographs aim to produce a reaction to that pain, "the *punctum*," defined by Roland Barthes as that detail that attracts the attention like a sting.⁸ At the same time, it seeks to provoke the connection between madness and pain felt and expressed by the author in the process of writing her thesis, the novel and the book, *La Castañeda*. Just as Elaine Scarry expresses in *The Body in Pain*, "pain more than any other phenomenon resists objectification in Language" (5), Rivera Garza emphasizes how difficult it was to deal with the subject of pain and suffering. While she recognizes that the concept of pain has little or no historical validity, she confirms its political and epistemological value in relocating "the suffering back in the center of the stage of a nation committed with modernity and progress at all cost. In this sense, the suffering as an agency acquires an alternative denomination, 'the tragic'" (*La Castañeda* 31). The tragic associated with pain constitutes another motif imbedded in mental illness. For Rivera Garza, suffering is a dignifying category that bestows a moral status. Both her academic texts and the novel underline the tragic dimension of the mental illness as a reflection of the individual and society. However, the author is careful not to fall in the trap of romanticizing madness or using it as a metaphor for feminist empowerment. On the contrary, the suffering inscribed in the photographs and the medical archives provide the "space-off," to reveal the invisible part of the photo that is inferred by the viewer. The "space-off" complements Barthes' *punctum* as strategies to achieve what Caminero Santangelo considers fundamental in the literature of madness: "to reconfigure that space from within—to reveal 'the space-off'" (10).⁹ Rivera Garza accomplishes just this by using photography as a predominant discursive technique in the novel.

Although the photographs described in the novel were not visually registered, the author did publish the photographs in the book *La Castañeda*. The reader could finally see physically the pain and the suffering associated with the mentally ill that Rivera Garza so emphasized in the novel. The confrontation with the face of the mad provides another way to look into the narrative, as the reader could see that the mad and the marginalized shared the opprobrious conditions in which they were maintained by the institution. Like in the case of Diamela Eltit and Paz Errázuriz's *El infarto del alma*, the Castañeda inmates photographs evidenced what was at the core of the modernization project, to isolate and discard the individuals who did not fit the new idea of the nation.

Photography as a medium becomes the textual discourse that plays with combinations of light and darkness, black and white, fixed images and blurred ones. One significant element is the set of oppositions as a reflection of white and negative snapshots. This technique is used to subvert the redefinition of boundaries between history and micro history, inside and outside, glorification and marginalization, progress and decay; reason versus unreason, order against chaos, and language versus silence. In all of them, the textual lens reveals, reflects and refracts the angles of the story that have not been told. The narrative style parallels snapshots in a technique described by Jorge Ruffinelli in these terms:

> Su novela se desenvuelve en torno a momentos particulares, aparentemente (o realmente) disgregados entre sí, sin la necesidad de esforzarlos a formar parte de un hilo cronológico tal como entendemos convencionalmente el discurso histórico [35].
>
> The novel unfurls around small, particular moments, apparently (or really) disconnected from one another, without forcing them to become a chronological sequence within conventional historical discourse.

Following Walter Benjamin's method, according to Ruffinelli, the story focuses on the particular, not the general, and is told in non-chronological sequences, in an attempt to disarticulate time and space and to focus on the ethereal, the perpetual/fixed image that defeats both (36). This is particularly true in chapter seven of the novel, which places the protagonists outside of the major events of History in the "micro" level of history, in the individuality and concreteness of minor daily events:

> Matilda Burgos y Joaquín Buitrago se han perdido todas las grandes ocasiones históricas. Cuando la revolución estalló, ella estaba dentro de un amor hecho de biznagas y aire azul, y él en la duermevela desigual de la morfina. *Ninguno* se enteró de la fecha en que Pascual Orozco tomó Ciudad Juárez, ni el día exacto en que el presidente Díaz salió exiliado. [...] *Ninguno* de los dos formó parte de la muchedumbre que festejó la entrada de Francisco I. Madero en la Ciudad de México, y ninguna de las balas de la Decena Trágica los hirió. *Nunca* vieron a Victoriano Huerta en cantina alguna y, aunque oyeron los rumores y presenciaron el desorden, no se molestaron en leer los periódicos con las noticias de la invasión norteamericana. Cuando Emiliano Zapata y Francisco Villa se ofrecieron la silla presidencial el uno al otro, respetuosamente, hacienda gala de buenos modales, Matilda estaba absorta viendo las burbujas del agua en punto de

ebullición en una olla de barro, y Joaquín solo usaba su cabeza para recrear el fantasma cruel de Alberta [emphasis added, *Nadie* 175].

Matilda Burgos and Joaquin Buitrago have missed all the grand historic occasions. When the Revolution broke out, she was in the midst of a love made of barrel-shaped cactuses and blue air, and he was in the wavering daze of morphine. On the day Pascual Orozco took Ciudad Juárez, *neither* of them was aware of it, or the exact day on which Porfirio Díaz fled into exile. [...] *Neither* of them was part of the crowd that celebrated the entrance of Francisco Madero into Mexico City, and *none* of the bullets of the Ten Tragic Days in 1913 wounded them. They *never* saw Victoriano Huerta in any cantina whatsoever, and although they heard the rumors and witnessed the chaos, they *did not* bother to read the newspapers with the headlines about the American invasion. When Emiliano Zapata and Francisco Villa offered each other the presidential chair, each making a show of good manners, Matilda was absorbed in watching the bubbles of water about to boil in a clay pot and Joaquín was using his head only to call up again the cruel ghost of Alberta [emphasis added, *No One* 191].

In this passage the alternative hermeneutic is achieved through the contrasting elements, which prove that the totality can only be perceived through the individual. It also reflects the two sides of a snapshot—white versus black—by contrasting the big events of History with everyday occurrences. The negative anaphora, "neither, none, never, nor" along with the emphasis on absences, emptiness, and open spaces—the "space off"—accomplishes the purpose of interweaving the semantic with the visual in a disarticulation of language, order and truth. The last line of that paragraph emphasizes this opposition: "Los dos anduvieron siempre en las orillas de la historia, siempre a punto de resbalar y caer fuera de su embrujo y siempre, sin embargo, dentro, muy dentro" (*Nadie* 176) ["Both were in the wet, messy banks of history, ready to slip and fall out of its spell and yet always inside it. Very much inside it" (*No One* 192)].

Light and Darkness

The contrast of light and darkness in the novel has been analyzed by several critics as an analogy between the two characters, Joaquín and Matilda. According to Encarnación Cruz Jimenez, "Frente a la oscuridad que caracteriza a Buitrago tenemos la luz que caracteriza a Matilda. Si Buitrago se oculta detrás de la cámara, Matilda se sitúa frente a ella y se comporta con socarronería y altivez" (13) [Confronting the darkness that characterizes Buitrago, we have the light that characterizes Matilda. If Buitrago is hidden behind the camera, Matilda stands before it and behaves with sarcasm and arrogance]. Miguel Zugasti, on the other hand, suggests that the light surrounding Matilda is like an aura that individualizes her but goes unnoticed for the rest of mortals except Joaquín (698–99). However, I contend that Rivera Garza goes beyond the binary opposition of light and dark, sane and insane. All throughout the narrative the author uses different gradations of light reflected in walls, corners and roofs in order to play with what Nelly Richard calls "discontinuities of the visual field" (*Masculine and Feminine* 36). Chapter one ("Reflections, Gradations of Light, Images") registers this strategic disarticulation of fixed categories and interpretations. Joaquín's room ceiling is a vivid representation of a visual cartography that is composed through the storyline interposed in the cracks of his pain, morphine addition and obsession with Matilde's story. The same applies to Joaquín and Matilda. Their fluid dynamic character development does not allow for fixed categorizations. Rivera Garza achieves this visual cartography through an array of discursive resources. By using heteroglossia and the photographic artifice as textual strategies, the author exposes facts through real life stories transcending the fragile line of memory. It is her way of registering her testimony: look at the world through the other's eyes.

How do you become a photographer of the mad? Joaquin's camera lens registers and preserves history, not the official one, but the micro history, the one that has gone untold, unseen and unwritten. Joaquin has learned to see and hopes that through his photographs, someone will learn to see too. In the novel the scopic field expands through the lens of those considered insane, as they are the ones who have a wider angle of vision. Therefore, madness is symbolically as blurry as an out-of-focus photograph.

Photography and language work as the mechanisms to accentuate the ambiguity and contradiction that shape the writing of history. While photography manipulates the image to create and visualize the idea of the mad, language reflects the strategies used to control those who are excluded from society. In both cases a dynamic of power and control defines the way class, gender and nation were built in Mexico at the onset of the 20th century. These mechanisms are useful not only to analyze the history of that particular nation or time, but to establish parallels and similarities with the onset of the 21st century throughout Latin America.

Rivera Garza's technique is compelling and provocative. The series of inquiries across the novel unfold in more unanswered questions. The last section reproduces texts and manuscripts from Matilda (Modesta) Burgos, including the following question, "¿Cómo se convierte uno en una loca?" (*Nadie* 247) ["How does a woman go crazy?" (*No One* 228)]. The reader will have to answer with other questions of the same sort: was Matilda ever a crazy woman? Did she become insane in the asylum? Was she considered mentally ill because of her sexual behavior? Who are really the crazy ones in the story? Probably the only feasible answer is her response when she returns to the asylum: "La tautología es la reina de su corazón" (*Nadie* 198) ["Tautology is the queen of your heart" (*No One* 218)]. As Emily Hind concluded, this is the contradiction of the novel. Not only Matilda has turned mad through the narrative, but the language, too, has become irrational: "La idea de que las palabras tienen un solo significado coincide con la propuesta de que las palabras no tienen significado" (198) [The idea that the words have only one meaning coincides with the proposal of words having no meaning]. Therefore, the concept of tautology eliminates all semantic meaning—the disconnection between signified and signifier—and reflects the opposition of language and silence, darkness and light, reason and unreason which lies at the core of the novel. It may be also the answer to the series of questions scattered across the novel: there is not a real answer after all.

CHAPTER FIVE

A Poetics of Madness

Laura Restrepo's *Delirio*

Elvira Sánchez-Blake

> *La locura es el territorio donde se pierden no solo las personas sino las sociedades.*
>
> Madness is that territory where not only people but also societies become lost.
>
> (Laura Restrepo, interview with Roger Santo Domingo, 2014)

Delirio by Laura Restrepo delivers a powerful statement about Colombian society, a society entrapped by multiple forms of insanity at the turn of the millennium. Restrepo creates in her narrative a poetics of madness casting insanity in multiple directions, from the individual to the collective, from the social to the political, and from the country to the continent. Reason and unreason are expressed in all fashions by multiple actors in a polyphony of voices that transcend time and space.[1]

Laura Restrepo, a Colombian journalist, writer and political activist, is the author of *Historia de una traición* (1986) later republished as *Historia de un entusiasmo* (*History of Enthusiasm*, 1997), *La isla de la pasión* (*Isle of Passion*, 1989), *Leopardo al sol* (*Leopard in the Sun*, 1993), *Dulce compañía* (*Angel of Galilea*, 1995), *La novia oscura* (*The Dark Bride*, 1999), *La multitud errante* (*A Tale of the Dispossessed*, 2002), *Olor a rosas invisibles* (*The Scent of Invisible Roses*, 2002), *Delirio* (*Delirium*, 2004), *Demasiados héroes* (*Too Many Heroes*, 2009) and *Hot Sur* (2013). As activist and journalist, Restrepo has been both witness to and participant in the tumultuous times Latin

America has experienced since the Cuban Revolution. She was a political militant in Argentina during the Dirty War and later a member of the peace commission that negotiated with the M-19 rebel movement during President Belisario Betancur's administration (1982–1986) in Colombia. Her participation in this endeavor resulted in exile. She continued her militancy from Mexico and Spain until peace with this group was negotiated and she returned to Colombia. Throughout her political and literary career, Restrepo has advocated for demilitarization and peace in Colombia and other Latin American countries. Her novel *Delirio* (2004) has garnered numerous literary recognitions including the prestigious Alfaguara Prize (2004) and the Grinzane Cavour literary prize (2006) in Italy for best foreign fiction.

In *Delirio,* Restrepo takes an ethical stance on truth. To do so, she employs madness as a cultural metaphor to portray a society at its limits by inverting the variables of real-unreal and hyperreal,[2] true and false, ethical and unethical. The author transcends those limits through a poetics of madness, defined as the aesthetic literary project that exposes multiple forms of insanity in content and form. Through an amalgam of narrative techniques and literary resources, *Delirio* unveils the repercussions of individual conflict within the social fabric of the nation.

In this chapter I explore madness from the sociological perspective by focusing on the intersection of reason and unreason as a reflection of a society in crisis. First I analyze the narrative structure: plot, voices, characters and the depiction of diverse types of insanity at individual and societal levels. Second, I focus on the textual cartography of the novel, including rituals and mythic references, symbolic associations, intertextualities and literary techniques, to reveal the hermeneutics of the text.

Project of Madness

Since its publication in 2004, *Delirio* has been extensively studied from an array of perspectives by critics of all latitudes, including the psychoanalytical, the clinical, the phenomenological, the anthropological and the sociological. It has been classified among magical realism, the fantastic, and even as part of the so-called "narco-literature" genre. Most critics, however, have overlooked the deep overtones and subterfuges of this complex narrative. I contend that Restrepo's own project of madness underlies her textual strategy as a framework that manifests throughout the narrative.

In "Quijote and The Real thing,"[3] Restrepo addresses the symbolic connection between madness and modernity. She asks, "Why should modern man end up recognizing himself in the words of a lunatic?" Her answer is "Because madness was the only conceivable name for tearing to pieces the old models, transgressing the limits of the known and accepted, of moving beyond whatever it is that *conventional rationality has succeeded in codifying*" (emphasis added, "Quijote" n.p.). Restrepo compares both Cervantes's and Shakespeare's use of mad characters in their literary works to sustain

> The concept of the madman gradually came to be a hallmark of modernity, or otherness, of a subjective, ironic vision of the world. In sum, it encompasses a freedom—to err, to make a fool of oneself and others, to doubt, to fail; which is to say, freedom to human foibles to get their own way ["Quijote" n.p.].

For Restrepo, it is through Don Quijote and Hamlet that culture acquired great power and with it the ability for language to shape reality, and to supplant it. However, the opposite is true in contemporary times. She argues, "what for Don Quijote was madness is today a standard component of modern man, those who mistrust this faint element we call *reality*, and even doubt its very existence" (emphasis in the original, "Quijote" n.p.). The inversion of variables between the real and unreal is evident in this proposition:

> We feel more comfortable trusting in the symbolism of the *real* and in its interpretations. We are no longer very interested dealing with reality as raw matter as we feel on more solid ground when we do battle with our own creations—systems of signs that constitute culture itself [emphasis in the original, "Quijote" n.p.].

Thus, madness as a cultural mediator lies at the core of the author's project and the systems of signs that compose the structure of the novel provide a helpful framework for understanding the intention of *Delirio* from the start. In the title, Restrepo formulates her proposal, as delirium is a concept defined by Foucault as the sum of all forms of madness:

> It is in that delirium, which is both body and soul, language and image, and grammar and physiology, *that all cycles of madness end and begin.* [...] Delirium is both madness itself, and beyond each of its phenomena, the silent transcendence that constitutes it, in its truth [emphasis added, *History of Madness* 238].[4]

The epigraph complements the author's intention by suggesting the deep overtone of her literary project: "Sabiamente, Henry James les advertía a los escritores que no debían poner a un loco como personaje de una narración, sobre la base de que el no ser el loco normalmente responsable, no habría verdadera historia que contar" (*Delirio* n.p.) ["Wise Henry James had always warned writers against the use of mad person as central to the narrative on the ground that as he was not morally responsible, there was no true tale to tell" (*Delirium* n.p.)]. In this quote Restrepo detaches responsibility from the insane protagonist, while at the same time indulging in a freedom that allows the author to render the proposition submitted in the title.[5] Madness becomes the resource, the tool and the artifice through which the story, its characters and the aesthetics create a *tour de force* that is *Delirio*.

In the novel, the narrative unfolds along vertical and horizontal axes constituting a dialectic of madness. The vertical axis reflects the individual and personal level, while the horizontal axis represents the social and collective dimensions. These axes crisscross in Agustina, the delirious character who condenses the sum of all madness. The plot combines past, present and future in a series of events centered upon a simple quest, the search to discover how and why Agustina lost her sanity. Gravitating around Agustina are her mother's and family's system of falsehoods, and her grandfather Portulinus's dementia (the vertical axis). Counteracting this level is Midas McAlister, the link to the underworld of drug trafficking and money laundering in Bogotá's high-class circles (the horizontal axis). The most stable character is Aguilar, Agustina's partner, who acts as the detective in a quest to discover the source of Agustina's crisis.

The structure of the novel is articulated through layers of narrations that are superimposed on each other to form a puzzle. These layers intersect and overlap with each other as they assemble the pieces into a unit constituting a sort of kaleidoscope. Restrepo uses stream of consciousness as a narrative technique through which multiple and interchangeable voices collide to produce a delirious effect akin to the main character's state of mind. As whole, the summation of stories reveals an array of unstable characters attempting to survive in a territory where chaos is the norm. Restrepo guides the reader through this quest by providing clues imbedded in symbolic associations and riddles. The role of the reader is to be the active agent in the process of assembling the pieces of the puzzle in order to decipher the enigma at the root of Agustina's madness. Restrepo creates poetic associations between several layers of individual, family and social madness in order to deliver a powerful message about the source of Colombia's turmoil.

To better understand the connection between madness and society, I draw from R.D. Laing's existential phenomenology. As a member of the antipsychiatry movement that flourished in the sixties with the aim of counteracting psychoanalytical theories and practices, Laing proposed that madness was determined by the social context.[6] "Laing argued that mental illness was not the result of inherited weakness (as evolutionists had claimed) or of faulty or incomplete development (as Freud suggested), but rather, a special strategy that a person invents in order to live an 'unlivable situation'" (Caminero-Santangelo 8).

Laing establishes a connection of psychosis with the perception of the real and unreal in *The Divided Self*. For him, the psychotic is the name we have for the other person in a disjunctive relationship of a particular kind (37). Laing coined the term "the false self system" to describe the psychosis that withdraws from reality to become another self or to live in another reality. Laing distinguishes between three forms of psychosis. First is the "normal" person pretending to be what he is not: one who dissociates himself from what he does, an evasion technique that makes him feel alien (102). The second is the "false self," referring to someone who acts in compliance with the intentions or expectations of others. The third form of psychosis is "impersonation," a form of identification where a part of the individual assumes the identity that he is not (109). Another type of psychosis is the individual engulfed in his "inner" or "true" self, trying to maintain his identity and freedom by being "unembodied," and thus "never grasped, pinpointed or possessed" (*The Divided Self* 94–95). Many of the cases in what Laing calls "the falsehood system" are of people not necessarily considered insane. On the contrary, under the appearance of the falsehood system most individuals seem to be "normal" (148). The idea of mental alienation from rational consciousness, according to Laing, constitutes a split between the true self and the false being whose chief functioning processes are determined by the need to adjust to the demands of society and the family as its offshoot (280). Following Laing's perspective, I address the diverse mental disturbances presented in *Delirio*.

Agustina's Childhood

During childhood, Agustina discovers that she possesses a gift of second sight, *el don de los ojos*. This gift is a sort of clairvoyance that usually manifests itself when she perceives the danger of her father lashing out at her brother Bichi. To protect her brother, she devises a strange ritual that combines purification through water with the contemplation of secret photographs, revealing the father's affair with his wife's sister. According to Maria Akrabova, "this mix of the 'high' (religious references, societal norms, law of the father) and the 'low' (sexual transgressions, injustices and lies) would be the most distinctive marker of the internal tangle and confusion that leads to Agustina's instability and to her delirium" (192).

Women with the gift of sight are a recurrent motif in literature and a topos through biblical and mythological storylines. Women's supernatural vision is connected to a source of punishment. In Greek mythology, Cassandra's prophetic gift allows her to foresee the destruction of Troy. However, she is unable to forestall the tragedy and is declared mad. I propose that in *Delirio*, Agustina's visual powers are the source of her misfortune, much like the case of Cassandra in Greek mythology. From the first paragraph, Agustina, like Cassandra, associates her gift of sight with trouble and punishment:

> Agustina siempre anda pronosticando calamidades, él ha tratado por todos los medios de hacerla entrar en razón pero ella no da su brazo a torcer e insiste en que desde pequeña tiene lo que llaman un don de los ojos, o visión de lo venidero, y sólo Dios sabe lo que eso ha trastornado nuestras vidas [*Delirio* 11].
>
> Agustina is always predicting some catastrophe; I've tried everything to make her see reason, but she won't be swayed, insisting that ever since she was little she's had what she calls the gift of sight, or the ability to see the future, and God knows the trouble that's caused us [*Delirium* 1].

Although Aguilar is the narrating voice in this section, Agustina's second sight is presented as her most peculiar characteristic: "porque los poderes de Agustina eran, son, capacidad de los ojos de ver más allá hacia lo que ha de pasar y todavía no ha pasado" (*Delirio* 16) ["because Agustina's powers were her eye's ability to see beyond, to what's still to come, to what hasn't come yet" (*Delirium* 6)]. Agustina's powers develop in adulthood into the ability to foresee what for others is concealed. However, there are threats that her power cannot control, dangers from the outside. From childhood she understands that the external world is a constant hazard and something from which she needs to be protected. The source of protection is her father, the center of authority and power. A father she adores and fears at the same time. Agustina's powers have a vulnerable point—an Achilles heel—which for her is the presence of blood. She learns this during childhood when she witnesses the death of a poor man at the front door of her house. The vision of his dying bleeding body made her aware of a weakness towards blood. Agustina understands that blood powers are superior to hers, but she also discovers that water can control the will of blood, a clue that will be fundamental later in her mental crisis.

Agustina's childhood storyline sets the map for understanding the source of her delirium. As Carmenza Kline has argued, Agustina's mental insanity is the product of three factors: the intrinsic (genetic and inherited aspects), the extrinsic (the physical, geographic, sociocultural and physical environment) and the inner world (the affective, emotional and behavior process) (116–117). All these elements, imbricated in contradictions, will foster her insanity in adulthood.

Midas

Midas McAlister, a cynical, corrupt and slimy character, reveals the radiograph of a society entrenched in violence and corruption. Midas, whose name evokes a mythical king obsessed with gold, is the one who unveils the plain truth about Agustina's family's clandestine business, the underworld of drug trafficking and money laundering and the whole scheme of falsehood of the Bogota social elite. Midas is the trickster who through his arts of deceitfulness and imponderable ambition believes that he reached a step up the social ladder, only to be thrown from grace by one simple mistake against his own people. Midas's storyline is the one where Restrepo excels in conveying irony, sarcasm, tone and humor, all in one voice that reveals the intricate underworld network hidden beneath an appealing facade. This network includes the drug lords and the oligarchs with their covert operations. One particular character who merits special attention is the DEA agent, Rony Silver, who benefits from both sides, prosecuting and extraditing drug lords while also receiving juicy bribes from them.

Midas McAlister introduces the infamous Pablo Escobar figure, who by now has evolved from the most powerful drug lord in history into the most iconic and mythical, and even heroic character, at the turn of the century. The novel discloses Escobar's explicit operations during the eighties and the mockery he made of Colombian society, turning it upside down. The blatant reference to Escobar as "Su Majestad, el rey don Pablo, soberano de las tres Américas y enriquecido hasta el absurdo gracias a la gloriosa War on Drugs de los gringos" (*Delirio* 80) ["His majesty King Don Pablo, ruler of the three Americas and absurdly rich thanks to the gringos' glorious War on Drugs" (*Delirium* 66)], reflects not the glorification of Escobar, but an explicit denunciation of the U.S. handling of the drug war. In fact, U.S. drug policies have created more illicit money, corruption and violence without reducing consumption or trade.

Madness is expressed at this level through the inversion of roles and values and the decomposition of society at the personal, national and international levels. Midas's storyline exposes the rise of individuals emerging from centuries of resentment and marginalization. In the attempt to climb the social ladder, Midas explains how he went to an elite boys school in Bogotá and learned nothing of trigonometry or chemistry, only how to behave like Agustina's oldest brother, Joaco. In the painful process of gaining acceptance in the higher circles, Midas comes to realize the particular skill that he has, but that Joaco and other members of the high class lack: the art of making money. This revelation reflects the phenomenon of many young people who succeeded in making money the easy way through illegal business. As a result, the economic structure of Colombian society changed, transforming higher circles on the poor side and the lower ones on the richer side. However, it did not impact the main principle of social mobility, because, as Midas firmly expresses, "así te hayas ganado el Nobel de literatura como García Márquez, o seas el hombre más rico del planeta como Pablo Escobar [...] en este país no eres nadie comparado con uno de los de ropón almidonado" (*Delirio* 155) ["even if you won the Nobel Prize in literature, like García Márquez, or you're the richest man on the planet, like Pablo Escobar [...] in this country you're nothing compared to one of those people with the starched christening gowns" (*Delirium* 138)].

At this level, vision is evident when Midas reveals to Agustina that the social injustice lying at the root of Colombia's conflict is not only the economic exploitation and inequality that have ruled through centuries, but also the politics of exclusion and marginalization produced by ignoring the existence of the lower classes. Aguilar remarks, "Tu familia ni siquiera registra a Aguilar [...] decir que tu madre lo odia es hacerle a él un favor, porque la verdad es que tu madre no lo ve siquiera, y a la hora de la verdad tampoco lo ves tú" (*Delirio*, 155) ["Your family doesn't even register Aguilar [...] to say that your mother hates him is to flatter him, because the truth is your mother doesn't even see him, and when it comes right down to it, you don't either" (*Delirium* 138)].

Paradoxically, it is Midas's inability to see his own kind, blinded by his false claim of belonging to the upper class that leads to his deadly sin. He denies Escobar's cousins entrance to his gym's aerobic center because of their evident low social standing and poor upbringing. Failing to recognize his own people, he excludes them in the same fashion he had been excluded. Worse still, he misjudges Escobar's moral codes, assuming that after all, he is a businessman first. As it turns out, Escobar was above all a family man, one who had succeeded in forcing his visibility by violent means against the elite class. In the end, Midas falls from grace from Escobar's circle and from his high class false friends. He returns to the origins he had denied and fled from all along: his mother's humble house on the outskirts of Bogotá, where no one would ever find him. Ironically, he finds refuge by concealing himself among the "invisible" sector of society. Thus, Midas conveys the epitome of "impersonation" described by Laing: he is the apparently normal individual pretending to belong to the upper class, managing a façade business of money laundering in a false society where no one is who they pretend to be.

Portulinus

Agustina's grandfather, Nicolas Portulinus, reflects the duality between the visible and invisible and the real and hyperreal. He is described as a German musician immigrant who established himself at mid-century in the small town of Sasaima. Portulinus suffers from delusion, an ailment that prevents him from seeing the real world as it is. The interplay of events and discourse in this storyline joins times, spaces and individuals. Portulinus lives simultaneously in Sasaima and in Germany. He loves and hates his wife Blanca, and is confused by his sexual orientation and feelings toward his piano student Abel, who is transformed into Farax in his illusory imagination. Lastly, his confusion of the Sweet River of Sasaima with the Rhine River of his childhood in Germany becomes an obsession, understood in connection with the constant reminder of his sister Ilse's tragic drowning in the Rhine, driven by insanity. His dementia carries him in a fatal flow of confusion until he is no longer able to distinguish real from unreal. Entrapped by his delusion, he throws himself into the Sweet River. His daughter, Eugenia, witnesses his disappearance and feels guilty because Portulinus was in her care at the time of his death. However, her mother, Blanca, convinces her that her father did not drown, but instead, returned to his hometown in Germany. As Eugenia learns to cope with traumatic events by the interpretation she makes of them, she substitutes the unreal for the real. This survival mechanism later proves decisive, when she becomes Agustina's mother.

Portulinus's insanity may be explained as the "divided self" psychosis described by Laing in which the inner world is separate from the outer world. Seeking protection from dangers, the self withdraws and creates a public fiction that confronts the world in its place (Laing 94). In the novel, Portulinus's storyline provides the background for understanding the genealogy of Agustina's delirium. At the same time, this underscores the roots of Colombia's violence and armed conflict. Sasaima, the pleasant little space presented in the story as both the origin of Agustina's family and the pleasant countryside summer home, also represents a drastic departure from the nostalgic idyllic locus in favor of political conflict and family disarray. This turn mirrors the history not only of the Londoño family, but of the nation as a whole.

Aguilar

Agustina's partner, Aguilar, acts as the detective in charge of assembling the puzzle by discovering the facts that link all pieces to the central storyline. Aguilar follows clues to Agustina's childhood through dialogues with Aunt Sofi. They travel to Sasaima in search of the grandparents' journals and letters. Through this process, he discovers Agustina's family history of insanity, crucial for understanding her delirium. In the end, the connections between times (past, present and future) and places (Germany, Sasaima) will be decisive in deciphering Agustina's mental state.

Agustina's delirium is the result of a series of events that impinge upon her own sensibility. She has been the recipient of the scheme of lies surrounding her. She is the collateral victim of her father's wrath resulting from his inability to accept Bichi's homosexuality. She cannot bear her mother's passivity when faced with the proof of her father's infidelity, the photos that Bichi displays to all the family. Agustina's mother's preference for continuing the farce in a world of appearances and falsehood destroys Agustina's grasp on reality. She is broken further by the horror of discovering a crime cover-up at Midas's gym as a result of money laundering and drug trafficking. Powers of sight signal misfortune and are at the root of her mental collapse. Agustina falls into delirium for being the only one able to "see" beyond the apparent normal surface of the murder of a stripper hired by Midas to entertain his rich buddies. Unable to cope with the impression of discovering and seeing it, she loses her mind. According to Akrabova, at that moment,

> [s]he begins to "reconstruct" the events leading to the murder, while in fact recalling metaphorically the instances of violence in her own life: and while the particularities differ significantly, the commonality of trauma and repression, victimization, and injustice turns to be the most important hidden truth, the elusive "absolute" that transcends the particular, the universal experience that connects each and all individual experiences [192].

It is at this point that all elements constructing Agustina's personality in childhood—rituals, sight powers and fears—intersect in producing an electric shock that precipitates her mental demise. The traces of blood, which she claims to see through her second sight, remind her of the paralyzing effect blood has on her powers and block her reasoning. Agustina's fragile mind is not able to cope with this farce. She gradually becomes unable to distinguish right from wrong, true from false, and is trapped by the falsehood system.

Following Laing's theory of psychosis, Agustina becomes the "unembodied self," an individual who experiences the self as divorced or detached from the body. Instead of being the core of one true self, the body is felt as the core of a "false self" (Laing 71). Agustina shuts out the outer world as a defense mechanism. She partially abandons the body, withdrawing into mental activity. She also experiences the self as an entity localized somewhere in the past: the inner self associated with the protection of her house—the safe space—in contrast to external dangers: the lepers,[7] the *chusma* (rabble), the "Others." Agustina's crisis also derives from a realization that the "home" represented by her family is a false system of lies and hypocrisy. Then she totally closes off, retreating into the inner self in an effort to deflect threats from the external world.

The Enigma

The resolution of the novel is perplexing and enigmatic. When Aguilar traces Agustina's family past, visiting Sasaima to find the grandmother's journal and letters, Agustina takes him to the Sweet River of her childhood. The river produces a parallel effect to Achilles's River Styx, mentioned in the childhood rituals. In this case the purifying stream washes away the "spilled blood." Metaphorically, water has the power to clear up the effect of delirium, portending Agustina may recover her sanity. Upon their return to the city, Aguilar begins to comprehend the source of his wife's insanity by realizing that the only way to overturn it was by looking into Agustina's "naked soul." This opportunity arises when Agustina asks him to wear a red tie for Bichi's arrival. If Aguilar is able to understand Agustina's complex sensibilities—including the importance she gives to rituals, colors, and amulets—by wearing red, he may be empowered to see the world through Agustina's eyes.

Thereby, Aguilar is inclined to access Agustina's inner world and decipher the logic of madness. The last line of the novel suggests that Agustina's recovery is possible when Aguilar stands in front of her and asks: "Señorita Londoño, ¿Le parece suficientemente roja esta corbata?" (*Delirio* 342) ["Miss Londoño, is this tie red enough for you?" (*Delirium* 320)]. Implicit in this act is also Aguilar's unconditional love, which as Carmiña Navia Velasco hints, is key to Agustina's healing. Aguilar provides the security she lost in her paternal home and the lack of a protective mother figure. Aguilar devotes himself entirely to Agustina, an unusual practice in the Latin American context, sacrificing his own career, refusing to commit her to an asylum, and caring for her even in the depths of Agustina's crisis (Navia Velasco 80).

As a mystery thriller, *Delirium* emulates Edgar Allan Poe's motif of "The Purloined Letter,"[8] a letter in plain view that nobody sees. Restrepo challenges the reader to see what is evident. The last scene may be the most enigmatic riddle posed by the author: did Agustina recover her reason? It is unknown and no longer relevant. As in Cristina Rivera Garza's *Nadie me verá llorar*, central questions about madness that the reader is encouraged to try to solve turn out to have no clear answer: meaning is made through the process of questioning, through the frustrated attempt to understand. Likewise, the reader's participation in the novel by attempting to solve the puzzle and restore order to madness remains suspended in time rather than being neutralized by a solution at the end of the novel.

While the prospect of the protagonist's cure is likely on the vertical axis by unraveling the family's genealogy of insanity, the revelation of the drug business and money laundering shatters along the horizontal axis with Midas as the only scapegoat. Correspondingly, Laing's falsehood system permeates the individual and social body in a dialectic of madness:

Midas pretends to be what he is not, while Agustina denies her true self; Portulinus lives in two selves, in two coexisting realities; Eugenia survives in her concealment through deceits and pretensions imposed upon herself and her family. This dialectic reveals the joint intricacies between individual and collective madness reflecting upon each other as a "space from which to explain and redeem Colombia" (Akrabova 191). According to Akrabova, Agustina as the mad character "serves as the metaphor for the craze of a society as a whole" (191). Aguilar, as the redeemer, is the one who discovers the secrets and hidden truths, and by doing so, provides the key for redemption: Agustina's possible cure lies in deciphering the codes beneath the logic of madness. Akrabova suggests that Colombia, as "a society caught in the frenzy of its compulsive denials," can only find relief in the "full disclosure of its painful truths" (191–92). Restrepo offers this redemption through the power of culture's symbolic system as mediator through literature. This would be achieved by decodifying the cultural symbolic system that in the words of Restrepo "conventional rationality has codified" ("Quijote" n.p.). I will now peer into the narrative structure to unfold the textual strategies in what I call the cartography of the novel.

Cartography of the Novel

Laura Restrepo draws from myth, ritual, riddles, Kabbalah, crossword puzzles, amulets, and ancient symbolism to formulate her project of madness through the symbolic systems that constitute culture. Along the way, she applies the metafictional paradox proposed by Patricia Waugh, to reveal the ontological status of the text: its quasi-referentiality, its indeterminacy and its existence as an alternate world (101).[9]

Rituals and Myths

Rituals and ceremonies invoking legends, myths and biblical admonitions of sacrifice, martyrdom and apocalyptic chastisement are pivotal to understanding deeper messages of *Delirio*. A ritual is an act within a system of beliefs that defines the sacred and profane in a given society. Rituals help people experience a shared sense of exaltation and fellowship. Ceremonies usually contain initiation rites, sacrifice, purification and redemption linked to supernatural forces (Durkheim).

According to Lilian Feder, "imaginative literature provides remarkable clues to the mental processes that produce the actual symbolization of the psychotic, for the poet, dramatist, and novelist explore and illuminate psychic conflict and confusion through the symbols they employ to depict these states" (6–7). One of these symbols is the connection between myth, ritual, religion and literature to explain human behavior, specially the "unconscious impulses against controls over individual demands and social constraints" (27). Feder draws from ancient ontological questions intrinsic to myth, ritual, religion, and literature. For this critic, literary characterizations and expressions of madness reflect cultural links between manifestations of psychosis and the modalities of social life patterns, such as rage, despair, confusion, and alienation (Feder 28–29). This explains why themes of insanity in Greek myths have been long appropriated by both scientific and literary analogies. References to Dionysus, the Erinyes, Oedipus and other mythical characters constitute common terminology to designate types of mental disturbances and behaviors at the root of literary and philosophical discussions.[10]

In *Delirio*, rituals associated with Agustina's childhood are not simple descriptions of games, they are the initiation rites, symbols and forces that predetermine her adulthood sensibility and ultimately, her breakdown. During their secret ceremony, Bichi and Agustina are empowered because the rite is their supreme moment of rule and command, what Agustina calls "our victory ritual" (*Delirium* 85). The ritual consists of washing their bodies free of sins, dressing themselves, and preparing for the supreme moment, watching the secret photographs at the center of the ceremony. Finally, they repeat the oath, never to reveal their secret because it will trigger the curse over Agustina and her family's fate. When Bichi breaks this pact by revealing the photos to the family, the ritual bends to another dimension. Through "the great revelation," Bichi attains a supernatural stature as a knight confronting and defeating his father, who in turn becomes as tiny as a mouse. However, for Agustina the broken pact suppresses her powers, because "the mystery had been laid bare and the furies unleashed" (*Delirium* 237). In addition, the revelation does not carry the expected result. Eugenia's denial of the evidence about her husband's infidelity with her own sister and her preference to maintain appearances only exacerbate the family split opening the pathway to Agustina's insanity. As predicted, the family curse comes true after the great revelation. When Agustina loses sanity in adulthood, the ritual ceremony reproduces in her frantic state: water, dressing, the photo album, her obsession with her father's return, and the threat of punishment. The same elements of her childhood rites are present, only this time, no one understands them and her solitary performance's lack of context and meaning undercuts the main symbolism of the ritual.

The connection of Agustina's character with the mythic Cassandra is not casual. As explained by Feder, frenzy states appear in several works of ancient literature. As Plato suggested in *Phaedrus* (244 BC), "madness appears through prophecy and has led them to purification and sacred rites, and thus, has brought a means of release" (Feder 54). For Feder, one of the essential features of prophetic powers is generally associated with madness or at least, a type of frenzy, as in the case of Cassandra (84). Feder claims that in ancient Greece "prophecy was regarded as a special form of madness, a perception of reality unavailable to the rational mind" (85). Thus, Cassandra is represented as a mad, frenzied, wild animal or "possessed by a god" (87). In *Agamemnon*, Cassandra calls to Apollo, the divine source of her oracular powers—being the agent of both suffering and wisdom—who induces the irrational mental unconscious state in which unconscious knowledge is released (Feder 88). In Cassandra's frenzy, she expresses wisdom beyond conscious reasoned logic. The images she sees convey past, present and future. "Her visions articulate the violence inherent in the state and the warnings that Trojans had refused to hear" (Feder 88). Cassandra's rages through her prophetic visions parallel Agustina's frenzied state delivering wisdom and truth when her visual powers are in action.

Rituals are also relevant to understanding Agustina's relationship with her father in childhood. The father represents power, authority, and a sense of security from external threats. A nightly ceremony they perform, which involves locking all doors of the family house, is portrayed as a sacred protocol by Agustina as she becomes the holder of her father's keys. In adolescence, she discovers the secret for undermining her father's power. Agustina finds out that she can get her father to pay attention to her by dating boys and by challenging his authority. Prompting parental jealousy thus becomes the key to reversing the power relationship. However, she can never fully appropriate her father's attention, and her obsession resonates in her delirious state. The dissected identity of Agustina's two selves in her delirium reproduces childhood fears and terrors in what might be considered the climax of her insanity. It is also through the revelation of Agustina's relationship with her father in her youth that these ceremonies make sense. The announcement of Bichi's return counteracts Agustina's terror and obsessions. Hernando Escobar Vera suggests that equilibrium can be restored by Bichi's return, breaking the spell and the curse over the family misfortune: "Bichi's return as an androgynous incarnation invokes the advent of this utopia, and delirium's end, the possibility of a new society."[11] Agustina's potential cure might be restored through the combination of ritual elements inscribed in the narrative: sacrifice, purification and redemption.

The ritual experience also appears in Midas's story line through purification, secrecy and sacrifice. The purification ceremony takes place at L'Esplanade aerobics center, the front for laundering big money from the drug business. When Midas breaks the tacit pact with Escobar, his spell is broken. Just as Agustina becomes the sacrificed victim, Midas's expulsion from Escobar's circle also marks his banishment and alienation from society. Only by telling his truth to Agustina, as the narrative suggests, might Midas find peace and reconciliation.

Kabbalah, Riddles and Crosswords

If myths and rituals open the key for inner layers of signification, textual devices such as labyrinths, Kabbalah riddles, crossword puzzles, intertextualities and metareferentialities are blended into the text to reveal the novel's cultural framework. Some of these textual strategies are essential to understanding how madness is interwoven into the narrative's symbolic system.

The narrative is a journey through intertwined texts with multiple characters and constantly alternating voices. The linguistic structure of the Agustina storyline indiscriminately mixes the "I" and the "she" subject pronouns as a strategy to distinguish between the more intimate first-person point of view and the more distant third-person perspective.[12] Conversely, Midas's storyline uses the "tú" voice (informal "you") as he constantly addresses his narratee, Agustina, in a colloquial and playful monologue resembling typical *Bogotano* patterns of speech. Portulinus's storyline plays with journal entries, alternating first and third-person voices from Blanca to Portulinus without explicit identification of the speaker. All these linguistic devices are delivered through stream of consciousness in the attempt to challenge and to submerge the reader with the delirium effect.

Kabbalah riddles are key to understanding Portulinus's dementia. His storyline constantly points to the mystery behind the framework of constellations, the music of the spheres, the power of numbers, and the unfolding of crystals (*Delirium* 38–39). Number symbology plays an important role in his narrative level. While the number three and its multiples signal instability, the number two restores peace and equilibrium. "Two is a number that makes it possible for him to shield himself [...] from the unbearable duality that interposes itself like a void between the sky and the earth, beginning and end, the male and female" (*Delirium* 38). But, when Abel/Farax comes into his life, the love-hate triangle shatters his mind and destroys the binary equilibrium. Also, the number three as the source for instability corresponds to Agustina's childhood ritual phases; three messages are left on the answering machine revealing Agustina's whereabouts at the onset of her delirium; and three is the number of times Agustina is confronted with blood, nullifying her powers.

Crossword puzzles represent the textual framework of scattered pieces to be assembled by the reader, but are also the palimpsest beneath the narrative. This is evident in several passages where puzzles are posed as riddles. When Agustina develops a passion for crossword puzzles. Aguilar asks, "Qué revelación podrá obtenerse de un crucigrama, qué combinación de palabras que sea fundamental, o qué clave que te permita comprender algo que te concierne de vida o muerte" (*Delirio* 85) ["What revelation might be had from a crossword puzzle, what fundamental combination of words or what clue might allow me to understand something that a moment ago meant nothing to me and that's suddenly of life-or-death importance" (*Delirium* 71)].

Crossword puzzles are also part of Portulinus's relationship to reason and unreason. The preoccupations or obsessions that plague Portulinus revolve around a multitude of puzzles and riddles that he must solve as though it were a matter of life and death:

> Por ejemplo, las órdenes que los espíritus mandan a través de algo que él llamaba la tabla de letras, [...] o el entrevero de palabras que se establece en los crucigramas, los mensajes escondidos , las voces que hablan en secreto, o el contenido de un libro abierto al azar, o la oculta lógica de los pliegues que se forman en las sábanas durante una noche de insomnio o la significativa manera como los pañuelos se amontonan dentro del cajón de los pañuelos o peor aún, del hecho inquietante de que un pañuelo aparezca, por decir algo, en el cajón de las medias [*Delirio* 92].

These include orders sent to him by the spirits through something that Portulinus calls the letter board [...] or in the jumble of words formed in crossword puzzles, the messages hidden in the notes of Portulinus's own compositions, the contents of the page of a book opened at random, the occult logic of the wrinkles in the sheets after a night of insomnia or the insignificant way handkerchiefs pile up in the handkerchief drawer, or even worse, the disturbing appearance of a handkerchief in the sock drawer [*Delirium* 78].

In one of the crossword references Aguilar is trying to solve, the word "palimpsest" triggers a fundamental clue, one suggesting that the text we are reading derives from superimposed layers of texts to be traced in order to resolve the puzzle presented by the novel. The palimpsest corresponds to intertextualities referenced across the narrative. For instance, Blimunda, José Saramago's clairvoyant character in *Memorial do convento*, is Agustina's alter ego and possibly her source of inspiration.[13] Bertha, the iconic madwoman character in Charlotte Bronte's romantic novel *Jane Eyre* who is concealed in Rochester's mansion, is referenced in relation to the protagonist's state of mind. Allusions to the "Death and the Maiden" composition by Shubert trigger immediate associations with the theater masterpiece by Ariel Dorfman depicting a woman losing her grip after torture interrogations during Chile's dictatorship. Ultimately, rhetorical devices resembling mad characters' disconnected monologues are reminiscent of Portuguese authors: António Lobo Antunes's style in *Que farei quando tudo arde?* (*What Can I Do When Everything's on Fire?*, 2001), and José Saramago's technique, especially in *Ensaio sobre a cegueira* (*Blindness* 1995).

On a discursive level, the narrative abounds with references to madness and its multiple manifestations. As another metafictional tactic, the novel explains itself in its own self-referentiality. In the novel, madness is described as "voracious" and as something that "can swallow" (*Delirium* 12). It is compared to the flow of a river, to the spread of contagious illness like the flu and to a chain reaction (*Delirium* 36). Madness may enter through the eyes and the skin (*Delirium* 36); it might be pedantic, hateful and tortuous (*Delirium* 105), but it is also theatrical, melodramatic and exhausting (*Delirium* 105). Finally, Agustina's crisis reaches its peak the night a bomb destroys the Security Police headquarters in Bogotá.[14] When Aguilar finds Agustina in the most acute episode, he concludes, "esta noche ella y la locura son una" (*Delirio* 209) ["tonight she and the madness are one" (190)]. Not only are Colombia's madness and Agustina's madness parallel, they are one and the same, thus following Foucault's definition of delirium, where "all cycles of madness end and begin." At the same time, while Aguilar acknowledges his wife's mental condition, he foresees hope at the end of it all when he asserts, "porque detrás de tu locura sigues estando tú" (*Delirio* 209) ["because you're still there behind your madness" (*Delirium* 190)], signifying the potential to overturn both individual and collective madness. This potential is not realized within the novel, and thus extends beyond the end of the novel into the reader's reality.

The Mirror Effect

Textual strategies conforming the poetic of madness in *Delirio* generate a mirror effect that contains madness in multiple and polyvalent forms. In the novel, the layers of narration converge as if they were a series of pictures spread across a table for the reader to find corresponding matches. Stories mirror one another in an array of reflections involving distortions, refractions and decompositions. The novel thus acts as a mirror, reflecting the truth and falsehoods of society in a dialectic of reason and unreason, while the author-narrator positions herself behind the mirror as the holder of truth[15] The mirror's reverse side presents another face of reality, revealing the falsehood systems in a society that has substituted the hyperreal for the real.

In "Quijote and the Real thing," Restrepo asks,

> Was Don Quijote considered insane because he altered his perception of reality? He saw giants instead of windmills, beautiful damsels in place of rustic peasants. However, his madness revealed a subtle truth behind the surface of the world. Quijote was always on the borderline of reason and unreason, true and falsehood. [...] But who decides which reality is the "real one? Is it the author or the spectator? ["Quijote" n.p.].

Reason and unreason become blurred, signifying that Agustina may be the only one who truly sees reality as it is. Just as Don Quijote saw giants (the un-real) instead of windmills (the real) and was labeled insane, Agustina is now the only one who sees windmills, implying that society has inverted the variables switching the real for the hyperreal.

In mythical terms, *Delirium* may be compared with the tragedy of Cassandra, to conclude that Agustina falls into madness upon deciphering a truth connecting past, present and future. She is unable to cope with the truth and she falls into madness—a self-inflicted chastisement—in the same fashion that Cassandra is punished upon telling her truth. Laura Restrepo assumes Agustina's clairvoyant powers to forewarn of what may become of a country and region that insists in denying its own true self:

> Y vinieron los utileros y alzaron con todo y ya cayó el telón, hasta el mismo Pablo un fantasma, y fantasmal por completo este país; si no fuera por las bombas y las ráfagas de metralla que resuenan a distancia y que me mandan sus vibraciones hasta acá, *juraría que ese lugar llamado Colombia hace mucho dejó de existir* [emphasis added, *Delirio* 327].
>
> The stagehands have carried everything away and now the curtain has fallen, even Pablo is a ghost, the whole country itself is ghostly, and if it wasn't for the bombs and the bursts of machine-gun fire that echo in the distance, the tremors reaching me here, *I'd swear that the place called Colombia had stopped existing long ago* [emphasis added, *Delirium* 305].

Colombia's succumbing to social madness becomes the text's warning alarm: an urgent need to halt the spiral of madness swallowing the country, region and continent by negating their own realities. Restrepo is fighting the dementia and the intricate powers surrounding the violence produced by not being able to apprehend and confront plain reality. *Delirio* becomes the synthesis and the disjunction of all forces traversing the novel, just as it reflects different types of mental insanity, both symbolic and real. This is the enigma at the core of the novel. Through a poetics of madness, Restrepo provides rationality to Colombia's reality, signaling a path for redemption. This redemption can be achieved only by disclosing painful truths. In this current period of conflict resolution (2014), Colombia is disclosing the secrets behind three decades of violence. In the process, cultural systems of production play a fundamental role in creating channels for building memory and for survival, through testimonial narratives and artistic projects including theater, music, poetry and social media.[16] The creation of the Center for Historical Memory and recent efforts for truth and reconciliation are evidence that the nation as a whole is undergoing a transformation through sacrifice, purification and redemption.

CHAPTER SIX

Literary Agency

Irene Vilar's Life-Writing

LAURA KANOST

The story begins with a double bind.
(Irene Vilar, irenevilar.com, n.d.)

Puerto Rican Irene Vilar's first memoir, *The Ladies' Gallery: A Memoir of Family Secrets* (1996, originally titled *A Message from God in the Atomic Age*), begins with an epigraph from "The Siren" by Franz Kafka: "The Sirens, too, sang that way. It would be doing them an injustice to think that they wanted to seduce; they knew they had claws and sterile wombs, and they lamented this aloud" (xviii). The epigraph bears witness to the existence of a ghosted original Spanish text; only Gregory Rabassa's English translation of Vilar's text has been published, but her Spanish title was the first part of the Kafka quotation: *También las sirenas cantaban así.*[1] This quotation also serves as a warning to the reader: sailors met their death because they misread the Sirens' song, hearing seduction where there was only a futile and destructive lament. The epigraph establishes the book's central themes of reading, writing, vicious cycles, and the lure of death, and it prefigures Vilar's frequent and self-conscious use of intertextuality. Ironically, Vilar's second memoir, *Impossible Motherhood: Testimony of an Abortion Addict* (2009), casts the first memoir as a misreading by the author of her own life. At the heart of both memoirs is the relationship between personal experiences of depression and self-harm, larger political questions, and writing. This chapter examines Vilar's re-writing of the madwoman figure as intellectual in *The Ladies' Gallery* and the subsequent complication of this persona through the mixed codes of confession and *testimonio* in *Impossible Motherhood*. Although Vilar's latter memoir presents the former as a fiction created under the influence of her dominating ex-husband, in both works the mentally ill subject effectively utilizes writing as a form of self-care.

The Author

Irene Vilar was born in Arecibo, Puerto Rico in 1969 and has lived on the U.S mainland since early adulthood. Vilar's life-writing is driven in part by her memories of her mother's struggles with depression and eventual suicide, and of the absent presence of Vilar's maternal grandmother, Lolita Lebrón, an icon of Puerto Rican independence activism known for her participation in a 1954 attack on the U.S. House of Representatives. The two memoirs explore the complex relationship between writing, identity, and a search for individual, familial, and national well-being. In addition to writing, Vilar is a literary agent and has worked as an editor in the academic publishing industry (series editor for Women and Jewish Studies at Syracuse University Press, founder and series editor of The Americas book series at University of Wisconsin Press, and series editor of The Americas at Texas Tech University Press). She was named a Guggenheim fellow (joining Peri Rossi, Eltit, and Restrepo) in 2010.

The Ladies' Gallery

Vilar concludes her first memoir with an epilogue that expands on the earlier Kafka quotation, noting that there were three Sirens, each one enfolding three stages of life, and they built their nests out of the bones of the doomed sailors who followed their song (319–20). The parallel to the book's three subjects, Irene, her mother, and her grandmother, is clear. Vilar closes the epilogue with another warning to the reader: "The song of the Sirens is the great paradox that suicides and madmen know. It is the paradox, too, of every book on suicide written by suicides: they make their nests from the skeletons of dead authors. It's contagious—beware" (323). The Sirens' song thus can be read as an impulse to self-destruction or disintegration that some, like the sailors, cannot help but follow. At the same time, however, Vilar compares herself as a suicide survivor and memoir writer to a Siren whose act of singing perpetuates itself through its readers even as it rests on the reconfigured remains of literary precursors. Within a cycle of death and destruction there is also life and creativity. This use of the Siren imagery, like *The Ladies' Gallery* as a whole, brings together issues of mental illness, family relationships, and literary creation and consumption.

These components are interwoven in *The Ladies' Gallery* with reflections on the lives of Irene Vilar, her mother, Gladys Mirna Méndez Lebrón, and her maternal grandmother, Lolita Lebrón. The work begins with and repeatedly returns to an italicized chronological narrative strand that follows Irene's Syracuse psychiatric hospital stays and concurrent pregnancy. This strand, too, finally brings *The Ladies' Gallery* to a close—with Irene's release from the hospital, a miscarriage, and her beginnings as a writer.[2] Resembling the Künstlerroman, the text as a whole tells the story of Irene's development as a young artist and intellectual. With its intricate structure, copious intertextual references, and keen observation of the texts at work in everyday life, Vilar's first memoir demands to be read as literature. Through this self-consciously literary approach to disability life-writing, *The Ladies' Gallery* asserts the subjectivity of the life-writer and the mentally ill person, implicitly taking part in cultural conversations on literariness, disability, and subjectivity, as well as contributing a unique representation of mental illness. Vilar would add new dimension to this representation of her life in 2009 with *Impossible Motherhood*, a memoir that follows the development of self-understanding and the ability to resist patterns of self-harm through the creation and revision of her own life narratives.

The broad term "life-writing" is particularly apt in describing *The Ladies' Gallery*, since, even more than a conventional memoir, it represents a combination of autobiography, biography, and literary and political reflection. Moreover, this text challenges the two conventional subdivisions of autopathography identified by disability life-writing scholar G. Thomas Couser. Couser distinguishes between illness narratives, which often "disengage the body from the self in the way that medical discourse often tends to do," and full-life narratives, which foreground the corporeal nature of identity by integrating "illness narrative into a larger life narrative" (14). The illness narrative portion of *The Ladies' Gallery* is visually marked as separate through the use of italics, and yet through its persistent recurrence it structures the entire work, thus signaling the interconnected relationship between the illness experience and all the other strands of the memoir. A reader expecting a conventionally self-contained illness narrative will be continually interrupted as the hospital strand alternates with a nonchronological, kaleidoscopic view of Vilar's identity filtered through her family, her country, and her literary activity. Similarly, although the epilogue ultimately refers to *The Ladies' Gallery* as "a book on suicide," the suicide attempt that results in Irene's hospital stay is not included in the illness narrative strand, and its full recounting is delayed until the very end of the memoir. The narration of Irene's mother's suicide is withheld until midway through the book. By contextualizing her hospitalization within her own life story as well as the stories of her mother and grandmother, Vilar represents mental illness as one pivotal life experience among many. Cristina Mathews notes in her study of melancholy and mourning in *The Ladies' Gallery*: "In negotiating a life-affirming relationship to the death wish of her grandmother, the death of her mother, and her own attempts to die, Irene does not delineate clear boundaries between herself and the other women who have helped to form her" (247). The interweaving of illness narrative and full-life narrative, autobiography and biography produces a form of life-writing that fosters awareness of the interplay of body and its context to identity, along with a recognition of the convention of treating experiences of bodily variation as interruptions or exceptions to a life story. Mathews writes: "the dissolved narrator at the beginning of her italicized hospital stay does not emerge as a unified subject at the end, but instead the subject attempting to feign coherence at the start of the plain text section is balanced by the emergence, at the end of the italicized section, of a healthy subject comfortable with multiplicity" (258). Vilar's second memoir, *Impossible Motherhood*, further complicates the relationship between the writing self and multiple narrator positions by pointing to omissions and misrepresentations in *The Ladies' Gallery* that only become apparent and representable to her after the process of publishing her first memoir is complete.

The first memoir is insistently self-referential and full of intertextual references, emphasizing the writer's awareness of her participation in literary and intellectual tradition. Vilar thus stakes a claim for her book as literature, despite the reluctance of literary scholars to include life-writing in the canon. Perhaps even more significantly, Vilar positions herself as a self-aware intellectual and literary author while simultaneously highlighting her experience as a woman with a mental illness. This combination forms a powerful statement, considering that the conventional association of madness with uniquely unfettered artistic creativity does not include such

Latin American Women and the Literature of Madness

calculated intellectual activity. Likewise, the reading of women's madness as a raging symptom or desperate protest of gender oppression, exemplified by Sandra Gilbert and Susan Gubar's *The Madwoman in the Attic* who embodies both her creator's rage and the diseased textual body of patriarchal society and its literature, only serves as a metaphor for rebellion. The madwoman as she has been defined ultimately cannot speak, as Marta Caminero-Santangelo has compellingly argued, since the metaphorical resistance ascribed to madness can provide only the illusion of effective power. Twentieth-century Western thought has defined madness as a form of otherness that is associated with subversiveness, yet removed from the space of subjectivity. *Madness and Civilization*, Foucault's "archaeology" of the ideas and practices associated with madness in Europe from the Middle Ages through the 19th century, states that "the language of delirium can be answered only by an absence of language, for delirium is not a fragment of dialogue with reason, it is not a language at all; it refers, in an ultimately silent awareness, only to transgression" (262). Likewise, Shoshana Felman's *Writing and Madness* argues that literature appropriates the language of madness, and is defined by its contradictions: "this reclaiming of the margins both of knowledge and of power come[s] to represent the literary claim par excellence" (2–3), and yet "it is somewhere between their affirmation and their denial of madness that these texts about madness act, and that they act themselves out as madness, i.e., as unrepresentable" (252).

The Ladies' Gallery forges a different relationship between mental illness and writing. Vilar casts herself not as a madwoman, but as an intellectual who deftly moves in and out of countries, libraries, psychiatric hospitals, and memories. Vilar uses the discomfort and ambiguity of her social position as the catalyst for a self-consciously literary and intellectual text that affirms her capacity to speak. The marked literariness of *The Ladies' Gallery* is established from the outset with the Kafka epigraph evoking the perils of reading, and it is strengthened throughout with numerous references to other literary texts and constant discussion of themes of reading and writing. Vilar's frequent literary references suggest that her understanding and expression of her life experiences are mediated through cultural discourse, and thus underscore her own participation in cultural discourse as the author of *The Ladies' Gallery*.

In order to interpret and communicate her range of experiences, Vilar calls on a broad knowledge of world literature, asserting her own domination of literary codes and inviting readers to do the same. The following

Six. Literary Agency (Kanost)

are but a few examples of this tendency. Irene explains, "In college one has the Borgean sense that it is possible to be many without even trying to be one (since everything is there for you to choose)" (8). When the hospital has a Valentine's Day decoration contest, Irene observes, "In my room there are so many hearts on the floor already that all that's left is for them to start beating, as in a Cortázar story" (115). As a little girl, Irene read *The Lives of the Saints*; looking back, she reflects, "I wasn't devout, I was only a girl searching for the key to something in books, even though I didn't know quite what: nostalgic, a mini–Madame Bovary with no object in mind and, to top it off, from the Caribbean" (199). Recalling her childhood travels and role models, Irene comments that she was "like one of those characters in the Spanish picaresque novel: educated en route, so to speak, the missing one, the adapted or adopted one" (210). In addition to comparisons such as these, the memoir mentions numerous other writers, often in the context of Irene's literary coursework, among them Woolf, Joyce, García Márquez, Homer, Chuang Tzu, Cervantes, Barthes, Kristeva, Nabokov, Sontag, Paoli, Santa Teresa, Kierkegaard, and Gordimer. In particular, Irene identifies with "women writers at war with life"—Pamela Djerassi Bush, Sylvia Plath, Julia de Burgos, Alfonsina Storni, Virginia Woolf, and Violeta Parra—saying, "Irene was there all the time, before Irene had been born, and, as Borges would say, behind the mask of other names" (37). By explicitly comparing herself to both literary characters and writers, Vilar flouts the marginality of life-writing within the literary canon and the objectification of people with mental illnesses. It is hardly surprising that she went on to become a literary agent whose clients include Ernesto Cardenal and Mayra Santos-Febres.

The noticeable accumulation of literary references throughout *The Ladies' Gallery* positions Irene Vilar as a subject who exercises the authority to read and write within and about a literary tradition. Even as she struggles with depression and suicide, Irene is writing a diary, taking copious notes for a future book, and reading and writing about literature, psychology, and other subjects for her university classes and in her leisure time. Quite literally, she refuses to cede her place as a literary scholar:

> The last few times I went to the library, I went to the fourth floor, to the PQ section where the Latin American and Spanish literature collection was shelved. I read haphazardly, and if I found some interesting phrase, I would memorize it, or try to, because it was very hot in those cubicles on the fourth floor, and that voice of mine would begin to babble, and it

would be as if they'd put my head in an oven and it had exploded, like an eggplant you bake without perforating the skin [81].

As a markedly literary mental illness narrative, Vilar's self-portrayal in *The Ladies' Gallery* rewrites the conventional concept of madness as a pathology of language or a space removed from language altogether.

This resistance is particularly prominent in the chronological strand of *The Ladies' Gallery* that narrates Irene's experiences while being treated for psychosis in two Syracuse psychiatric hospitals. Mostly using the present tense, this illness narrative gives the impression of being taken from a journal kept during that time. Sometimes presenting a sense of helplessness or disorientation, and other times expressing shrewd analytical observation of her surroundings, the hospital narrative is consistently articulate, self-aware, and critical. Irene constantly calls on her literary competency to analyze and "read" the social dynamics and power structures of the hospital; as she notes upon arrival, "I was slowly becoming a spectator of my own fable" (15). When she meets her first doctor, Irene observes her taking notes, and wonders, "What about? My silence, certainly. Well? What does my silence mean to her? She's waiting for me to tell her I'm in love. Should I play the adolescent, sick Juliet they imagine me to be?" (16). Just as Irene reads others, she is clearly aware that others are interpreting her, always through the lens of cultural discourse:

> [Irene] becomes a patient, an unfinished being. The doctors know it; and from the first day, Dr. O. knows that I read novels and psychology books. She didn't like me to read Melanie Klein. (What would she have preferred? Romances of chivalry?) They know a lot about me, they have it written down in a file with my whole history, and when I am finally able to see it, I am startled to read the things I'd said and the things they'd heard. They didn't know what name to give me: Hispanic female, senior at SU, functioning with HX of maternal suicide [38].

During an evaluation, she considers representing herself as a patient to be a conscious act of creativity on her part: "Hell, I know quite well what he expects of me and I'm ready to help him. I see myself inventing a diagnosis of my soul for him, as if it were a matter of literary composition" (276). As a psychiatric in-patient, Irene is keenly aware of her participation in a network of readers, writers, and texts.

Along with this unconventional representation of the psychiatric patient as self-conscious reader and writer, Vilar also diverges from tradition in her portrayal of the psychiatric hospital as a space that interfaces with mutable individual bodies and cultural discourses. *The Ladies' Gallery* presents a complex portrayal of several psychiatric hospitals, which changes with time and according to the situation. When Irene first arrives at Hutchings Psychiatric Hospital, the primary characteristics of the place seem to be a sense of enclosure and detachment, qualities typically associated with the asylum: "We all go about half-bewildered by all the sun pouring in through the window. Last night it was the moon that bewildered us. We move along corridors that lead through rectangular parlors into yet other corridors. The sound of steps on the white tiles is loud, along with the squeak of litters and wheelchairs, but nothing from outside can be heard [...] these walls enclosing us are hermetic" (14–15).

Later, en route from Hutchings to University Hospital, Irene wonders, "How does someone come back from a mental hospital?," again evoking physical and social isolation (34). She finds, however, that at University Hospital, "the people are less crazy, more sad. Hutchings was closer to an asylum, with restraints everywhere" (62) whereas "at University Hospital the contrasts are not so great. The patients are anorexics, manic-depressives, an occasional drug addict, all generally middle- or upper-middle class, awash in social tedium. [...] But contrasts or no contrasts, they all look as if asleep" (64). These early impressions of Hutchings and University Hospital reveal an awareness of and partial identification with the conventional image of the "total institution" (Goffman), a closed and controlling space, removed from society.

As Irene's hospital stay continues, however, the emphasis shifts to a strategic view of the hospital as a permeable space providing needed, temporary shelter. Upon leaving the hospital for the first time, she remembers, "I wasn't frightened. You can always come back, I told myself. And leave again" (84). Later, she reflects, "Sometimes (as in my case) being hospitalized is a great comfort. The empty monastery walls and the silence invite rest. [...] I wonder if Mama could have been saved by something like this, an empty place, a 'peaceful house'" (175). Viewed in this light, the ability to take up residence in the psychiatric hospital is a flexible coping mechanism rather than a loss of agency. Considering the utility of this vantage point, Irene notes: "Noah's ark: Proust said of Noah that probably he never saw the world so clearly as from inside the ark, though it was closed and there was darkness on the earth" (257). Ultimately, in Irene's experience, the psychiatric hospital can be a hermetic enclosure full of restraints, but also a temporary respite and window of perception.

To these facets, Vilar adds the contrasting experience of her activist grandmother Lolita, for whom the psychiatric hospital was a dehumanizing place of politically-motivated torture. Vilar recounts how, after sending the prophetic "Message from God in the Atomic Age" to President Eisenhower, Lolita was abruptly removed from her Alderson, West Virginia prison cell and transported to St. Elizabeth's Hospital in Washington, D.C.: "Orderlies and guards dragged her into a room, shoved her onto a platform in the center, and seated her on a chair. All around her were people sitting in easy chairs, as if in a theater. They stood up in a threatening way. Were they going to burn her? 'Well, it was a circus, and it was my job to amuse them'" (263). The comparison recalls the medieval tradition of displaying asylum residents for public entertainment (Foucault). For Lolita, the asylum-as-spectacle blends with the asylum-as-political-apparatus as she undergoes interrogation and is subsequently subjected repeatedly to what she calls "electric torture" (264). When her daughter Gladys comes to visit her, Lolita is angry to be seen in this position by an adult daughter she hardly knows, and tells Gladys repeatedly "how they were trying to drive her crazy but hadn't succeeded. They were making her hear 'electronic voices,' injecting her, experimenting with her" (266). In contrast to Irene, then, Lolita experiences the psychiatric hospital as a nightmarish total institution and instrument of political oppression. *The Ladies' Gallery* juxtaposes St. Elizabeth's, a monolithic structure that ruthlessly strips its occupants of identity and agency, with University Hospital, a structured yet maneuverable space that can be utilized as a coping mechanism.

Central to this flexible representation of Irene's hospital experience are references to her body. Vilar's memoir reflects on hospitalization as one among many life events that she experiences both physically and intellectually. Irene's corporeal perception of mental illness highlights the spatial negotiation of the psychiatric hospital and contributes to the book's overall implicit concept of mental illness as a disability.

Physicality is salient in the memoir's opening paragraphs, as Irene awakens in the hospital to a sensation of overwhelming depression: "Face up, the beginning of another day is unbearable. You feel that nothing is ending and nothing is beginning. Maybe if you close your eyes and get away from the light of day you can put an end to that anguish. I tried to move. Starting with my arms and then my hips, back, and head. Finally, I managed to move my legs and, with the greatest effort, I succeeded in turning onto my side" (10). As Irene describes it, this intense anguish of depression is a bodily experience as much as a mental and emotional one. As the narration continues, the strange sense of bodily disconnect becomes the focus: "I got a good grip on the edge of the bed so I wouldn't slip and lose the position that it had taken me so long to reach. Yes, I would stay in that position with my nose pressed against the wall and my right wrist bent under the weight of my thigh. [...] For some reason my body took on grotesque postures, as if challenging me or mocking my clumsiness. Whose huge foot was that hanging from the light?" (10–11). A similar physical disorientation is prominent in Irene's narration of her arrival at the hospital. She explains having a "larval feeling," an understanding that "something in my body had broken down. The orderlies straightened up the bent thing; it walked. I thought they were taking me to an operating room, to cure me, to remove death from inside me" (12). Irene's emotional crisis and physical displacement are experienced as a sense of partial disembodiment or corporeal distress, as evidenced by the shift here between internal and external perspectives.

Just as Irene experiences mental illness through her body, she is aware that her mental illness influences how her body is perceived by others. Throughout her hospital stay, Irene notes how the psychiatric patients' bodies are viewed as different. She herself observes the altered physical presence of her fellow patients, "young people full of lethargy, turning about and shuffling along the corridor" (15). She feels as though others approach her body differently now that she occupies the role of patient: on Irene's first morning in Hutchings, "the nurse arrived from the end of the hall and, with a tug, pulled off the blanket, leaving me uncovered. Get up, she said, as if she were talking to an insect, or a corpse" (11). Similarly, Irene observes upon arrival at University Hospital that the nurses "don't look at me, or they look through me as if I were transparent, or just an idiot" (61). The self-inflicted wounds marking Irene's wrists as she reenters University Hospital are yet another physical manifestation of her mental illness. Reminiscent of Luft's spatial imagery in *The Red House*, Vilar's frequent use of sensory imagery throughout *The Ladies' Gallery* implies that mental illness is experienced through the body.

Despite the limits that the hospital often places on her physical agency, Irene constantly affirms her subjectivity and exerts her intellectual power by critically analyzing her situation within the hospital dynamics. Irene narrates the beginning of her first hospital stay as an experience of powerlessness:

> Two orderlies come out of nowhere, take me by the arms, and escort me to the room of the day before. They give me a small glass full of shiny pills and another with orange juice. The lithium journey was about to start. Vilar! I walk toward where the voice is coming from, slowly. Two orderlies take me to a room with a lot of machines, another orderly connects me to a dozen cables. They disconnect the machines, fill out a form that was lying on top of a pile of papers. You're okay. You're normal. They take me to another ward [16].

By placing herself as the grammatical object in much of this section, Irene emphasizes the ways in which hospital procedures objectify patients.

Much more frequently, however, Irene narrates her experiences in the hospital with a more overtly critical approach that asserts her own intellectual agency. In one scene, for example, the narration presents Irene's thoughts during an evaluation, which focus on her own assessment of the hospital's procedures and structures: "Why do they need seven people for a psychological evaluation? This room has a problem with its design. They forgot to put in windows. Besides, how ridiculous it is to make me sit in a chair, just me, in the middle of the room" (154). On another occasion, Irene returns her doctors' analytical gaze with her own, observing and thus neutralizing the uneven visual power dynamic implicit in clinical observation: "Among psychiatrists, psychologists, and social workers there is a game of looking: seeing who can be the most intense. It's the same game we used to play as girls in school, sitting face-to-face, staring at each other to see who could hold her look the longest without laughing or blinking" (173). She goes on to observe that, after several therapy sessions, the typical patient soon "takes on that insistent doctor's stare, which gives the same look to a table as to a person, since everything is equally suspicious" (174). Not only is the doctor's authoritative gaze demystified by being likened to a common child's game, it is also appropriated not just by Irene but other patients as well—a tactic also enacted by Matilda en *Nadie me verá llorar* and the hospital residents in *Infarto del alma*.

Irene's study of psychology books is another means by which she exerts her intellectual agency in the hospital. She repeatedly states that her doctors disapprove of these readings, and their multiple requests that she stop suggest that she continues her studies throughout her hospitalization. Irene's familiarity with psychological discourse allows her to read and negotiate her doctors' recommendations. She senses, for example, that her doctor believes it would be therapeutic for her to complete her pregnancy rather than aborting it, and she recognizes the underlying 19th-century rationale: "for Dr. O. motherhood must have been the antidote for sadness. Underneath it all, the old version of hysteria" (314). Armed with this knowledge, Irene decides to lie about her intentions in order to be discharged from the hospital: "I left like Odysseus, the way one always leaves a labyrinth, traps, encirclements: by means of a subterfuge. I said I was going to have the child" (317). The classical reference further underscores Irene's intellectual agency.

This complex representation of the physical and intellectual power dynamics of the psychiatric hospital extends to the book's political dimension. *The Ladies' Gallery* reinterprets the cliché metaphorical use of the insane asylum as a political microcosm by exploring the details of instances in which international politics literally were intertwined with an individual's psychiatric hospitalization. Irene's multifaceted experience of hospitalization stands in stark contrast to Lolita's confinement at St. Elizabeth's decades before, in which psychiatric treatment was literally inextricable from the larger political and punitive contexts. The motherless and homesick Irene's hospitalization in New York could certainly be read as an allegory about the dysfunctional neocolonial status of Puerto Rico—and more directly, Benigno Trigo's reading affirms that the work "describes and underscores the catastrophic effects of the loss of national identity on her and on her family. The losses of the colonial process turn Lebrón and Vilar into melancholy writers bent on regaining what is lost by identifying it and by silencing their own voices" (111). The complex contextualization of this political dimension to Irene's mental illness does not allow for a simplistic metaphorical reading. Representing mental illness as a disability, *The Ladies' Gallery* avoids using madness and the asylum as essentializing metaphors detached from the contexts of politics, culture, and individual experience. Instead, Vilar's literary appropriation of the genre of autopathography contextualizes a mental illness within a life story, and situates it within a network of fluctuating physical, spatial and intellectual planes. Vilar stakes a powerful claim for the literary legitimacy of life-writing and for the integrity of subjectivity throughout a mental illness.

Impossible Motherhood

Vilar's second memoir, *Impossible Motherhood: Testimony of an Abortion Addict*, revises this claim, registering ways in which narration—including her first memoir—and the accumulation of additional life experiences change the writer's perception of who she was and who she is. In *Impossible Motherhood*, written in English and later translated into Spanish, Vilar's previous work serves as the primary intertext; rather than constantly engaging literary and intellectual tradition in dialogue, this second memoir primarily dialogues with the first. The structure, too, is mainly chronological, less markedly literary. Yet the second part of the title inscribes this work within the marginal literary discursive traditions of Latin American *testimonio* and North American self-help memoir. *Impossible Motherhood* profoundly interrogates the relationship between narrative, performance, and self. Through multiple life narrations, including the process of writing *The Ladies' Gallery* and work with a therapist, Irene in *Impossible Motherhood* is able to interrupt a harmful cyclical performance of creation and destruction through fifteen pregnancies and abortions. Vilar downplays the role of political and social forces in this personal drama throughout much of *Impossible Motherhood*, but bookends the work with discussion of context, a reminder that the personal is political, just as the political is personal.

Within this frame, constant references to omissions and distortions in *The Ladies' Gallery* highlight Vilar's agency as life-writer or *testimonio* speaker in crafting a narrative of her experiences. These references hold readers back from identification with the implicit reminder that this version, too, may contain omissions and distortions of its own. The story, the identity, is hers alone. *Impossible Motherhood*, I argue, utilizes what Doris Sommer has called a "rhetoric of particularism" employed by writers who "assume that they are in control of their subject and that access to it is limited" (15): "it is the eloquence of marking frontiers, limiting access, distinguishing the speaking subject from the target of speech" (124). The subject of *testimonio*, Sommer argues, is "plural but particularist":

> The testimonial 'I' in these books [*testimonios* by Rigoberta Menchú, Domitila Barrios, and Claribel Alegría] doesn't invite us to identify with it. We are too foreign, and there is no pretense here of universal or essential human experience. That is why, at the end of a long narrative in which Rigoberta has told us so much, she reminds us that respectful limits still hold. They bind her too, as she takes care not to conflate her community with herself. Personal identity depends on, doesn't replace, the collective [Sommer 129].

Through what I will call a rhetoric of mixed messages, Vilar invites readers to witness her self-narration but frustrates any attempt to assimilate it.[3]

Six. Literary Agency (Kanost)

Even more clearly than *The Ladies' Gallery*, *Impossible Motherhood* features a warning to the reader early on: "My testimony was fated to be misunderstood" (1). The narrator proceeds to assert that her story is both inseparable from its political context—"shrouded in shame, colonialism, self-mutilation, and a family history that features a heroic grandmother, a suicidal mother, and two heroin-addicted brothers"—and a story of personal accountability and redemption, "an account of my addiction, a steady flow of unhappiness, the X-ray of a delusion, and ultimately, the redeeming face of motherhood" (5). This account follows a chronological structure, beginning with a brief discussion of Irene's mother's history and Irene's childhood, but focusing primarily on the development and dissolution of a dysfunctional relationship with her first husband during her young adult years. Hunger, poverty, and self-harm—including multiple suicide attempts and abortions—are recurring themes in this part of Irene's life. *Impossible Motherhood* foregrounds the partiality and mutability of life narrative by making constant corrections and additions to the earlier account given in *The Ladies' Gallery*. Readers must notice that the meaning of Irene's life—her relationships, her mental illness, her identity, her writing—is not stable, but changes with a shifting vantage point.

> My first book was a memoir that today reads to me as proof of the lie I have at times made of my life. I told a clear-cut story of three generations of woman in one family [...] intent on self-destruction against the backdrop of political struggle. The transference horror script I lived out with the man I loved and became pregnant by multiple times, as I wrote my life down during those years, is absent in that memoir, tucked away under the noble rug of family history. The story I told was true, but it could have been truer [34].

The narrator of *Impossible Motherhood* now sees *The Ladies' Gallery* as a reading of her own life imposed by her ex-husband, a reading she had internalized. The narrator views the persistent intertextuality of *The Ladies' Gallery* as yet another way that Irene's first husband exerted authorship over her life: the intertexts were "books my master brought me," the references organized on note cards "a failed attempt to be enough or have enough to repay him for including me in his life" (78). The writing of *The Ladies' Gallery* looks now like the internalization of an identity imposed by a colonizing authority:

> Forget [...] your fantasies to give birth to somebody else for fear of having to birth your own self. A big project begins here for you today. You have a

mother and grandmother's suicidal fantasies to break free from. I'm going to help you. What you have is a beautiful problem, it's what poetry is made of, so don't feel bad my young Alfonsina. I'm going to show you the ocean and you'll see how everything painful shrinks at the horizon [86–87].

Yet the narrator also views her appropriation of this prescribed role as manipulative, a way to "exploit his weakness—from the romantic and modernist traditions, nursed by exile and extermination—for women at the brink of self-annihilation. [...] I very quickly assumed an Alfonsina Storni persona. I became a writer tangled up in the giant octopus of family history and suicide so that he could only love me more" (87). The *Impossible Motherhood* narrator now exposes the many silences in *The Ladies' Gallery* that testify to the power dynamic through which it emerged:

In the published book there is no promiscuous teenager shaming her way through Mexico, or in love with her literature professor, bowing her way through life for fear of looking it in the face. [...] There are no abortions either, except for a 'miscarriage' mentioned in passing at the end. Instead, the memoir follows a college girl coming undone as the mourning for her mother catches up with her. Pressures from the adult world that include underperforming in college, splitting with a boyfriend, the burden of an adolescent body, depression, and the progressive slowing down into inertia are narrated in broad terms, in passing. Only the suicide attempts are given in detail, but even these are lacking an identifiable referent that inspired them. It's as if the movement toward self-annihilation was happening in a vacuum, the vacuum of a history attractive enough in its tragic sense to be understood as the reason for it all. My misery at the center of the book is historically romanticized, and the personal, domestic truths of a self's struggles are for the most part missing [99].

Paradoxically, however, the narrator of *Impossible Motherhood* views the process of writing the externally imposed narrative of *The Ladies' Gallery* as a way of emerging from this power dynamic: "My days took on an independent quality, a relevance and direction of my own making. [...] In these heightened moments of creativity and validation, I evaded the drama of pregnancy and abortion and 'remembered' to take my birth control pills" (115). "The translation—and the passage of time since I had first written the book—revealed substantial fissures in the story. [...] My ideas for how to tackle them differed from what he thought should be done. The editing process created a new tension between us that sometimes felt competitive and other times patronizing" (116). "One day I shocked myself by hating his ideas and edits. When I asked him to let me be, I could not believe my words" (118).

The narration in *Impossible Motherhood* emphasizes the roles of writing—formulating identity—and, to a lesser extent, sailing—performing self-reliance—in Irene's developing ability to stop hurting herself. Through the writing process and the narrative process of therapy, she reinterprets her story as one of addiction, drawing parallels to the heroin addiction experienced by two of her brothers, her father's alcohol addiction, and her mother's Valium addiction. The narrator points to an MFA writing workshop as a pivotal point leading toward that reformulation of her self-narrative: "By the end of the workshop, I knew the task ahead of me was to give up my idealized memory. But a whole year would go by before, under the right circumstances, in the strange land of self-reflection, my memory ripped open so that I could see 'the happiest years of my life' as the story of an abortion addict" (168). Although the role of therapy in this process receives only brief attention in the narrative, it is viewed as fundamental:

> In my last session with Joan, we looked back at my progress, how my grief, which had been gridlocked, had become more fluid in the last year. How my emphasis in therapy began to change. Instead of talking about my ex-husband I came to spend long sessions describing my life story. I remembered my childhood in Palmas Altas differently from the one I had recalled when writing about it in my memoir.
>
> We discovered that the distance I put between my country and family and myself for close to two decades had not been all his doing. [...] I chose him. I made him the runway of my flight. I owned him as much as I owned my dreams and my nightmares [179].

In the account of how Irene finally strikes out on her own, leaving Syracuse and the pain she experienced there, she almost immediately meets and marries Dan, becomes the stepmother of his children, and starts trying to get pregnant for the sixteenth time. Their large wedding in Puerto Rico becomes a chance to reconcile with Lolita, who had considered *The Ladies' Gallery*—in particular its representation of Irene's mother's suicide—a betrayal of the nationalist cause. The new relationship and pregnancy do not magically erase Irene's troubled past, however: "'I can't be a mother. I can't do it. I want to abort.' I couldn't believe I said it, but I had. I wanted to abort the child I had begged God for for over seven months. I felt I was going insane. [...] What was wrong with me? I had a family I loved. [...] And yet, I was sad" (198). The coping mechanism Irene adopts is to write another book: "How can I give testimony to the horror

I precipitated upon a girl fifteen different times? [...] As I wrote the words down, I felt delivered from a damned life and I imagined, at last, the face of my daughter" (200).

In the final chapter, the particularist rhetoric of mixed messages snowballs as Vilar develops the concept of her abortion "addiction" in terms of performance and power, self-mutilation, and post-traumatic stress. The repeated pregnancies begin as a rehearsal of the empowering role of mother—forbidden to her by her first husband—alternating with exercising the power to end the pregnancy, simultaneously a form of self-harm and an addiction: her body "would come to crave" "the drama of life and death" (202). Vilar describes the pregnancies and abortions in terms of a "high" related to performing control: although Irene never craved the moment of the abortion itself,

> at times the high took place before pregnancy, waiting for a missed period, my body basking in the promise of being in control. At other times it was the pregnancy itself, the control I embodied if only for a couple of months, and still other times it was leaving the abortion clinic, feeling that once again I had succeeded in a narrow escape. The time of my drama was my time, no one could interrupt it, and what was more important, I could not interrupt it to meet others' needs. Feelings of inadequacy, helplessness, and disorder faded in the face of the possibilities of my reproductive body. An excitement, hyperarousal, almost euphoria surrounded my maternal desire. The craving gave structure to the confusing morass of events that made up my life. [...] It was a violent, intensely emotional drama that kept me from feeling alone. [...] Soon it was no longer about the control I had craved before. Getting pregnant began to be simply a habit. [...] I needed another self-injury to get the high [202–03].

Performance and narrative have become both a process and a framework for understanding herself and her history: "I had no control over my mother's decision to abandon me. But I had control over my body. [...] Repeat abortions 'remembered' an element of the experience of death and abandonment. If my mother chose death over me, I chose to tell the story fifteen terrifying times" (206). Although the narrator is confident about this interpretation, other readers have found it troublingly incoherent. "The narrative becomes a rushed, unconvincing jumble of explanations and epiphanies as it attempts to draw together Vilar's thoughts about her own mother and motherhood, as well as her feelings of shame and her need for redemption" (Thompson 151). The epilogue discusses Irene's experiences as a mother and how they have affected her sense of self. Speaking directly to her daughter, she says that writing this book has been one way "to protect you from me" (219). "Reflecting the tone and conventions of much 'mommy lit' (a direct address to the child, effusing warm confidence balanced by pensive concerns for her future), the conclusion of *Impossible Motherhood* argues that motherhood cured her by providing an identity. This more socially acceptable identity of 'mother' authorizes the memoir's otherwise unacceptable testimony of abortion" (Thompson 151). Alluding to *testimonio* but confining its discourse to a framing device, Vilar affirms individual ownership over a life story linked to collective political concerns, but resists the tendency, exemplified by her ex-husband and grandmother, to politically coopt her personal experiences. Even within the initial claim "this testimony [...] does not grapple with the political issues revolving around abortion" (2), the word "testimony" signals the political dimension of the story. Further, the next paragraph goes on to discuss the "alarming results of a rigid fundamentalism combined with poverty and ignorance" and cite Latin American abortion and mortality statistics, concluding that *Roe v. Wade* "acknowledged and addressed the fact that the human missteps leading to the painful reality of abortion, like the psychological ones afflicting me or the economic ones pursuing so many, are beyond control" (4).

In the final chapter, Vilar adds the testimonial frame back to the conclusion of her narrative by again drawing explicit connections between her personal drama and the ways Puerto Rican women, including her own mother, have been objectified and abused by the U.S. government:

> I can't think about my mother and in general Puerto Rican women without thinking about "choice." [...] Choices are framed by larger institutional structures and ideological messages. [...] Views of U.S. social scientists in turning fertility and reproduction into the source of the "Puerto Rican problem." The Puerto Rican mother was either victimized by her macho husband and countless children, longing to be rescued from her own ignorance, or a relentless dangerous mating machine that needed to be stopped. [...] Throughout my mother's childbearing years, from 1955 to 1969, Puerto Rico was a human laboratory for the development of birth control technology and population control policies [204].

According to the narrator, Irene's mother's lack of choice in the medication and surgery imposed on her reproductive system according to U.S. government policy directly affected her mental health and the way she performed—and abandoned—her role as Irene's mother:

> Most of the conscious memories I have of my mother belong to the time after her hysterectomy. Depression and mood swings fastening her to a chair or sending her away in the middle of the night. Migraines curled her blood-clotted body in bed. Irritability slapped a daughter for asking a question. Bloating and fat gain in the hips and thighs shamed her in the mirror. [...] Self-medicating with Valium and acting out a ransacked, frantic, if vacant, sexuality, my mother came undone while I watched [205].

The bookend structure suggests that the loss, economic hardship, uprootedness, self-destructive sexual behavior, depression, anxiety, suicide, writing, and motherhood that Irene experiences must be read within their gendered neocolonial context, and yet they are not reducible to it.

As a *testimonio*, Irene's personal story represents the dysfunctional relationship between the medically and politically regulated biological processes of women's bodies, their social roles, their socially encoded family relationships, and their mental health and sense of self, within the contexts of *machismo* and U.S. neocolonialism in Puerto Rico.[4] The call for action inherent to the *testimonio* genre, however, is not clear here. *Impossible Motherhood*, with its scandalous title and a cover image of tally marks representing abortions reminiscent of a score being kept, is certainly a call for dialogue about the relationship between abortion and other aspects of women's lives, including poverty, gender roles, relationships, and mental health. The way the book highlights the transformative role of writing as a coping mechanism and affirmation of identity also implies a call for women to take up narrative as an empowering tool. Yet in stating, "My testimony is not unique," the narrator elaborates, "many other women were hungry to come to terms with a past scarred by cowardice and the need to cloak themselves in someone else's power. Many had a history of repeat abortions. They, like me, were eager to find a language to articulate an experience they had seldom spoken about" (4). By defining the testimony as representative of a collective need to articulate and thus overcome personal shortcomings, Vilar mixes the codes of Latin American *testimonio* and North American neoconfessional, disturbing reader expectations.

Leigh Gilmore defines neoconfessional as "reviving key elements of American autobiographical narrative for new audiences, reawakening national fantasies of individualism, and promoting new normativities in life narrative that displace histories of racial and gendered violence with tales of individual hardship and redemption" (658). She clarifies the differences between *testimonio* and neoconfessional:

> Unlike testimonials that bear witness to human rights abuses and are more directly political in their aims, the American neoconfessional primarily bears witness to personal pain. By locating the cause, experience, and end of suffering within the framework of the individual rather than in histories of violence that require political critique and legal and social remedies, and that compel readers to negotiate identification and witnessing, neoconfessionals displace the analysis of wrongdoing away from questions of justice [659].

Megan C. Brown argues that narratives of addiction within the neoconfessional genre "function as lifestyle instruction, telling readers how to recognize, assess, and respond to 'shortcomings.' These memoirs have much to say, to be sure, about physical and psychological selfcare, but they also teach readers about the biopolitically linked matters of normative productivity, efficiency, and the management of relationships, particularly as these function within the context of U.S. neoliberalism" (360). Through her mixed genre messages in *Impossible Motherhood*, Vilar juxtaposes *testimonio* discourse with this individual accountability discourse of U.S. neoliberalism. She examines her life struggles through a Latin American lens and a U.S. lens, and asks readers to do the same. Her self-perception is not reducible to either one.

For Mary Thompson, Vilar's mixed rhetoric is an appeal to both prolife and pro-choice readers, with troubling consequences:

> The memoir suppresses and deploys Vilar's ethnic and gender identity either to build sympathy with a pro- choice feminist audience or to express shame to an antiabortion audience responsive to the rhetoric of personal accountability.
> The rhetorical strategy adopted in the memoir toward its audiences, I argue, is fashioned through omissions and strategic emphasis in addition to Euro-American feminist allegories of female rebellion and metaphors of illness that stand in for more meaningful political consciousness and discourses of ethnicity and gender [Thompson 134].

While I have read Vilar's appropriation of the madwoman figure as a revision of a metaphorizing cliché that denies women the capacity to speak as intellectuals through and about mental illness, Thompson argues that Vilar's representation of herself as a writer as a strategic performance of the madwoman "suppresses her ethnicity in order to enhance feelings of identification and sympathy in her prochoice readers" (141).[5] Thompson argues—circularly—that because, as Susan Sontag as demonstrated, pathologies such as addiction have negative cultural connotations, Vilar's representation of abortion as related to these pathologies reinforces negative cultural connotations of abortion (146). Furthermore, "her sense of a personal victory over U.S. imperialist population- control ideologies in Puerto Rico (represented by her mother's ruin) is achieved by ignoring the politics of class privilege in determining the right to motherhood on the mainland" (Thompson 153). While I respect Thompson's detailed reading and shrewd analysis of Vilar's rhetoric, I do not believe it is fair to criticize Vilar both for appropriating Anglo-American feminist discourse (through the trope of the madwoman) and also for not dialoguing enough with Anglo-American feminist discourse (on the intersectionality of class and women's reproductive issues). Although Thompson finds *Impossible Motherhood* damaging to feminist goals in its mixed messages, she concludes, "the importance of Vilar's work (beyond its restorative role in her personal life) lies in her effort to bring this difficult subject into mainstream conversation" (155).

Vilar's particularist rhetoric of mixed messages in *Impossible Motherhood* engages readers, disturbs their expectations, and evades their interpretive frameworks. "'The ultimate goal,' Vilar says, 'was to write a testimonial that was empowering to young women, by giving them a model for thinking about their actions and their unconscious actions'" (Roig-Franzia); "'Hay que empezar a hablar de depresión y aborto sin tantos tabúes, como se habla de cualquier otro tema de salud pública,' explica Vilar" ["We have to start talking about depression and abortion without so many taboos, like we talk about any other public health issue"] (Cruz). To read *Impossible Motherhood* as a *testimonio*, we must accept that the call to action is to engage in dialogue about these public health issues and their intertwined personal and political dimensions, and to develop self-awareness and mental health through narrative. The narrative that Vilar has constructed in *Impossible Motherhood* is unsettling because it weaves personal accountability, shame, and redemption through motherhood into a political *testimonio* and refers constantly to the distortions and omissions in her previous life narrative. The discomfort resulting from this rhetoric of mixed messages constantly reminds the reader that his or her own position is different. As Vilar writes on her website, "You will never understand. I will never forget. Yet here we are. You and I. 'No one bears witness for the witness' wrote Paul Celan. Where can we look for the witness for whom there is no witness? I'm hoping she is you."

Irene Vilar's life-writing is an intensely personal exploration of the relationship between writing and mental illness. Like the other writers featured in this volume, Vilar utilizes literary techniques to represent what has been considered outside of language. Intertextuality, complex narrative structure, sensorial imagery, genre mixing, and scrutiny of the processes of reading and writing converge in Vilar's work to form a vivid self-portrait of a writer whose identity is inseparable from her experience of mental illness. At the same time, Vilar's work examines the role of writing as a tool for the cultivation of well-being on both societal and personal levels. A troubling mix of *testimonio* and sensational neoconfessional stirs public dialogue on traditionally silenced experiences—mental illness and abortion—and their political contexts. Vilar represents the writing process both as an empowering way of connecting with a literary tradition, and as a path to individual self-understanding. Her writing challenges readers to engage in dialogue and invites them to form their own life narratives in the process, no matter how rocky, of developing personal well-being.

Conclusions

This volume has charted a map of the kaleidoscopic territory of madness in literature by women writers in turn-of-the-millennium Latin America. A poetics of madness emerged as we plotted the strategies that these writers use to represent madness on individual and societal levels. These works position the reader in the role of cartographer, puzzle-solver, staging an encounter between madness and reason that ends either by restoring reason or by questioning the relationships between madness and reason, text and reader. As we have discussed, Laura Restrepo's *Delirio* and Cristina Peri Rossi's *La nave de los locos* encourage the reader to bridge madness and reason by learning how to read mad discourses and restore coherence. In contrast, *Nadie me verá llorar* by Cristina Rivera Garza, *Exílio* by Lya Luft, and *El infarto del alma* by Diamela Eltit and Paz Errázuriz, invite the reader to solve a puzzle that turns out to be impossible because the texts conspicuously withhold missing pieces. Lastly, in *The Ladies' Gallery* and *Impossible Motherhood: Testimony of an Abortion Addict* by Irene Vilar, the memoir narrators themselves have assembled a puzzle of their own experience of mental illness, narrating that very process. Thus, the works we have considered in this volume perform different relationships between literary author/reader and madness: literature can teach us how to listen to and interpret madness, show us the limitations of this approach, and be appropriated as a way to interpret and emerge from one's own mental state.

When women write about madness in contemporary Latin America, they write from a specific position. They negotiate both patriarchal and feminist discourses that have placed women outside of rationality, global postmodern fragmentation and relativism, a regional postboom shift toward

Conclusions

social engagement. Similarly, a history of Western thought has defined madness as a manifestation of social control, and an immediate reality in which mental illness is stigmatized and women are more likely to struggle with mental health than men due to the multiple stressors of socially defined roles, poverty, and political strife. Women write within a culture that traditionally expects them more than men to suffer *ataques de nervios* or *susto* in distressing situations. They write within a regional literary tradition whose foundational 19th-century texts utilize madness to mark their transgressions of prescribed social norms.

It is from this commonality that the writers we have studied here have participated in the development of what we are identifying as a poetics of madness in Latin American women's writing. We refer to "poetics" in the sense of "a cultural process of activity in an ever changing theoretical structure by which to order both our cultural knowledge and critical procedures" (Hutcheon 4). "Madness," as we have maintained, is a problematical and controversial concept, one that triggered multiple ethical and philosophical predicaments in the process of writing this book. A poetics of madness, then, is the confluence of textual analysis and cultural construct that leads us to inquire within the individual, the social and the political in order to better comprehend what lies behind the apparent rational discourses of the irrational.

One of the main challenges we confronted across the textual analysis was the dual edge of madness as a concept, as a category and as a clinical definition. We were aware of the risk of falling into essentialist and reductive categorizations, a risk that we tried to avoid at all costs. In the process, we found that there is not a single approach or definition for madness, but rather, multiple theoretical views that confront, dispute and refute one another. To deal with this contentious relationship between different theoretical constructions, we chose to align with Foucault's *History of Madness* and to extract from complementary perspectives in accordance with the focus of each work. Throughout this critical examination, then, Foucault guided the inquiry, complemented by North American, European and Latin American approaches.

This book focused on literary works by women in the context of postmodern Latin American narratives. In *La nave de los locos*, Uruguayan Cristina Peri Rossi represents madness through characters traveling on a ship of fools to challenge patriarchal domination and to denounce politics of exclusion and marginalization. The depressed protagonist in Lya Luft's

Conclusions

Exilio is unable to cope with the social pressures placed on contemporary Brazilian women. Diamela Eltit and Paz Errázuriz in *Infarto del alma* portray with words and photographs the utterly marginalized residents of a psychiatric hospital, alluding to political oppression in Chile. Cristina Rivera Garza in *Nadie me verá llorar* considers madness as a reflection of power dynamics in the transformation of Mexico at the turn of the 20th century. In *Delirio*, Laura Restrepo depicts individual and collective madness in Colombia, a country affected by violence, political corruption and social decay. Irene Vilar's memoirs, *The Ladies' Gallery* and *Impossible Motherhood: Testimony of an Abortion Addict*, narrate experiences with mental illness that are at once personal and collective, reflecting the neocolonial status of Puerto Rico and the oppression of women in Puerto Rico and the mainland U.S. As our analyses have maintained, these narratives demonstrate how power relations, gender exclusions and social marginality result from cultural constructs and reflections of politics over the body and the self.

These authors and their works provide a mapping of the literature of madness in various countries of Latin America. From Uruguay, Chile and Brazil in the southern cone, to Colombia in the northern part of South America, and Mexico—geographically located in North America, but culturally related to Central and South America—ending in Puerto Rico, to represent the Caribbean in connection to the Hispanic world and to U.S. territorial politics. The mapping of these narratives of madness helped to explore how these authors raised critical awareness about social and political issues affecting the region in recent history. Our objective was to compare, contrast and analyze insanity as a literary device correspondent with postmodern and feminist critical theories. This selection was done after careful investigation from a myriad of choices dealing with the subject. A future project could consider the literature of madness in a variety of genres such as performance and theater, poetry, and virtual and cybernarratives in the new millennium.

By approaching madness as a cultural construct, we revealed the political concerns that are inevitable consequences of using madness as a metaphor for societal ills. We further sought to draw attention to the real relationship between this construct and the ways individuals experience mental illness, a position informed by the discipline of critical disability studies. We were able to conclude that regardless of the region of origin, literature of madness by women tells us that social expectations on traditional feminine gender roles of submission and domesticity are triggers for mental instability and disturbance. We discovered that madness is a fluid category, one that goes hand in hand with trauma and pain, disability and illness, gender identity, and the liminal zone that exists between reason and unreason in conflictive societies.

The narratives studied cover a period from the 1980s to the 2000s. Therefore, we could map a corpus of concerns representing this period and the transformation these issues experienced through time. For instance, in 1984, the depiction of a sexual cross-dressing performance in *La nave de los locos* submitted a groundbreaking proposition about dismantling fixed gender categories. This message does not have the same effect today in the midst of a revolution toward greater freedom of sexual and gender identities. The same could be said about Lya Luft's *Exílio*, where a woman becomes trapped by depression due to her failure to live up to the conflicting demands placed on her as a professional and as a mother and wife in an oppressive society. Most of the narratives focused on madness as a social and political allegory to depict the maladies affecting the region in the new era. Several of these works look at the relationship between women's family roles as mothers and daughters and their experiences of mental illness. For Irene Vilar, mental illness is a political and familial—matrilineal—legacy; the hospital residents in *Infarto del alma* have been removed by the state government from the family structure through isolation and forced sterilization; and the protagonist in *Exílio* has gone into exile from her family and professional identity.

As a whole, findings along our textual cartography reflect women's transformations and challenges during the last three decades in a territory marked by individual domestic battles, participation in political activism and commitment to social causes. This is the poetics of madness that emerges through the selection of the texts for this book as part of the gender-politics dynamic in a continuing flow of transformation and change.

This study has identified a collection of common motifs and techniques that the writers draw upon to represent literary, societal, and individual madness.

The Visible and the Invisible

Many of the narratives analyzed for this book posit a question about the role of vision in the literature of madness. We found that the dynamics of the visible and invisible, prisms and mirrors, gaze and sight, are recurrent motifs, as if there were a particular connection between vision and madness, or as if madness were the result of being able to apprehend reality from an alternative perspective.

Cristina Peri Rossi uses vision in different forms to widen the range of the scopic field: the voyeur who watches, the masculine gaze being reverted and by cinematic intertextualities. *La nave de los locos* is a text about people wandering in madness reflecting the insanity of their surroundings. Characters observe the world turning mad. They are the observers, and the ones being observed. At the same time, the text operates as a mirror. Peri Rossi plays with the images people expect to see of themselves, playing with distortion, fragmentation, parody, pastiche, and the allegory of the tapestry of creation as the metaphor of a harmonic universe. While the reader watches the characters driven by their circumstances, he/she reflects him/herself in the text as a mirror refracting the madness of its own world.

In *Nadie me verá llorar*, Rivera Garza uses photography to subvert the redefinition of boundaries between macro History and micro history, visibility and invisibility. Photographs are used as an artifice to represent the "space off" and the *punctum* produced by the pain inscribed in the narrated image. Photography is also the medium to interrogate the dynamics between the inside and outside of official discourse and the power relationship between the included and excluded in society and political institutions.

While in *Nadie me verá llorar,* photographs are symbolic representations inferred from the reader's perspective, in *Infarto del alma*, photographs are visually present in the text. They constitute powerful discursive tools that interpellate the reader through a testimonial gaze and the denunciation that this gaze implies. Simultaneously, the combination of the text and photographs of the Putaendo Psychiatric Hospital unveils troubling issues of consent and authority. *El infarto del alma* bears witness through its photographs to the social bonds between the marginalized hospital residents, and through its text, to the intellectual reflections that the presence of the residents apparently catalyzed.

In *Delirio*, Restrepo uses myth, ritual and vision to expose the blurriness between reality and hyperreality and to transcend the borderline separating reason and unreason. Agustina's clairvoyance follows the assertion by Gilbert and Gubar that many literary works use women's powers of sight to illustrate how "those cut off from political power may exploit their passivity by becoming instruments compelled by higher forces" (473–474). Correspondingly, Agustina's sight is essential to revealing a society that has replaced the real with the hyper real. Joining vision with myth, Agustina invites comparison to the Greek tragedy of Cassandra. Unable to cope with the falsehood of her surroundings, Agustina falls into madness for seeing and for revealing an imponderable secret, just as Cassandra was driven to insanity for telling her truth. Similar to *La nave de los locos*, *Delirio* uses a mirror effect that conveys madness in multiple and polyvalent forms. Stories in the novel mirror one another through distortions, refractions and decompositions. Readers are invited to reflect and refract their own positions onto the reality they either want to acknowledge or to ignore.

Reason/Unreason

Following Foucault, narratives selected for this volume play with the dialectics of reason and unreason as a fundamental theme in the discourse of madness. For instance, *La nave de los locos* is a text about people wandering around in a journey with no destination, reflecting on the irrationality of the ones considered rational. The author plays with the constant reflection of reason and unreason to point out the absurdity of monolithic structures ruling the world. The allegory of madness deconstructs and subverts the so-called "rational discourses" contained in repressive dictatorial political regimes, religious institutions and gendered categorizations.

In *Delirio*, reason and unreason are manifested by multiple actors in a polyphony of voices—from the individual to the collective, from the social to the political—reflecting a society in crisis. Through the discourse of madness and irrationality, Restrepo infuses rationality into Colombia's conflictive situation. Restrepo draws on textual and linguistic strategies to convey a dialectic of reason and unreason. Culture as a mediator becomes the synthesis and the disjunction of all forces traversing the novel, channeling the discourses of madness.

Rivera Garza's series of questions across *Nadie me verá llorar* reflect the dynamics of reason and unreason. This is evident in the dialogical nature of the text and the oppositions between language and silence, darkness and light, white and black, inside and outside, History and microhistory. Contrary to Peri Rossi and Restrepo, where the new possibilities arise from the dialectic of reason and unreason, in *Nadie me verá llorar* the unanswered questions at the end suggest that there is not a real answer after all. Matilda's silence, a strategy she willfully chooses, erases all semantic meaning and with it, the reader's hope for redemption.

On Confinement

Many works discussed in this volume portray specially defined spaces—psychiatric hospitals, the ship of fools, and liminal spaces—that house those considered mentally ill or mad. These structures reflect the social stigma of mental illness and the disconnect between turn-of-the-millennium Latin American mental health care reform movements and actual attitudes and infrastructure.[1] Three of the works describe the conditions of inmates in psychiatric hospitals. Diamela Eltit and Paz Errázuriz document through photography the poor treatment of residents at the Putaendo Psychiatric Hospital in Chile, suggesting in the accompanying text that this marginalization reflects the patients' threat to the country's neoliberal economic project. Cristina Rivera Garza describes the Castañeda Psychiatric Hospital in Mexico and its evolution during the early 20th century. Irene Vilar's *The Ladies' Gallery* discusses her experience with psychiatric care in upstate New York. In the first two works, the asylum as the site of confinement for the mad and marginalized from society parallels the socio-political environment of the respective countries. In *El infarto del alma*, the visible mistreatment of inmates and the hospital as an institution depicted in the book can be interpreted as a metonymy for postdictatorial Chilean oppression and resistance. The same applies to Rivera Garza's portrayal of La Castañeda as a reflection of political and social transformation in Mexico at the turn of the century.

Through multiple narrative voices and images, both works create a privileged vantage point from which to contemplate the conflicting meanings that play a role in understanding mental illness. While *El infarto del alma* reflects on the relationship between self and other, *Nadie me verá llorar* underscores how medical discourse describes and naturalizes mental illness, and imagines the negotiations that take place between patients and doctors through this language. The use of photographs in both works—as a narrative artifice in *Nadie me verá llorar*, and as the visual predominant element in *Infarto del alma*—accentuates both the suffering and the agency inscribed in the individual, while provoking the reader/

Conclusions

viewer to contemplate the power dynamic between the portrayed, the portrayer, and the viewer. In both works, photographs underline the uneven power dynamic of the medical gaze, while also suggesting that, to an extent, the medical gaze can be returned by subjects who are active participants in their own assessment. As a medium and as a representation, photography thereby challenges the power dynamics of portrayals of madness.

In *The Ladies' Gallery*, psychiatric hospitals are presented in another light. In this memoir, the hospitals belong to the U.S. medical system, and their portrayal reveals ways in which the neocolonial status of Puerto Rico damages the health of its citizens. Rather than depicting the hospital as a confining and marginalizing space, Irene, the narrator, recalls her own experience in the hospital as one of temporary refuge. Vilar recounts negotiating the space and discourses of the hospital as a resource for coping with the life stresses that she, like her mother and grandmother, experienced as part of a patriarchal, neocolonial society, both on the island and on the mainland. In contrast, according to the memoir, Irene's political activist grandmother, Lolita, experienced the psychiatric hospital as an oppressive political apparatus.

In *Exílio*, the asylum-like liminal space suggested by the Casa Vermelha is ambiguous and indeterminate. The Casa Vermelha embodies marginalization and neglect, both through its decaying physical structure and through the suffering and isolation of its motley cast of residents. It represents and interrogates the traditional asylum and the more integrated approaches that began to take place in Brazil during the 1980s. Contrary to the psychiatric hospitals as the site for sociopolitical contention and resistance described in Eltit's and Rivera Garza's work, in *Exílio*, the emphasis is focused on the individual suffering from depression. As demonstrated in the chapter's analysis, *Exílio* evokes the intensely personal pain of depression through imagery involving the liminal spaces of the body, the boarding house and the forest. The spaces of liminality, while lonely and uncomfortable, also gain an empowering dimension as they serve as a vehicle for the communication of intensely personal sensations and pain.

In sum, these representation of mental institutions—the asylum, the clinic, the hospital or a refuge—reflect multiple dimensions of agency and control over the body and the mind, the individual and the collectivity. In some novels the asylum becomes the metonym of repressive political regimes, while in others, it replicates gender and social exclusion. As a whole, a Foucauldian vision of the asylum as a structure for socioeconomic and political control is enacted, with recognition of the agency, however limited, that individuals exercise as they negotiate that structure.

The Postmodern

Recent Latin America literature has contributed to the liberation movements opposing dictatorships and military regimes, while also reflecting key historical events in the region. Women's narratives combine both a feminist and political agenda. They denounce gender inequalities embedded into social and political issues. Many of them use madness to deliver messages about women's roles in society and how they intersect with political oppression. In these narratives, the figure of the middle class housewife gone mad (loca) by social restrictions is intertwined with socio-political exclusion as part of women's struggles for rights and dignity. The term "la loca" has distinct connotations from that of "madwoman." Debra Castillo distinguishes different cultural baggage in the term "la loca" in Latin America, where "madness and sanity are differently coded and valued" (7). As we have illustrated, connotations of madness are inherent to the particular cases examined in each chapter. In political terms, madness has been used as a label to stigmatize transgressive action. Such is the case for the political activism by the Mothers of the Plaza de Mayo in Argentina, who were officially deemed "locas" for crossing the traditional boundaries into public space. In addition, women who do not conform to societal norms of domesticity and passivity are also branded as "locas," as Vilar's memoirs and Luft's *Exílio* demonstrate.

With the rise of postmodernism in Latin America, women have acquired access to the literary and artistic terrain, capitalizing on the decentering of cultural power and the recognition of the margins and "other" discourses, as remarked by Nelly Richard. Our narrative selections have incorporated postmodern techniques in different fashions. While Cristina Peri Rossi's *La nave de los locos* may be considered a paradigmatic postmodern novel for its integration of fragmentation, discontinuity, parody, language games, chronological jumps, pastiche and ironic discourse, Rivera Garza's heteroglossia and dialogic strategies are pivotal in *Nadie me verá llorar*. Although Rivera Garza also draws upon textual fragmentation and temporal and spatial jumps across the narrative, her emphasis in dialoguing with the boundaries of historical discourse constitutes her most distinctive feature. More importantly, as a scholar, Rivera Garza deliberately appropriates theoretical approaches, transforming them into literary hermeneutical stances in her fictional work.

Other postmodern techniques such as self-referentiality and intertextuality are common denominators in many of these narratives. Intertexts operate as palimpsests, as in Restrepo's *Delirio*, or in the superimposed literary, artistic, and cinematic layers in Peri Rossi's *La nave de los locos*. Vilar's *Impossible Motherhood* also stands as a palimpsest, a text layered over *The Ladies' Gallery* that refers constantly to the first memoir's omissions and distortions. In other cases, intertextuality calls attention to author participation in universal intellectual traditions. This applies to *The Ladies Gallery*, in which Vilar assumes a powerful stance toward the intellectual community as a literary author who is a woman suffering from mental illness. Vilar rewrites the position of the "madwoman" as an eloquent intellectual, and then she rewrites it again, suggesting a never-ending process of reading and revision.

In most cases, the dialogical nature of intertextuality is a posture taken by the authors to demonstrate intellectual knowledge and the capacity to transcend regional and local cultural competencies. This is part of the strategies assumed by writers selected for this volume, to negotiate their positions as both local and universal literary authors, who exercise the authority to write about national and regional issues and also draw connections between the local and the global.

From a textual standpoint, mixed genres and discursive linguistic strategies are used in most of the novels. The mixing of genres in Vilar (*testimonio*/memoir/autobiography) and Eltit (*testimonio*/travel diary/essay) makes it difficult to categorize the narratives. More importantly perhaps, this may be interpreted as the authors' intention not to allow the reader—or the critic in this case—to categorize her texts. Madness as a discursive technique is apparent in *Delirio* through the stream-of-consciousness monologue with alternating narrative voices, thus intentionally emulating the delirium effect in the reader. Rivera Garza's use of discursive tactics to create semantic disruptions of meanings replicates the language of madness as a predominant protocol in *Nadie me verá llorar*. The same applies to Peri Rossi's and Luft's fragmentations and ruptures to imitate what might be called the schizophrenic text. All these forms of textual strategies conform to what Patricia Waugh called the metafictional paradox, one of the essential components of postmodernism.

Conclusions

Raising Consciousness

Foucault defined the literature of madness as a medium to raise the critical consciousness of humanity. Women writers in Latin America are using postmodern literary tools to this end. One of these tools is the rewriting of the allegory of madness as a literary artifice: to revert feminine marginalization, to reflect changes in women's positioning in society, to raise awareness about a world in crisis, and to denounce social and political struggles, including the stigmatization of mental illness within an often inadequate mental health care system. By exploring and analyzing these narratives, we have traced out a map of madness in contemporary Latin America.

Madness in the selected narratives for this volume is subversive and destabilizing, and it represents a counter-culture point of view. It is destabilizing because it challenges social normativities and power dynamics. It is subversive because, as most novels suggest, what separates reason from unreason lies in how cultural practices are understood and naturalized. At the core, the discourse interrogates and denounces the structures that oppress, shackle and regiment women's roles. These writers promulgate a countercultural discourse attempting to deconstruct and to revert fixed gender categories, socio-political power relationships and conventional cultural practices. Herein, the language of madness advocates a fluid and pluralistic dynamic of participation with different voices and marginal groups where the Other, the different and the minority, can indeed speak and be heard.

Appropriating a marginalized voice in literature is an ethical concern. As Marta Caminero-Santangelo points out, "Every time [feminist scholars] write another article or book about the emancipatory power of madness, they demonstrate just how fully they themselves can engage in public, rational forms of discourse" (180). Through their self-referentiality, intertextuality and mixing of genres, the works considered in this volume draw attention to their literariness and to their particular relationship to the voices they represent. Rather than neutralizing or ignoring the ethical concern, these works highlight it. They emphasize that the mad voices they project are literary constructions created in particular sociopolitical contexts, and challenge readers to participate in solving some difficult puzzles: what the voices are saying, why the writers imagined them this way, and how they are related to both societal madness and unique individual experiences of mental illness.

Conclusions

Through this volume we have journeyed, like sailors on a ship of fools wandering through a dark sea of conceptualizations and confrontations that are intermingled around the subject of madness. We co-authors of this enterprise assumed the command of this process by searching for the ship's wheel and the lighthouses to guide us in order to arrive at a good harbor. Our journey comes to a close, offering a map of cultural knowledge and critical understanding of the role of madness in Latin American narratives written by women at the onset of the 21st century.

Chapter Notes

Introduction

1. Silvia L. Gaviria and Marta B. Rondon point to a tendency in Latin America for preventive medicine for women to focus on prenatal care, reinforcing "the belief that the biological processes linked to procreation represent the most significant risk for women's health in developing countries, which distracts attention from other important threats" (363). Such as unequal access to opportunities (lower earning power, greater likelihood of being employed in the informal economy, less access to education) and unequal burdens of stress (childcare, work overload, poverty, political violence and forced displacement, culturally ingrained acceptance of violence towards women, pressure to conform to narrow standards for female beauty, lack of access to reproductive health care, and high rates of teenage pregnancy). They cite data showing that in Latin America, women are more likely than men to experience depression, anxiety, and post-traumatic stress disorder, and to attempt suicide, while men are much more likely to experience alcoholism (364).

2. Jacques Derrida refuted Foucault's fundamental claims in "Cogito and History of Madness" (1964).

3. In the introduction of the fifth edition of *Women and Madness: Revised and Updated* published in 2005, Chesler notes that much has certainly changed since she was a medical student, but clinical biases (sexism, racism, classism, homophobia, and more) are still threaded through textbooks, medical journals, and published studies: "For female patients, often-debilitating medical conditions like lupus and chronic fatigue syndrome are regularly dismissed as 'just' psychiatric illness; that psychiatric counseling for rape victims will invariably be used to further a 'nuts and sluts' defense when the rape goes to trial; and that class and race stereotypes (wealthy white women are bored, not depressed; women of color are 'stronger' than their less oppressed counterparts) run rampant in the white halls of psychiatric medicine" (quoted in Andi Zeisler's review for Powell's Books).

4. In *Rereading Women: Thirty Years of Exploring our Literary Traditions* (2011), Sandra Gilbert reflects on *The Madwoman in the Attic* and asks, "Why and how did these ideas become so urgently necessary to women in the sixties and seventies? Are those feminist concepts and practices still relevant today? Although these questions have been much addressed both in the media and by academics, they still compel attention from women and men alike, and for all of us, and our children, they retain their primordial urgency" (xiii).

5. For a more detailed analysis of madness in Latin American 20th-century narratives, see the work of Dora Georgina

Salamán Rocha, "La locura como identidad narrativa. *El obsceno pájaro de la noche* y *El otoño del patriarca*," Thesis, Universidad Iberoamericana, México, 2005.

Chapter One

1. I refer to Frederick Jameson's definition of the schizophrenic text (following Lacan's theory): "when the links of the signifying chain snap, then we have schizophrenia in the form of a rubble of distinct and unrelated signifiers" (25).

2. Peri Rossi's publications include Narrative: *Viviendo* (1963), *Los museos abandonados* (1968), *El libro de mis primos* (1969), *Indicios pánicos* (1970) *La tarde del dinosaurio* (1976), *La rebelión de los niños* (1976), *El museo de los esfuerzos inútiles* (1983), *Una pasión prohibida* (1986), *Cosmogonías* (1988), *Desastres íntimos* (1997). *El libro de mis primos* (1969), *La nave de los locos* (1984), *Solitario de amor* (1988), *La última noche de Dostoievski* (1992), *El amor es una droga dura* (1999); Poetry: *Evohé: poemas eróticos* (1971), *Descripción de un naufragio* (1975), *Diáspora* (1976), *Poemas* (1979), *Europa después de la lluvia* (1987), *Babel Bárbara* (1991), *Otra vez Eros* (1994), *Aquella noche* (1996), *Las musas inquietantes* (1999), *Estado de exilio* (2003); Essays: *Fantasías eróticas* (1991), *Cuando fumar era un placer* (2003) and Biography: *Julio Cortázar* (2001).

3. Personal interview, 8 June 2000.

4. Personal interview, 8 June 2000.

5. In this film, directed by Donald Cammell (1977), the character played by Julie Christie is raped by a diabolic machine. When Ecks watches the movie several times, he exposes a contradiction: his scopophilic fascination with the scene and the repulsion derived from its brutality (Fender Solano 39).

6. The English translations of these titles are "The Garden of Forking Desires," "A Fool and His Fire," "The Hydrangeas," "The Death of a Chinese Checkers Player" and "Women and Utopias" (*The Ship* 36–37).

7. Literary and artistic references to the ship of fools include "Triumphos de locura" (1521) a poem by Spanish Humanist Hernán López de Yanguas, *La nave de los locos* by Spaniard Pío Baroja (1925), *Ship of Fools* by North American Katherine Anne Porter, (1962) and *La nave de los locos* by Colombian Pedro Gómez Valderrama (1984). Other artistic expressions include musical concerts such as *Ship of Fools* by New Culture Quartet: World Museum/Narragonia (works 1983–1997).

8. It is important to differentiate the meaning of "folly" and "mad." The French word "folie" (from which "folly" is derived) "is more inclusive and common than the English word "madness": "folie" covers a vast range of meanings going from slight eccentricity to clinical insanity, including the connotations of "madness" and of "folly" (Felman 52). In the translations of the "Ship of Fools" to Latin, "Stultifera Navis" has the two meanings "fool" and "mad." In Spanish, "Nave de los locos" refers clearly to "mad" in contrast with "tonto" which would be the equivalent of "fool."

9. The first mention to Glaucus appears in Journey II: Ecks reads the *Illiad* passage where Glaucus (Paris's ally in the Trojan war) confronts Diomedes, "*Greathearted son of Tidis, why ask about my lineage?*" (*The Ship* 2).

10. See for instance Olivera-Williams (83).

11. My translation. The published English version reads, "He had read of this journey."

12. Ortega y Gasset (1883–1955) was a distinguished Spanish philosopher, social theorist, essayist and critic. Pio Baroja explicitly explains in his preface the intention of contesting Ortega y Gasset's *Ideas on the Novel* published in 1924.

13. This information is based on personal observation working as a reporter in Colombia.

14. "Extranjero" is translated sometimes as "stranger," but the literal meaning is "foreigner." The word in Spanish conveys the two meanings.

15. The Pantocrator represents more than the figure of Christ in the tapestry. Pantocrator from Greek, παντοκράτωρ, was originally applied to Zeus in Greek mythology meaning supreme power (ruler

of all). The image was specially used in Byzantine iconography to represent the power of Christianity over the world. Some of the oldest representations are located in Turkey (Hagia Sophia) and in the monastery of St. Catherine in the Sinai desert.

16. The specular composition of the two textual series contains 21 narrative segments (the journeys) and 12 descriptive fragments in italics (the tapestry). The narrative series represents the chaotic, fragmented exterior reality in contrast with the harmonic orderly structure of the tapestry (Dejaborn 129).

17. For a detailed analysis of the contrasting sequences of the tapestry see Ivernizzi Santa Cruz, "Entre el tapiz de la expulsión del paraíso."

18. The original title of this movie is *La caduta degli dei*, translated in German as *Götterdämmerung* and in English as *The Damned*.

19. Peri Rossi's own interpretation is valid when she asserts: "En *La nave* hay una riña de machos, una referencia a los viejos mitos. La respuesta se refiere a que la manera de amar es renunciando al poder del macho [...] es la renuncia al poder del *falo*" [In *La nave* there is a struggle of males, a reference to the old myths. The answer to the riddle means that to be able to love, you need to surrender male power [...] it is the surrender of *phallic* power]. Personal interview, 8 June 2000.

Chapter Two

1. I borrow the concept of liminality from anthropologist Victor Turner's discussion of rites of passage, during which the liminal individual is separated from society. Jeffrey Willett and Mary Jo Deegan have extended Turner's model to consider the social role of disability, suggesting that it entails a similar separation from society that is isolating but offers a different perspective enabling awareness of possibilities for change.

Chapter Three

1. Throughout this chapter, all translations are my own unless otherwise noted.

2. The pages of *El infarto del alma* are not numbered. All English quotations from *El infarto del alma* are from Ronald Christ's translation.

3. Eltit mentioned in an interview that the editor, Francisco Zegers, was responsible for the arrangement of the photographs and overall design of the book (294–95). It should be noted that the book design and placement of photographs in the English translation differ significantly from the original.

4. Errázuriz stated in an interview that the dictatorship prevented her from undertaking an earlier project focused on a different psychiatric hospital. ("De amor y desamparo," n.p.).

Chapter Four

1. In the prologue of *La Castañeda*, Rivera Garza explains: "Tengo una deuda de alrededor de quince años con este libro [...] primero fue una tesis de maestría y, años más tarde, de doctorado. Luego entre las páginas de este manuscrito salió otra cosa: su contrario. [...] La novela logró su cometido, en efecto, pero a costa de la vida del hermano siamés que, escondido o desfalcado, se dedicó a languidecer. Estamos, ustedes y yo, ante la restitución" (*La Castañeda* 12) [I have a debt of about 15 years with this text [...] first it was a master thesis, and years later, a doctoral dissertation. Then, among the pages of this manuscript it became another thing: its opposite. [...] The novel accomplished its task, indeed, but at the expense of the life of the Siamese brother that, hidden or bankrupt, decided to languish. We are, you and I, before the restitution]. All translations from this source are mine.

2. Carlos Fuentes's endorsement of Rivera Garza was pivotal for the recognition she acquired in Mexico literary circles. The original text in Spanish reads: "Estamos ante una de las obras de ficción más notables de la literatura no sólo mexicana, sino en castellano, de esta vuelta de siglo" ("El melodrama de la mujer caída").

3. In the original, "Este libro hace énfasis en las distintas maneras como las percepciones de los pacientes sobre sus

propias aflicciones han dado forma a la comprensión médica de los padecimientos mentales, así como a las interpretaciones de género y clase en el contexto de la construcción nacional" (*La Castañeda* 24).

4. In the original, "exploro las frases del libreto, las metáforas fundamentales y los elementos metafóricos que estructuran el padecimiento, [las cuales] se derivan de modos culturales y personales para organizar las experiencias de maneras significativas y para expresar esos significados de forma efectiva" (*La Castañeda* 15).

5. In the original: "En medio de los debates historiográficos que por lo regular enfatizan los procesos de construcción, reconstrucción o centralización del Estado, las narrativas polisémicas de los padecimientos mentales recuerdan de manera vívida la destrucción, el desmantelamiento y la dispersión; es decir, las fuerzas centrífugas que Bakhtin asoció con la heteroglosia" (*La Castañeda* 31).

6. This distinction is presented with capital letters in the macro level (History) and in lower case in the micro level (history) throughout the chapter.

7. In both the book *La Castañeda* and her thesis, Rivera Garza describes the architecture of the modern asylum as "monumental and unique" ("She Neither Respected" 659). She remarks that the hospital was built following European and United States models where "la arquitectura de la salud no solo incorporó nociones médicas de tratamiento y cura sino también acentuó el lugar simbólico del Estado como agente de modernidad" (*La Castañeda* 57) [health architecture not only incorporated notions of medical treatment and cure but also stressed the symbolic place of the State as an agent of modernity].

8. According to Roland Barthes in *Camera Lucida* photography should produce a reaction, a "*punctum*" understood as "that accident which picks me, bruises me, is poignant to me" (27). In contrast, the *studium* is that photograph that only causes a sort of "vague, slippery, irresponsible interest" of inconsequential nature (27).

9. As discussed in the introduction and in other chapters of this volume, Caminero-Santangelo's main claim is that insanity is the final surrender to dominant discourses of madness precisely because "it is characterized by the (dis)ability to produce meaning—that is, to produce representations recognizable as meaningful within society" (11).

Chapter Five

1. The terms madness and insanity are used in this chapter to distinguish between the concept and general symbolism (madness) and the mental illness and psychological condition (insanity).

2. Jean Baudrillard coined the term "hyperreal" to define systems constituted by models of the real without origin or reality. For this thinker, in this system meaning has lost is value, because "the real is no longer a question of imitation, nor reduplication, nor even a parody. It is rather a question of substituting signs of the real for the real itself" ("Simulacra and Simulations" n.p.).

3. "Quijote and the Real Thing: on Madness and Modernity" is the text of a lecture delivered by Laura Restrepo at the Latin American Studies Program Seminar Series at Cornell University on March 30, 2007. Excerpts from this lecture were published at http://www.pen.org/nonfic tion-essay/quixote-400-tribute. I am using the unpublished manuscript of the entire lecture as the source for this analysis.

4. In the same section, Foucault provides the definition of the word: "Delirium, from *Deliro*, to rave or talk idly; which is derived from *Lira*, a Ridge or Furrow of Land. *Deliro* is also to deviate from the Right, that is the right reason" (Robert James, *Medicinal Dictionary*, cited by Foucault, *History of Madness*, 237).

5. Gabriela Polit Dueñas contended that the epigraph of the novel does not propose "a protagonist responsible of her acts, but a victim of the other's acts" ("Sicarios, delirantes" 135). However, I believe this interpretation overlooks the goal of the literary project as a whole.

6. I acknowledge the controversial nature of Laing's theories as expressed in

the introduction. However, from the strictly theoretical perspective, Laing's *The Divided Self* provides the elements that allow the connection between individual and collective madness to sustain the argument developed in this chapter.

7. The lepers are a reference to the town of Agua de Dios, where a leper colony existed until mid-century in Colombia. This town is located 120 kilometers from Bogotá. During the years of Agustina's childhood (1960s), many people afflicted with leprosy returned to Bogotá. It was common to see street beggars displaying a sign: "I come from Agua de Dios. Help me." The novel also refers to scenes of lepers presented in the movie Ben-Hur, a popular film during the same time period. Agustina related both images as the symbol of her fear of the spread of this stigmatized contagious disease. Symbolically, leprosy represented the disease spreading throughout the nation collective self.

8. I refer here to the comparison made by Vania Barraza Toledo in the essay "La reestructuración y el desplazamiento social en el espacio urbano de Bogotá" (*El universo literario de Laura Restrepo* 288).

9. According to Patricia Waugh, "All literary fiction has to construct a 'context' at the same time it deconstructs a 'text' through entirely *verbal* processes. [...] Metafiction, in laying bare this fiction of literary conventions, draws attention to what I shall call the *creation/description/paradox* which defines the status of *all* fiction" (emphasis in the original, 88).

10. I am referring to Nietzsche's discussion of the Apollinian and Dionysian in *The Birth of Tragedy* and Freud's psychoanalytical theories based mostly on ancient myths and the number of sounded themes developed in the 20th century by existentialists, phenomenologists, and other movements, which draw from ancient myths to develop their theories.

11. In the original: "el retorno de Bichi como encarnación del andrógino, conlleva el advenimiento de esta utopía, el fin del delirio, la posibilidad de una nueva sociedad" (Escobar 200).

12. This tactic is less obvious in the English translation because of the morphological difficulty presented by conjugating verbs in different persons. For instance, in the Spanish version it reads: "Cuando *me fui* no le pasaba nada raro [...] salvo sus propias premoniciones, claro está, pero cómo *iba Aguilar a creerle* si Agustina, *su* mujer, siempre anda pronosticando calamidades" (*Delirio* 11). In the English version: "When *I* left, *I* swear nothing odd was going on [...] except for her premonitions, of course, but how *was I to* believe her when Agustina is always predicting some catastrophe" (*Delirium* 1). While the English version maintains the first person throughout the whole section, the Spanish shifts from the first to the third person in the same sentence.

13. For further analysis on the parallel between Agustina and Blimunda, see Sánchez-Blake, "La frontera invisible: Razón y sin razón en *Delirio*" (*El universo literario de Laura Restrepo*).

14. The bombing of the DAS (Departamento Administrativo de Seguridad) headquarters occurred on December 6, 1989. This event was one of the infamous Pablo Escobar's attacks against the State.

15. I refer to a statement by Laura Restrepo in which she compared the narrative technique with a mirror where the author is positioned in the back of the mirror to observe reality from the inverse side (interview with Daniela Melis).

16. Memory and truth have been fundamental tools in the process of reconciliation that Colombia is undergoing at the writing this book (2014). The Victims and Land Restitution Law1448 of 2011 and negotiations in Havana with revolutionary groups assign special emphasis to the right for truth, justice and reparation.

Chapter Six

1. In an interview with Ilan Stavans, Vilar discussed the circumstances surrounding the publication of her first memoir in translation only.

2. Throughout, I use "Irene" to refer to the character and "Vilar" to refer to the writer, in order to distinguish the two.

3. I borrow the phrase "mixed messages" from Vilar's own words quoted in a

news article: "She's unabashedly supportive of abortion rights, but says her addiction to the cycle of pregnancy and abortion meant that she wasn't really choosing to end her pregnancies. 'In a pathology, you don't have choice,' she says. 'I come from a culture that cultivates mixed messages,' she says, quiet for a moment on the couch in Alexandria. Then she softly starts to sing. 'Te amo muchisimo/Por tu bien te digo, 'Adiós.'— I love you very much. For your own good, I say goodbye. 'You see?' she says. 'Mixed messages, even in our songs'" (Roig-Franzia).

4. Vilar discusses the deliberate choice of the word "Testimony" in her title on her website: "I position myself in the Latin American tradition of testimonio and feminist methodology, attempting to enact new forms of agency and solidarity and alleviating the shame inflicted by trauma. [...] As speaker of testimony, I wish to stand as representative of women who have remained silent about the power struggles of their reproductive bodies, specifically of those whose bodies have acted out the emotional life and dramas of their families and countries. I wish to distance myself from the at times hyper individualistic mode of memoir writing, though I will inevitably remain forever such a writer."

5. In an online Q&A, Vilar described her appropriation of the madwoman figure as an intentional engagement of feminist discourse: "I was unable to channel my rebellion against the forced sterilization that took my mother away from me and alienating motherhood through political pamphlets or taking to the streets. And of course I did not know 'consciously' what I was doing. I was living in the moment. It is only in retrospect that I can link my addiction to abortion to my refusal to submit to my husband's belief that women should not have children. I recognize now that I projected on his views the ones pervasive in Puerto Rico— Women need to be contained in the home with multiple babies or should be made barren to control the growth of an undesirable population—My blinding desire for control was at the core of my neurosis. The feminist pamphlet 'the personal is the political' has been preceded for centuries by women who used their own bodies as a form of resistance against the system. They were called hysterics and were often locked up. There is a huge feminist literature showing how hysteria is the god mother of feminist theory—The academic in me knew this and I think my book belongs to that literature as well" (Vilar, "Nightmare").

Conclusions

1. A more detailed analysis of such representations can be found in Laura Kanost, *Political Asylums*, Diss., University of Kansas, 2007.

Bibliography

Akrabova, Maria G. "The Outsider as Catalyst: Marginality, Truth, and Violence in Three Novels by Laura Restrepo." *The Image of the Outsider in Literature, Media and Society.* Ed. Will Wright and Steven Kaplan. Proceedings of the Conference of the Society for the Interdisciplinary Study of Social Imagery, Colorado State University–Pueblo, 2008: 189–193. Web. 22 Sept. 2014.

Almeida, Sandra Regina Goulart. "The Madness of Lispector's Writing." *Brazilian Feminisms.* Ed. Solange Ribeiro de Oliveira and Judith Still. Nottingham: University of Nottingham Press, 1999: 101–15. Print.

Alvarado, Rubén, Alberto Minoletti, Elie Valencia, Graciela Rojas and Ezra Susser. "The Need For New Models of Care for People with Severe Mental Illness in Low- and Middle-Income Countries." *Improving Mental Health Care: The Global Challenge.* Ed. Graham Thornicroft, Mirella Rugger, and David Goldberg. Hoboken, NJ: Wiley, 2013. Web. 2 July 2014.

Antebi, Susan. *Carnal Inscriptions: Spanish American Narratives of Corporeal Difference and Disability.* New York: Palgrave Macmillan, 2009. Print.

Araújo, Helena. *La Scherezada criolla: Ensayos sobre escritura femenina latinoamericana.* Bogotá: Centro editorial Universidad Nacional de Colombia, 1989. Print.

ArboledaFlórez, Julio, and David N. Weisstub. "Conflicts and Crises in Latin America." Ed. Ahmed Okasha, Julio ArboledaFlórez, and Norman Sartorius. *Ethics, Culture and Psychiatry: International Perspectives.* Washington, D.C.: American Psychiatric Press, 2000: 2945. Print.

Aristotle. *Poetics.* Trans. and Intro. Malcom Heath. London: Penguin, 1996. Print.

Bakhtin, Mikhail. "The Discourse of the Novel." *The Dialogical Imagination. Four Essays.* Ed. Michael Holquist. Trans. Caryl Emerson and Holquist. Austin: University of Texas Press, 1981. Web. 1 Nov. 2014.

Baroja, Pío. *Memorias de un hombre de acción: La nave de los locos*, 3d ed. Ed. Francisco Flores Arroyuelo. Madrid: Cátedra, 1999. Print.

Barraza Toledo, Vania. "La reestructuración y el desplazamiento social en el espacio urbano de Bogotá en *Delirio* de Laura Restrepo. *El universo literario de Laura Restrepo: Antología crítica.* " Ed. Elvira E. Sánchez-Blake and Julie Lirot. Bogotá: Taurus, 2007: 273–291. Print.

Barthes, Roland. *Camera Lucida.* New York: Hill and Wang, 1981. Print.

Baudrillard, Jean. "Simulacra and Simulations." *Jean Baudrillard, Selected Writings.* Ed. Mark Poster. Stanford: Stanford University Press, 1988: 166–184. Web, 3 Aug. 2014.

Bibliography

Baugher, Joyce. "Feminist Vision: Visual Art, the Act of Writing, and the Female Body in the Novels of Clarice Lispector, Lya Luft, and Diamela Eltit." Diss. Tulane University, 2007. Print.

Brant, Sebastian. *The Ship of Fools*. Trans. Alexander Barclay. Edinburgh: William Paterson and New York: D. Appleton, 1874. Print.

Brown, Megan C. "Learning to Live Again: Contemporary U.S. Memoir as Biopolitical Self-Care Guide." *Biography* 36.2 (Spring 2013): 359–375, 483. Web. 7 July 2014.

Caminero-Santangelo, Marta. *The Madwoman Can't Speak: Or Why Insanity Is Not Subversive*. Ithaca: Cornell University Press, 1998. Print.

Cammell, Donald. Dir. *The Demon Seed*. MGM, 1977. Film.

Castillo, Debra. *Talking Back: Toward a Latin American Feminism Literary Criticism*. Ithaca: Cornell University Press, 1992. Print.

Castro-Klarén, Sara. "La crítica literaria feminista y la escritura en Latinoamérica." *La sartén por el mango: encuentro de escritoras latinamericanas*. Ed. Patricia E. González and Eliana Ortega. San Juan: Ediciones Huracán, 1985: 27–46. Print.

Cavani, Liliana. Dir. *Night Porter* [*Il portiere di notte*]. The Criterion Collection, 1973. Film.

Chesler, Phyllis. *Women and Madness*, 2d ed. Harmondsworth: Penguin, 1979. Print.

Corbin, Megan. "Neutralizing Consent: The Maternal Look and the Returned Gaze in *El infarto del alma*." *Lucero* 22 (2012): 55–75. Web. 30 June 2014.

Couser, G. Thomas. *Recovering Bodies: Illness, Disability and Life-writing*. Madison: University of Wisconsin Press, 1997. Print.

Crowther, Bosley. Review of *Ship of Fools*. *New York Times*. 29 July 1965. Web. 5 Aug. 2014.

Cruz García, Ana. *Re (de-) generando identidades: Locura, feminidad y liberalización en Elena Garro, Susana Pagano y María Amparo Escandón*. Bern: Peter Lang, 2009. Print.

Cruz Jimenez, Encarnación. "El Arte De Novelar De Cristina Rivera Garza." Diss. University of North Carolina at Chapel Hill, 2010. Web. 15 July 2014.

Cruz, Silvia. "Irene Vilar: 'He abortado 15 veces pero espero que mis hijas no tengan que hacerlo nunca.'" *La Vanguardia* 18 May 2012. Web. 10 July 2014.

Cummins Muñoz, Elizabeth. "Writing the Past: Women's Historical Fiction of Greater Mexico." Diss. University of Houston, Texas, 2007. Web. 10 Nov 2012.

Davis, Lennard. *Bending over Backwards: Disability Studies: Enabling the Humanities, Dismodernism and Other Difficult Positions*. New York: New York University Press, 2002. Print.

Dejbord, Parizad Tamara. *Cristina Peri Rossi: Escritora del exilio*. Buenos Aires: Galerna, 1998. Print.

de Lauretis, Teresa. *Technologies of Gender: Essays on Theory, Film, and Fiction*. Bloomington: Indiana University Press, 1987. Print.

Derrida, Jaques. "Cogito and History of Madness." *Writing and Difference*. London: Routledge, 1979. Print.

Domínguez, Carmen. "Las mujeres *en la nave de los locos* de Cristina Peri Rossi: Viajeras en perpetua huida." *Texto Crítico* 10 (2002): 159–167. Print.

Donoso, Claudia, and Paz Errázuriz. *La manzana de Adán*. Santiago de Chile: Zona, 1990. Print.

Durkheim, Emily. *The Elementary Forms of the Religious Life*. Trans. J. W. Swain. New York: The Free Press, 1965. Web. 15 Aug. 2014.

Eltit, Diamela. "Interrogando los signos: Conversando con Diamela Eltit." By Robert Neustadt. *Inti: Revista de literatura hispánica* 1.46 (1997). Web. 30 June 2014.

_____. *El padre mío*. Santiago de Chile: Francisco Zegers, 1989. Print.

Eltit, Diamela, and Paz Errázuriz. *El infarto del alma*. Santiago: Francisco Zegers, 1994. Print.

_____, and _____. *Soul's Infarct*. Trans. Ronald Christ. Santa Fe: Lumen, 2009. Print.

Bibliography

Errázuriz, Paz. "De amor y desamparo: Impactante ensayo fotográfico sobre los afectos en un hospicio chileno." By Daniel Molina. *Clarín.com Reseña N.* 23 March 2002. Web. 1 July 2014.
Escobar Vera, Hernando. "El retorno del andrógino: revuelta y utopía en *Delirio*." *Discusiones actuales sobre literatura iberoamericana*. Bogotá: Universidad Santo Tomás. Instituto Caro y Cuervo, 2011: 197–205. Print.
Etcheverría, Estefanía. "Amores de siquiátrico inspiran obra teatral y nueva exposición de Paz Errázuriz." *La Tercera*. 27 July 2012. Web. 1 July 2014.
Facio, Sara, Alicia D'Amico, and Julio Cortázar. *Humanario*. Buenos Aires: Azotea, 1976.
Feder, Lilian. *Madness in Literature*. Princeton: Princeton University Press, 1980. Print.
Felman, Shoshana. *Writing and Madness*. Trans. Martha Noel Evans and Felman. Ithaca: Cornell University Press, 1985. Palo Alto: Stanford University Press, 2003. Print.
Ferreira Pinto, Cristina. *Gender, Discourse, and Desire in Twentieth-Century Brazilian Women's Literature*. West Lafayette: Purdue University Press, 2004.
Fonder-Solano, Leah. "Intersections between Feminism, Film and Text: *La nave de los locos* by Cristina Peri Rossi." *Letras Femeninas* 29–2 (Winter 2003): 33–44. Web. 12 Aug. 2014.
Forcinito, Ana. "Voz, escritura e imagen: Arte y testimonio en *El infarto del alma*." *Hispanófila* 148 (2006): 59–71. Web. 30 June 2014.
Foucault, Michel. *History of Madness*. Ed. Jean Khalfa, trans. Jonathan Murphy and Jean Khal. London: Routledge, 2006. First published as *Folie et Déraison: Histoire de la folie à l'âge classique*. Paris: Librarie Plon, 1961.
_____. *Madness and Civilization: A History of Insanity in the Age of Reason*. Trans. Richard Howard. New York: Vintage, 1988. Print.
_____. "Of Other Spaces." Trans. Jay Miskowiec. *Diacritics* 16.1 (1986): 22–27.
Fuentes, Carlos. "El melodrama de la mujer caída." Review. *El País*, January 11, 2003. Web. 5 Nov. 2014.
Garcia, Carla Cristina. *Ovelhas na névoa: Um estudo sobre as mulheres e a loucura*. Rio de Janeiro: Rosa dos Tempos, 1995. Print.
Garland-Thomson, Rosemarie. "The Politics of Staring: Visual Rhetorics of Disability in Popular Photography." *Disability Studies: Enabling the Humanities*. Ed. Shannon Snyder, Brenda Jo Brueggemann, and Rosemarie Garland-Thomson. New York: The Modern Language Association of America, 2002: 56–75. Print.
Gaviria, Silvia L. and Marta B. Rondon. "Some Considerations on Women's Mental Health in Latin America and the Caribbean." *International Review of Psychiatry* 22.4 (August 2010): 363–69. Print.
Gilbert, Sandra M. *Rereading Women: Thirty Years of Exploring Our Literary Traditions*. New York: W.W. Norton, 2011. Print.
_____, and Susan Gubar. *The Madwoman in the Attic: The Woman Writer and the Nineteenth-Century Literary Imagination*. New Haven: Yale University Press, 1979. Print.
Gilman, Sander. *Disease and Representation: Images of Illness from Madness to AIDS*. Ithaca: Cornell University Press, 1988. Print.
_____. *Seeing the Insane*. Lincoln: University of Nebraska Press, 1996. Print.
Gilmore, Leigh. "American Neoconfessional: Memoir, Self-Help, and Redemption on Oprah's Couch." *Biography* 33.4 (Fall 2010): 657–79. Web. 10 July 2014.
Goffman, Erving. *Asylums: Essays on the Social Situation of Mental Patients and Other Inmates*. New York: Anchor, 1961. Print.
Gómez Valderrama, Pedro. *La nave de los locos*. Madrid: Alianza Editorial, 1984. Print.
Hart, Stephen M. *White Ink: Essays on Twentieth-Century Feminine Fiction in Spain and Latin America*. London: Tamesis, 1993. Print.
Hind, Emily. "Hablando histéricamente: La ciencia de la locura en *Feliz nuevo siglo doktor Freud* de Sabina Berman y *Nadie me verá llorar* de Cristina Rivera Garza." *Literatura Mexicana* 17.2 (2006). Web. 10 Nov. 2011.

Bibliography

Hutcheon, Linda. *A Poetics of Postmodernism: History, Theory, Fiction*. New York: Routledge, 1998. Print.
Ilarregui, Gladys, ed. *Femenino plural: La locura, la enfermedad, el cuerpo en las escritoras hispanoamericanas*. Alexandria: Los signos del tiempo, 2000. Print.
Invernizzi Santa Cruz, Lucía. "Entre el tapiz de la expulsión del paraíso y el tapiz de la creación: Múltiples sentidos del viaje a bordo de *La nave de los locos* de Cristina Peri Rossi." *Revista Chilena de Literatura* 30 (1987): 29–53. Web. 6 Nov. 2014.
Jameson, Frederic. *Postmodernism, or, The Cultural Logic of Late Capitalism*. Durham: Duke University Press, 1991. Print.
Kaminsky, Amy K. *After Exile: Writing the Latin American Diaspora*. Minneapolis: University of Minnesota Press, 1999. Print.
Kanost, Laura. "Pasillos Sin Luz: Reading the Asylum in *Nadie Me Verá Llorar* by Cristina Rivera Garza." *Hispanic Review* 76.3 (2008): 299–316. Web. 14 Feb. 2013.
_____. *Political Asylums*. Diss. University of Kansas, 2007. Print.
Kantaris, Geoffrey. "The Politics of Desire: Alienation and Identity in the Work of Marta Traba and Cristina Peri Rossi." *Forum for Modern Language Studies* [St. Andrew's] 25.3 (1989): 248–64. Web. 10 July 2014.
Kline, Carmenza. "Agustina y el delirio." *Cajón de Textos: Ensayos sobre literatura hispanoamericana*. Ed. Carmenza Kline. Bogotá, Fundación General de la Universidad de Salamanca sede Colombia, 2007: 111–123. Print.
Kramer, Stanley. Producer. *Ship of Fools*. Columbia Pictures, 1965. Film.
Lagos, María Inés, ed. *Creación y resistencia: La narrativa de Diamela Eltit, 1983–1998*. Santiago: Cuarto Propio, 2000. Print.
Laing, R.D. *The Divided Self*. Harmondsworth: Penguin, 1984. Print.
Lazzara, Michael J. "The Poetics of Impossibility: Diamela Eltit's *El padre mío*." *Chasqui* 35.1 (2006): 106–18. Web. 30 June 2014.
Levav, Itzhak, Helena Restrepo, and Carlyle Guerra de Macedo. "The Restructuring of Psychiatric Care in Latin America: A New Policy for Mental Health Services." *Journal of Public Health Policy* 15.1 (1994): 7185. Print.
Lorenzano, Sandra. "Cicatrices de la fuga." *Creación y resistencia: La narrativa de Diamela Eltit, 1983–1998*. Ed. María Inés Lagos. Santiago: Cuarto Propio, 2000: 93–110. Print.
Loss, Jacqueline E. "Portraitures of Institutionalization." *CR: The New Centennial Review* 4.2 (2004): 77–101. Web. 1 July 2014.
Luft, Lya. *Exílio*. São Paulo: Siciliano, 1991. Print.
_____. *Mulher no palco*. Rio de Janeiro: Salamandra, 1984.
_____. *The Red House*. Trans. Giovanni Pontiero. Manchester: Carcanet, 1994. Print.
Machado de Assis, Joaquim Maria. *O alienista*. São Paulo: Companhia das Letras, 2014. Print.
Marsiglia, Regina, et al. *Saúde mental e cidadania*. São Paulo: Mandacaru, 1987. Print.
Mathews, Cristina. "A Nest from the Bones of the Dead: Challenging the Mourning and Melancholia Dichotomy in Irene Vilar's *The Ladies' Gallery*." *Bilingual Review / La Revista Bilingüe* 28.3 (2004–2007): 245–264. Web. 2 July 2014.
Medeiros Costa, Maria Osana de. *A mulher, o lúdico e o grotesco em Lya Luft*. Sao Paulo: Annablume, 1996. Print.
Medina, Eduardo. "Nota histórica: De Manicomio Nacional a Hospital Psiquiátrico." *Revista chilena de neuro-psiquiatría* 39.1 (2001): 78–81. Web. 1 July 2014.
Medina-Sancho, Gloria. "*El infarto del alma*: Un tributo a la memoria afectiva." *Revista Iberoamericana* 71.210 (2005): 223–39. Print.
Melis, Daniela. "Una entrevista con Laura Restrepo." *Chasqui* 34.1 (2005): 114–129. Web. 15 April 2013.
Navia Velasco, Carmiña. *Escritoras latinoamericanas: Razón y locura*. Cali: Universidad del Valle, Colección La tejedora. 2012. Print.

Bibliography

Norat, Gisela. *Marginalities: Diamela Eltit and the Subversion of Mainstream Literature in Chile*. Newark: University of Delaware Press, 2002.
"Nuevas obras de Psiquiátrico continúan rescatando estilo arquitectónico original." *Diario El Observador*. 16 June 2014. Web. 30 June 2014.
Olivera-Williams, María Rosa. "La nave de los locos de Cristina Peri-Rossi." *Revista de Crítica Literaria Latinoamericana* 11.23 (1986): 81–89. Web. 12 Aug. 2014.
Paulino Bueno, Eva. "Maternidade, Mito e Ideologia na Ficção de Lya Luft." *Revista Iberoamericana* 66.192 (2000): 601–616. Web. 8 June 2014.
Pérez-Sánchez, Gema. *Queer Transitions in Contemporary Spanish Culture: From Franco to la Movida*. (SUNY Series in Latin American and Iberian Thought and Culture). Alband: State University of New York Press, 2007. Print.
Peri Rossi, Cristina. *La nave de los locos*. Barcelona: Biblioteca de bolsillo, 1984. Print.
_____. *The Ship of Fools*. Trans. Psiche Hugues. London: Allison and Busby, 1989. Print.
_____. *State of Exile*. Trans. Marilyn Buck. San Francisco: City Lights Books, 2008. Print.
Polit Dueñas, Gabriela. "Sicarios, delirantes y los efectos del narcotráfico en la literatura colombiana." *Hispanic Review* 74.2 (Spring 2006): 119–142. Web. 13 Aug. 2014.
Porter, Katherine Anne. *Ship of Fools*. New York: Back Bay Books, 1984. Print.
Quayson, Ato. *Aesthetic Nervousness: Disability and the Crisis of Representation*. New York: Columbia University Press, 2007. Print.
Restrepo, Laura. *Delirio*. Bogotá: Alfaguara, 2004. Print.
_____. *Delirium*. Trans. Natasha Wimmer. New York: Nan A. Talese, 2007. Print.
_____. "Don Quijote and the Real Thing: On Madness and Modernity." Lecture. Latin American Studies Program, Seminar Series, Cornell University. 30 March 2007.
Richard, Nelly. "Cultural Peripheries: Latin America and Postmodernist De-Centering." *Boundary 2. An International Journal of Literature and Culture* 20.3 (1993): 156–161. Web. 10 July 2012.
_____. *Masculine/Feminine: Practices of Difference(s)*. Durham: Duke University Press, 1979. Print.
_____. *Residuos y metáforas* (Ensayos de crítica cultural sobre el Chile de la Transición). Santiago: Cuarto Propio, 1998. Print.
Rivera Garza, Cristina. *La Castañeda: Narrativas dolientes desde el manicomio general. México, 1910–1930*. México: Tusquets, 2010. Print.
_____. *Nadie me verá llorar*. México: Tusquets, 1999. Print.
_____. *No One Will See Me Cry*. Trans. Andrew Hurley. New York: Curbstone Press, 2003. Print.
_____. "She Neither Respected nor Obeyed Anyone: Inmates and Psychiatrists Debate Gender and Class at the General Insane Asylum La Castañeda, Mexico, 1910- 1930." *Hispanic American Historical Review* 81:3–4 (Aug.–Nov. 2001): 653–688. Web. 13 July 2014.
_____. *The Masters of the Streets: Bodies, Power and Modernity in Mexico, 1867–1930*. Diss. Department of History: Houston University, 1995. Web. 10 June 2014.
Rogers, Charlotte. *Jungle Fever: Exploring Madness and Medicine in Twentieth-Century Tropical Narratives*. Nashville: Vanderbilt University Press, 2012. Print.
Roig-Franzia, Manuel. "Irene Vilar, a Mother At Last After 15 Abortions." *Washington Post* 30 Oct. 2009. Web. 10 July 2014.
Rotella, Pilar V. "A Recurrent Image: The Ship of Fools in Catherine Ann Porter and Cristina Peri Rossi." *Antípodas* VI-VII (1994): 143–154. Web. 5 Aug. 2014.
Ruffinelli, Jorge. "Ni a tontas ni a locas: notas sobre Cristina Rivera Garza y su nuevo modo de narrar." *Nuevo texto Crítico* 21.41–42 (2008): 33–41. Web. 27 July 2014.
Salamán Rocha, Dora Georgina. "La locura como identidad narrativa: *El obsceno pájaro de la noche* y *El otoño del patriarca*." M.A. Thesis. Universidad Iberoamericana, 2005. Web. 6 Oct. 2014.
Saldivia, Sandra, Benjamin Vicente, Robert Kohn, Pedro Rioseco, and Silverio Torres.

Bibliography

"Use of Mental Health Services in Chile." *Psychiatric Services* 55.1 (2004): 71- 76. Web. 1 July 2014.

Samuelson, Cheyla. "Writing at Escape Velocity: An Interview with Cristina Rivera Garza." *Confluencia* 23.1 (2007). Web. 10 June 2013.

Sánchez-Blake, Elvira E., and Julie Lirot, eds. *El universo literario de Laura Restrepo: Antología crítica*. Bogotá: Taurus, 2007. Print.

Sánchez Fernández, Leyshack. "La Narrativa de Cristina Peri Rossi." Diss. Universidade Da Coruña Facultad De Filoloxía, 2007. Web. 15 Aug, 2014.

Santo Domingo, Roger. "Interview with Laura Restrepo." BBC mundo.com. 4 Aug. 2004. Web. 14 Aug. 2014.

Scarry, Elaine. *The Body in Pain: The Making and Unmaking of the World*. Oxford: Oxford University Press, 1985. Print.

Shannonhouse, Rebecca, ed. *Out of her Mind: Women Writing on Madness*. New York: Modern Library, 2003. Print.

Showalter, Elaine. *The Female Malady: Women, Madness and English Culture, 1830-1980*. London: Virago Press, 1987. Print.

Snyder, Sharon, Brenda Jo Brueggemann, and Rosemarie Garland Thomson, eds. *Disability Studies: Enabling the Humanities*. New York: The Modern Language Association of America, 2002. Print.

Sommer, Doris. "Attitude, Its Rhetoric." *The Turn to Ethics*. Eds. Marjorie Garber, Beatrice Hansen, and Rebecca L. Walkowitz. New York: Routledge, 2000. 201–220. Print.

_____. *Proceed with Caution: When Engaged By Minority Writing in the Americas*. Cambridge: Harvard University Press, 1999. Print.

Sontag, Susan. *Illness as Metaphor and AIDS and its Metaphors*. New York: Doubleday Anchor Books, 1978. New York: Farrar, Straus and Giroux, 1990. Print.

Thompson, Mary. "Misconceived Metaphors: Irene Vilar's *Impossible Motherhood: Testimony of an Abortion Addict*." *Frontiers: A Journal of Women Studies* 35.1 (2014): 132–59. Web. 10 July 2014.

Tierney-Tello, Mary Beth. *Allegories of Transgression and Transformation: Experimental Fiction by Women Writing under Dictatorship*. Albany: State University of New York Press,1996. Web. 14 Aug. 2014.

_____. "Testimony, Ethics, and the Aesthetic in Diamela Eltit." *PMLA* 114.1 (1999): 78–96. Web. 1 July 2014.

Todorov, Tzvetan. *The Fantastic: A Structural Approach to a Literary Genre*. Trans. Richard Howard. Ithaca: Cornell University Press, 1975. Print.

Trigo, Benigno. "Memoirs for the Abject: Irene Vilar's *Memoria*." *Remembering Maternal Bodies: Melancholy in Latina and Latin American Women's Writing*. New York: Palgrave Macmillan, 2006: 111–132. Print.

Turner, Victor Whitter. "Social Dramas and Stories About Them." *Critical Inquiry* 7.1 (1980): 141–68. Web. 8 Dec. 2007.

Vaughn, Jeanne Marie. "The Latin American Subject of Feminism: Unraveling the Threads of Sexuality, Nationalisms and Femaleness." Diss. University of California, Santa Cruz, 1999. Web. 15 July 2014.

Vera-Franco, Bridget. "The Politics of Madness in Southern Cone Literature of the Dictatorship and Post-Dictatorship." Diss. University of California, Irvine, 2009. Web. 10 Aug. 2014.

Vilar, Irene. *Impossible Motherhood: Testimony of an Abortion Addict*. New York: Other Press, 2009. Print.

_____. "Impossible Motherhood." Blog post. *Irenevilar.com* 27 May 2009. Web. 28 Oct. 2014.

_____. *The Ladies' Gallery: A Memoir of Family Secrets*. Trans. Gregory Rabassa. New York: Vintage, 1998. Print.

_____. *A Message from God in the Atomic Age: A Memoir*. Trans. Gregory Rabassa. New York: Pantheon, 1996. Print.

―――. "Nightmare Addiction: Abortion." Online Q & A. *Washington Post* 30 Oct. 2009. Web. 10 July 2014.

―――. "Transcript of Conversation with Irene Vilar." *Conversations with Ilan Stavans.* WGBH. Web. 2 July 2014.

Visconti, Luchino. Dir. *The Damned [La caduta degli dei]*. Warner Bros., 1969. Film.

von Stenberg, Joseph. Dir. *The Blue Angel. [Der Blaue Engel]*. Universum Film A.G., 1930. Film.

Waugh, Patricia. *Metafiction: The Theory and Practice of Self-Conscious Fiction*. London: Routledge, 1984. Print.

Willett, Jeffrey, and Mary Jo Deegan. "Liminality and Disability: Rites of Passage and Community in Hypermodern Society." *Disability Studies Quarterly* 21.3 (2001): 137 152. Web. 26 Feb. 2013.

Williams, Gareth. *The Other Side of the Popular: Neoliberalism and Subalternity in Latin America.* Durham: Duke University Press, 2002. Print.

Zeisler, Andi. "Women and Madness: Revised and Updated, by Phyllis Chesler." Review. Powell's Books. 6 Aug. 2006. Web. 6 Oct. 2014.

Zugasti, Miguel. "Saludar al fracaso y platicar con él: *Nadie me verá llorar*, de Cristina Rivera Garza." *Cien años de lealtad. En honor a Luis Leal*. Vol. I. Ed. Sara Poot Herrera, Francisco A. Lomelí y María Herrera- Sobek. México: UCSB, UNAM, Instituto Tecnológico y de Estudios Superiores de Monterrey, Universidad del Claustro de Sor Juana, UC-Mexicanistas, 2007: 693–707. Web. 31 July 2014.

Index

abortion 40, 44, 45, 134–43, 162
abuse 11, 32, 37, 44, 65, 139, 141
addiction 88, 129, 135, 137, 138, 141, 142, 162
agency 15, 21, 22, 48, 49, 57, 58, 72, 73, 75, 97, 105, 116, 129–34
Akrabova, Maria 107, 112, 114
alcoholism 57, 62, 63, 137, 157
Alegría, Claribel 22, 134
The Alienist 68
O Alienista 68
allegory 3, 5, 9, 19, 26, 29–31, 33, 35–36, 40, 42, 50, 51, 85, 133, 141, 147–49, 154
Almeida, Sandra Regina Goulart 55
Alvarado, Rubén 70
Ángel, Albalucía 22
Antebi, Susan 1, 18
El anticuario 19
antipsychiatry 13–14, 106
anxiety 17, 19, 58, 140, 157
Anzaldúa, Gloria 22
Aponte Alsina, Marta 22
Araújo, Helena 20–22
Arboleda Flórez, Julio 18
Argentina 20–21, 102, 152
Aristotle 4
art 4, 7, 10, 34–35, 43
asylum 2, 7, 14, 26, 52–53, 57, 66–69, 71–72, 74–75, 77–80, 82, 85–88, 90–94, 101, 113, 129–30, 133, 150–51, 160
autopathography 124
The Autumn of the Patriarch 19

Bakhtin, Mikhail 84–85, 160
Balet, Jan 40
Baroja, Pío 39, 158
Barraza Toledo, Vania 161
Barthes, Roland 85, 97, 127, 160
Baudrillard, Jean 160
Baugher, Joyce 54
Belli, Gioconda 22
Berman, Sabina 22
The Blue Angel 46–47
body 4–5, 12, 16–17, 21–22, 47–48, 58–61, 74, 78–79, 94, 97, 104, 108, 112–13, 124–26, 130–31, 136, 138, 140, 146, 151
The Body in Pain 16, 58, 97
Bombal, María Luisa 59
Boom 19
Bosch, Hieronymus 4, 35–36, 40
Boullosa, Carmen 20, 22
Brant, Sebastian 6, 25, 35–37, 40
Brazil 2, 3, 5, 19, 24, 25, 52–68, 146, 151
Brontë, Charlotte 119
Brown, Megan C. 141
Brueghel 4, 35, 40
Burgos, Modesta 85, 93, 101
Butler, Judith 48

Cambio de armas 19
Caminero-Santangelo, Marta 14–15, 77, 80, 97, 106, 126, 154
Carpentier, Alejo 19, 23
Cassandra 107, 116, 120–21, 149
La Castañeda 82, 84, 85, 90–92, 95–97, 159–60
Castellanos, Rosario 20
Castellanos Moya, Horacio 19
Castillo, Debra 20–21, 152

Index

Castro-Klarén, Sara 21
Catholicism 21, 37
Cervantes, Miguel de 4, 6, 104, 127
Chesler, Phyllis 11–13, 157
chess 33–34, 45
Chile 3, 5, 19, 20, 23, 24, 25, 59, 69–81, 119, 146, 150
Cien años de soledad 19
clairvoyance 106, 119, 121, 148
class 5, 11, 12, 20, 21, 37, 70, 79, 82–84, 87–89, 95, 100, 105, 109–110, 129, 142, 152, 157
Colombia 2, 3, 5, 24, 26, 39, 40, 102–21, 146, 149, 158, 161
Com meus olhos de cão 19
coping 111, 112, 121, 129, 130, 137, 140, 146, 149, 151
Corbin, Megan 74
Coronación 19
Cortázar, Julio 19, 72, 127, 158
Couser, G. Thomas 124
creativity 11, 12, 15, 123, 125, 128, 136
criminal 26
critical disability studies 71, 146
crónica 76
Cruz, Silvia 142
Cruz García, Ana 22
Cruz Jiménez, Encarnación 99
Cummins Muñoz, Elizabeth 89, 94

D'Amicio, Alicia 72
The Damned 46–47, 159
Davis, Lennard 79
death 6, 48, 54, 60, 62, 67, 72, 96–97, 108, 110, 122–23, 125, 131, 138
Death and the Maiden 119
deconstruction 29, 30, 37, 43, 48, 50, 80, 89, 149, 154, 161
deinstitutionalization 61, 70
Dejbord, Parizad Tamara 41, 49, 159
de Lauretis, Teresa 83–84
Delirio 2, 26, 64, 89, 102–121, 144, 146, 148, 149, 153, 161
delirium 5, 20, 91, 104, 107, 108, 111, 113, 116, 117, 118, 120, 126, 153, 160
dementia 105, 110, 118, 121
demilitarization 103
Demon Seed 32, 46, 49
depression 5, 17, 25, 55–62, 66–68, 122, 123, 127, 130, 136, 140, 142, 145, 147, 151, 157
Derrida, Jacques 157
La diabla en el espejo 19

Díaz, Porfirio 26, 89, 99
dictatorship 5, 18, 19, 20, 21, 25, 26, 30, 36, 48, 50, 54, 71, 80, 89, 119, 149, 150, 152, 159
Dietrich, Marlene 45–48
disability 1, 16–18, 53, 55–57, 60, 68, 71, 72, 79, 124, 130, 133, 146, 147, 159
discontinuity 29, 30, 152
discourse 4–9, 12, 14, 15, 19, 23–25, 27, 29, 30, 31, 34, 43, 44, 50, 69, 71, 73, 75, 78, 80, 83–85, 89, 93, 94, 98, 110, 124, 126, 132, 139, 141, 142, 144, 145, 148–52, 154, 160, 162, 163, 165
disorder 4, 13, 17, 29, 44, 47, 70, 92, 138, 157
distancing 25, 53, 58, 63, 67
domestic 2, 19, 21, 93, 136, 147
Domínguez, Carmen 177, 164
Don Quixote (Quijote) 103, 104, 114, 120, 160, 167
Donoso, Claudia 71, 164
Donoso, José 19
Dorfman, Ariel 119
dream 29, 32–37, 42, 44–46, 49, 60, 73, 74, 78, 137
drug trafficking 19, 105, 108, 111
Durkheim, Emily 114, 164

Eltit, Diamela 2, 3, 5, 19, 20, 22, 25, 69–81, 89, 97, 123, 144, 146, 150, 151, 153, 159, 164, 166–68
Ensaio sobre a cegueira 119
Erasmus of Rotterdam 4, 6, 36
Errázuriz, Paz 5, 25, 69–81, 89, 97, 144, 146, 150, 159, 164, 165
Escobar, Pablo 108, 109, 161
Escobar Vera, Hernando 117, 165
Etcheverría, Estefanía 165
ethics 17, 56, 80, 103, 145, 163, 165, 168, 154
ethnography 85
exile 20, 29, 31, 38, 40–43, 50, 51, 55–57, 64, 68, 99, 103, 136, 147, 166, 167
Exílio 25, 41, 52–68, 144, 146, 147, 151, 152, 158, 164, 166

fable 61, 128
Facio, Sara 72
fairy tale 52, 53, 61, 66
fantastic 25, 31, 53, 57, 58, 62–67, 103
Faverón, Gustavo 19
The Feast of the Goat 19
Feder, Lillian 115–16

Felman, Shoshana 8, 9, 13, 15, 30, 31, 50, 126, 158
The Female Malady 12–14, 72
feminism 2, 3, 11, 14, 15, 21, 24, 27, 30, 31, 49, 50, 97, 141, 142, 144, 146, 152, 154, 157, 162
Ferreira Pinto, Cristina 54
La fiesta del Chivo 19
film 32–34, 36–39, 46, 47, 49, 83, 158, 159, 161
El fin de la locura 19
focalization 85
folly 6, 37, 38, 158
Fonder-Solano, Leah 165
Forcinito, Ana 69, 72, 75, 77, 165
Foucault, Michel 4, 6–8, 10, 15, 26, 35, 40, 60, 72, 78, 79, 85, 89, 90, 94, 104, 120, 126, 130, 145, 149, 154, 157, 160, 165
fragmentation 20, 26, 30, 50, 69, 144, 148, 152, 153
Freud, Sigmund 7, 13, 49, 106, 161, 165
Fuentes, Carlos 83, 159, 165

Gallegos, Rómulo 23
Gambaro, Griselda 22
Gamboa, Federico 86
game 30, 32–35, 45, 50, 115, 132, 152
Garcia, Carla Cristina 55, 57
García Márquez, Gabriel 19, 109, 127
Garland-Thompson, Rosemarie 72
Gaviria, Silvia L. 157
gaze 7, 46, 47, 49, 50, 72–75, 80, 88, 132, 148, 151
gender roles 5, 11–13, 20, 21, 25–27, 29, 46–50, 55–57, 82–84, 86, 87, 89, 95, 100, 125, 140, 145–47, 149, 151, 152, 154
genre 20, 24, 27, 39, 41, 53, 62, 67, 75–77, 85, 103, 133, 140, 141, 143, 146, 153, 154
Gilbert, Sandra M. 12–14, 20, 126, 148, 157
Gilman, Sander 9–11, 72
Gilmore, Leigh 140
Goffman, Erving 129
Gómez Valderrama, Pedro 39, 40, 158
Gubar, Susan 12–14, 20, 126, 148, 157

Hart, Stephen M. 37, 39
heteroglossia 83–85, 89, 95, 100, 152
heterotopia 60–61
Hilst, Hilda 19
Hind, Emily 88, 101

history 4, 8, 10, 12, 15, 18, 21, 26, 36, 73, 79, 82–85, 88–91, 94, 95, 98–100, 111, 135, 136, 138, 145, 146, 148, 149, 160
History of Madness 4, 6, 7, 35, 36, 72, 78, 90, 94, 95, 104, 145, 157, 160
Hopscotch 19
hospital 1, 5, 25, 69–81, 82–101, 124–33, 146–48, 150–51, 159, 160
Humanario 72
Hutcheon, Linda 89, 145
hyperreality 26, 103, 110, 120, 148, 160
hysteria 13, 133, 162

I, the Supreme 19
Ilarregui, Gladys 22
Illness as Metaphor 16, 78
illness narrative 91
Impossible Motherhood: Testimony of an Abortion Addict 26, 27, 122–25, 133–43, 144, 146, 153
El infarto del alma 25, 69–81, 89, 95, 97, 132, 144, 146–48, 150, 159
Informe sobre ciegos 19
Insensatez 19
intertextuality 32–35, 45, 46, 50, 85, 103, 117, 119, 122, 124, 125, 135, 143, 148, 153, 154
Invernizzi Santa Cruz, Lucía 40
irony 24, 30, 49, 68, 104, 108, 110, 122, 152

Jameson, Frederic 158
Jane Eyre 119
journey 25, 29–51, 82, 117, 132, 149, 155
juxtaposition 4, 21, 25, 71, 75, 78, 80, 89, 130, 141

Kabbalah 114, 117, 118
Kafka, Franz 122, 123, 126
Kaminsky, Amy K. 56
Kantaris, Geoffrey 50
Kleinman, Arthur 91
Kline, Carmenza 108
Kristeva, Julia 22, 127

The Ladies' Gallery 2, 26, 122–37, 143, 144, 146, 150, 151, 153
Laing, R.D. 13, 14, 106, 110–13, 160, 161
language games 30, 152
Lazzara, Michael J. 71
Lebrón, Lolita 27, 123, 124, 129, 133, 147, 151
leprosy 161

Index

lesbian 60, 64, 87
Levav, Itzhak 18
life-writing 122–43
liminality 19, 25, 38, 53–68, 147, 150, 151, 159
Lispector, Clarice 22, 55
la loca criolla del ático 21
Loss, Jacqueline E. 69, 73, 77
Luft, Lya 2, 3, 22, 25, 52–68, 144
Lumpérica 19, 71

Machado de Assis, Joaquim Maria 68
machismo 140
Madres de la Plaza de Mayo 21, 152
The Madwoman Can't Speak, Or Why Insanity Is Not Subversive 14–15, 77, 80, 97, 106, 126, 154
The Madwoman in the Attic 12–14, 20, 126, 148, 157
La manzana de Adán 71
Marsiglia, Regina 57, 61
master narrative 19, 23, 30
Mathews, Cristina 125
Medeiros Costa, Maria Osana de 54
Medina, Eduardo 70
Medina-Sancho, Gloria 72, 77
melancholy 125, 133
Melis, Daniela 161
memoir 26, 53, 59, 122–44, 146, 151–53, 161, 162
Memorial do convento 119
memory 21, 52, 65, 71, 80, 96, 100, 121, 137, 161
Méndez Lebrón, Gladys Mirna 27, 124, 130
mental health care 18, 57, 70, 150, 154
A Message from God in the Atomic Age 122
mestizo/a, mestizaje 22, 27
metafiction 24, 114, 119, 153, 161
metaphor 9, 14, 16–18, 22, 26, 30–32, 37, 43, 44, 49, 50, 56, 59, 71, 72, 78–80, 85, 91, 97, 103, 112–14, 126, 133, 141, 146, 148
metonymy 30, 59–61, 71, 150–51
Mexican Revolution 26, 84, 86, 89, 90, 99
Mexico 1, 2, 5, 20, 24, 37, 82–101, 103, 136, 146, 150, 159
military regime 5, 20, 21, 25, 29, 31, 49, 69–71, 80, 151
mirror 4, 7, 19, 36, 39, 43, 44, 50, 53, 58, 66, 68, 111, 120, 140, 148, 149, 161

modernity 82, 87, 88, 97, 103, 104, 160
modernization 86, 90, 98
monster 12
moral insanity 91–93
mother 21, 22, 25–27, 52–57, 62–66, 76–79, 93, 105, 109–13, 122–25, 129, 132–44, 147, 151, 152, 162
multi-temporal heterogeneity 23
mutilation 25, 59, 135, 138
mythology 3, 9, 10, 11, 23, 30, 34, 45, 103, 107, 108, 114–17, 120, 148, 149, 158, 159, 161

Nadie me verá llorar 2, 26, 64, 72, 82–101, 113, 132, 144, 146, 148–150, 152, 153
narco-literature 19, 103
narcotráfico 167
Das Narrenschiff 36
national identity 133
nature 12, 94
La nave de los locos (novel by Peri Rossi) 2, 9, 25, 29–51, 86, 89, 144, 145, 147–49, 152, 153, 158
Navia Velasco, Carmiña 23, 86, 113
neocolonial 5, 27, 133, 140, 146, 151
neoconfessional 27, 140, 141, 143
neoliberalism 80, 141, 150
The Night Porter 46
No One Will See Me Cry 2, 26, 64, 72, 82–101, 113, 132, 144, 146, 148–150, 152, 153
nonlinear narrative 26, 82, 88, 96, 152
Norat, Gisela 80

El obsceno pájaro de la noche 19, 158
Olivera-Williams, María Rosa 44, 158
One Hundred Years of Solitude 19
order 7, 26, 29, 43, 44, 47–49, 74, 78, 79, 88, 90, 98, 99, 113
Other Weapons 19
El otoño del patriarca 19, 158
El otro 81
El padre mío 19, 71

pain 4, 16, 17, 25, 54, 58–60, 62, 92, 96, 97, 100, 137, 141, 147, 148, 151
palimpsest 49, 118, 119, 153
parable 25, 29, 45
parody 24–26, 30, 47, 50, 86, 148, 152, 160
particularist writing 25, 27, 53, 58, 67, 134, 138, 142

Index

Los pasos perdidos 19, 23
pastiche 24–26, 30, 148, 152
patriarchy 12–14, 19, 37, 43, 48, 49, 54, 126, 144, 145, 151
Paulino Bueno, Eva 54
Pedro Páramo 19
pen 12
Pérez-Sánchez, Gema 48, 165
performance 32, 45, 47–50, 86, 87, 134, 138, 141, 146, 147
performativity 22, 46, 47, 49
Peri Rossi, Cristina 2, 3, 5, 9, 20, 22, 25, 29–51, 67, 86, 89, 123, 144, 145, 148, 149, 152, 153, 158, 159
phallocentric 33, 39, 49
photography 10, 25, 26, 69, 71–76, 78, 80, 83, 84, 87, 88, 95–98, 100, 107, 115, 146, 148, 150, 151, 159, 160
physician 7, 8, 86, 88, 92, 94
Pinochet, Augusto 20, 69–71
Plato 10, 116
Plaza de Mayo 21, 152
poetics 2, 4, 15–17, 27, 71, 89, 102, 103, 121, 144, 145, 147
poetry 25, 31, 36, 37, 40, 41, 54, 83, 115, 121, 136, 146, 158
Polit Dueñas, Gabriela 160
Poniatowska, Elena 20, 22
Por la patria 19, 71
Porfiriato 86, 89, 90
Porter, Katherine Anne 38, 40, 46, 158
postboom 19, 31, 144
postmodernism 1–4, 20, 23–25, 29–31, 34, 50, 89, 144–46, 152–54
poverty 78, 80, 85, 90, 91, 95, 108, 109, 135, 139, 140, 145, 157
power 3–10, 13–17, 19, 22–24, 26, 27, 29–31, 33, 36, 39, 40, 43, 45–50, 58, 59, 64, 67, 68, 72, 75, 76, 78, 80, 82, 92–94, 97, 100, 102, 104, 105, 107, 108, 111–16, 118, 121, 125, 126, 128, 131–33, 136, 138, 140, 142, 143, 146, 148, 149, 151–54, 157
pregnancy 40, 44, 60, 124, 132, 134–38, 157, 162
Prichard, James 92
prostitution 44, 85–87, 96
psychiatric hospital 1, 5, 18, 25, 57, 61, 69–101, 124, 126, 128–30, 133, 146, 148, 150, 151, 159
psychiatry 7, 11, 13, 14, 17, 18, 55, 68, 70, 72, 82, 84, 89, 92, 93, 106, 132, 157

psychoanalysis 7–10, 13, 14, 31, 34, 48, 54, 103, 106, 161
psychosis 11, 69, 106, 111, 112, 115, 128
Puerto Rico 2, 3, 5, 20, 24, 26, 27, 122, 123, 133, 137, 139, 140, 142, 146, 151, 162
punctum 97, 148, 160
puzzle 4, 88, 105, 111, 113, 114, 117–19, 144, 154

Quayson, Ato 70
"Quijote and the Real Thing" 103, 120, 160

rape 11, 14, 32, 46, 49, 157, 158
Rayuela 19
reader 4, 6, 7, 25, 26, 30–36, 38, 43–48, 50, 53, 57, 58, 62–68, 71, 73, 74, 80, 82, 84, 85, 88, 92, 95–97, 101, 105, 113, 117, 118, 120, 122–24, 126, 128, 134, 135, 138, 140–44, 148–50, 153, 154
The Red House 25, 41, 52–68, 144, 146, 147, 151, 152, 158, 164, 166
redemption 114, 117, 121, 135, 138, 140, 142, 150
El reino de este mundo 19
religion 10, 21, 22, 30, 34, 36, 37, 43, 48, 50, 91, 107, 115, 149
Restrepo, Laura 2, 3, 5, 22, 26, 89, 102–05, 108, 113, 120, 121, 123, 144, 146, 148, 149, 153, 160, 161, 163, 166, 168
Richard, Nelly 23, 24, 72–74, 77, 100, 152, 165, 167
riddle 4, 30, 32, 33, 35, 44–48, 105, 113, 114, 117, 118, 159
ritual 10, 38, 103, 107, 112–18, 148
Rivera, José Eustasio 23
Rivera Garza, Cristina 2, 3, 5, 22, 25, 26, 72, 82–101, 113, 144, 146, 148–53, 159, 160
Roa Bastos, Augusto 19
Rogers, Charlotte 4, 23
Roig-Franzia, Manuel 142, 162
Rotella, Pilar V. 38
Ruffinelli, Jorge 98
Rulfo, Juan 19

Sábato, Ernesto 19
Salamán Rocha, Dora Georgina 158
Saldivia, Sandra 70
Samuelson, Cheyla 84
Santa 86
Santo Domingo, Roger 102

Index

Saramago, José 119
satire 6, 36, 68
Scarry, Elaine 16, 17, 58, 59, 62, 97
schizophrenia 9, 30, 71, 153, 158
scopophilia 49, 158
self-care 123, 141
self-mutilation 135, 138
self-referentiality 24, 119, 125, 153, 154
sexuality 11, 13, 20, 21, 47, 49, 63, 80, 86, 87, 91–93, 101, 110, 111, 140
Shakespeare, William 4, 6, 104
La Sherezada criolla 20
The Ship of Fools (film) 37
ship of fools (motif) 3, 5, 6, 29, 32, 33, 35–37, 40, 42, 49, 50, 67, 145, 150, 155, 158
The Ship of Fools (novel by Cristina Peri Rossi) 2, 9, 25, 29–51, 86, 89, 144, 145, 147–49, 152, 153, 158
The Ship of Fools (novel by Katherine Anne Porter) 37
The Ship of Fools (poem by Sebastian Brant) 25, 37
Showalter, Elaine 12–14, 72
sight 7, 26, 34, 100, 106–109, 111, 112, 116, 147–49
"The Siren" 122
Sommer, Doris 25, 27, 53, 58, 67, 134
Sontag, Susan 16, 72, 78, 79, 127, 141
Soul's Infarct 25, 69–81, 89, 95, 97, 132, 144, 146–48, 150, 159
Souza Leão, Rodrigo de 20
space-off 83, 96, 97, 99, 148
spatial imagery 25, 53, 55, 59, 131
State of Exile 29, 40, 41, 51
sterilization 74, 80, 147
stigma 13, 16–18, 70, 79, 80, 145, 150, 152, 154
Storni, Alfonsina 127, 136
stream of consciousness 105, 117, 153
subjectivity 15, 53, 58, 63, 70, 75, 77, 80, 124, 126, 131, 133
suicide 46, 53, 56, 57, 62, 63, 123, 125, 127, 128, 135–37, 140
synecdoche 16

Tapestry of Creation 29, 30, 32, 33, 37, 43, 44, 49, 50, 148, 158, 159
tautology 101
testimonio 27, 75, 77, 78, 122, 134, 139–43, 153

theater 6, 36, 49, 81, 87, 93, 119, 121, 130, 146
therapy 11, 13, 72, 78, 132, 134, 137
Thompson, Mary 138, 139, 141, 142
Tierney-Tello, Mary Beth 49, 72, 77
Todorov, Tzvetan 53
Todos os cachorros são azuis 20
total institution 129, 130
translation 29, 41, 52, 54, 60, 61, 69, 81, 86, 122, 134, 136, 158, 159, 161
trauma 4, 18, 68, 71, 111, 112, 138, 147, 157, 162
travel 5, 33, 35, 39, 41, 42, 51, 73, 75–77, 111, 127, 145, 153
Trigo, Benigno 133
tuberculosis 16, 79
El túnel 19
Turner, Victor 159
La última niebla 59

uncertainty 4, 25, 40, 53, 58, 63, 65, 67, 114
Uruguay 2, 3, 20, 24, 29–51, 145, 146

Vaca sagrada 19, 71
Valenzuela, Luisa 19, 20, 22
Vargas Llosa, Mario 19
Vaughn, Jeanne Marie 33, 34, 43, 44
Vera Franco, Bridget 42
Vilar, Irene 2, 3, 5, 22, 26, 53, 59, 122–43, 144, 146, 147, 150–53, 161, 162
violence 5, 18, 20, 22, 24, 26, 32, 42, 44, 46, 47, 49, 91, 108–12, 116, 121, 138, 140, 141, 146, 157
virgin 21
vision 7, 26, 34, 100, 106–109, 111, 112, 116, 147–49
Volpi, Jorge 19
La vorágine 23
voyeurism 47, 49, 50, 148

Waugh, Patricia 114, 153, 161
Willett, Jeffrey 159
Williams, Gareth 72
Women and Madness 11, 157
Woolf, Virginia 12

Yo el supremo 19

Zeisler, Andi 157
Zugasti, Miguel 100

www.ingramcontent.com/pod-product-compliance
Lightning Source LLC
Chambersburg PA
CBHW032103300426
44116CB00007B/872